THREE PREVIEWS OF THIS ANTHOLOGY

"As a social work librarian, I am always on the lookout for sources of information that help researchers and social workers understand people. Transplanted Lives does just this through a presentation of 13 personal narratives of college-age Jewish persons living in communist Hungary and attempting to escape to the free world following the 1956 Uprising. 12 of the individuals successfully emigrate and tell their stories of young Jews living in marginal conditions as refugees in their adopted countries. The personal histories in this insightful book will help readers come to a better understanding of the lives of displaced persons. I would recommend Transplanted Lives to anyone wanting to read about the experiences of refugees in America and also for gaining a better understanding of what it is like to be a marginalized person, viewed by society as outside the norm.

Each narrative in the book has its own unique story and yet they all contain a mix of joy, optimism, unease, and sadness. Several times I laughed out loud while reading this book, but also sensed a heartache and unsettledness in each account.

At a time when events such as the Syrian refugee crisis in Europe and the Black Lives Matter movement in the United States are featured so prominently in the news, reading these stories of survival helped to expand my point of view and remind me of all the privileged opportunities I take for granted. This book inspires me to be more gracious and humane and I believe many readers will have a similar experience through the personal connections the authors forge between the reader and their experiences portrayed in this work."

Paul Belloni
Bibliographer for Psychology, Education, & Social Service Administration
The Social Service Administration Library
The University of Chicago

"The manuscript makes very interesting reading. The stories that your contributors tell are engaging and easy to identify with. Some are very moving. Some, sad and tragic.

They illuminate from a very personal perspective common phenomena known from immigration research such as dilemmas that trouble young immigrants vis-a-vis their new homeland and the old country. Also, conflictual relationships with parents who stayed behind.

It was interesting to find in almost all stories illustrations of a well-known resilience factor in migration - social support. Or the detrimental effects of the lack of human contact and support. In many of the stories, the success in the new country was made possible by one person or a family who extended help to the young immigrants.

I believe the manuscript is a welcome contribution to the documentation of immigrants' narratives. It offers a rare perspective on the specific emigration wave from Hungary as well as more personal and experiential materials that are a very important part of documenting and understanding migration in general.

Wish you much success in publishing the book."

Julia Mirsky, Ph.D., Professor
Head of the Project for Research and Education on Migrants' Lives in Israel
בישראל ומהגרים עולים על וחינוך למחקר הפרויקט ראש
The Spitzer Department of Social Work
Ben-Gurion University of the Negev
POB 653, Beer-Sheva 84105, Israel

"Not only as a clinical psychologist, but also as a life-long Chicagoan whose ancestry includes many blood relatives who were Russian Jews lost in the Holocaust, I had many personal as well as professional reactions to reading this book of haunting accounts of emigres.

First, like few accounts I have read, these first-person stories not only give the day-to-day details of what life is like for (probably) most refugees from any troubled parts of the world, but gives the reader something quite special. The aspects of immigration common to all of these people is told from a point of view that most of us rarely experience when we think about and hear about the numerous "immigration" events in our world. We literally "feel" what is like to be torn from the dire circumstances of the life we have known and to be transported someplace different – perhaps better and yet with its problems. And to see this, as it were, from the inside looking out.

And, second, although as a clinical psychologist I am in a field in which (like many) we learn to place people in categories, reading this book I was struck by what to me is significant truth: There is no such thing as a standard human being. The individuality and uniqueness of each of these individuals, in spite of the similarities of their ordeals, shine through.

Bravo.

Dr. Sander I. Marcus
Licensed Clinical Psychologist
Center for Research and Service (IIT Department of Psychology)
IIT Lewis College of Human Sciences
Illinois Institute of Technology
Chicago, IL

TRANSPLANTED LIVES

TRANSPLANTED LIVES

The adventures of young Jewish immigrants

from post-Fascist and Communist Hungary

to the Free World

following the 1956 Uprising

— Struggles and successes

Edited by Susan V. Meschel and Peter Tarjan

CreateSpace

TRANSPLANTED LIVES

All rights reserved © 2016 Susan V. Meschel

This anthology contains the recollections of the adventures of young Jewish immigrants from post-Fascist and Communist Hungary to the Free World following the 1956 Uprising

Struggles and successes with languages, customs and careers

The majority of the essays in this collection are first person accounts with some editing.

ISBN: 1537066765

This collection of essays is dedicated to the memory of Andrew Handler.

Our friend, the late Andrew Handler was one of the graduates of the only Jewish High School in Hungary in the 1950s; an institution barely tolerated by the communist government, but provided first-rate preparation for university studies. *"Andris"* became a professor of history at the University Miami and authored several scholarly works on Hungarian Jewish subjects. With Susan Meschel, he compiled, edited and published two sets of personal accounts about the survivals of a group of their cohorts during the Nazi Holocaust,[1] followed by their experiences after the war under the Communist regime and their association with Zionism.[2] Many of the contributors graduated from the same high school and were unable to continue their studies for being "bad cadres"—meaning, they were not sufficiently tied to the proletariat, which the government was dedicated to nurture. As Handler and Meschel, most of the contributors left Hungary in 1956 following the anti-Communist and anti-Soviet Uprising that provided an opportunity for them to seek better lives outside the country of their birth that treated them as pariahs during Nazism and undesirables during Communism.

In 2011 Handler and Meschel reached out to many of the same people—and a few others with similar backgrounds—to share their stories of their "transplantation" beginning with their escape and

---

[1] YOUNG PEOPLE SPEAK – Surviving the Holocaust in Hungary; FRANKLIN WATTS, INC, New York - 1992.
[2] RED STAR, BLUE STAR – The Lives and Times of Jewish Students in Communist Hungary (1948-1956); EASTERN EUROPEAN MONOGRAPHS, BOULDER, CO - DISTRIBUTED BY COLUMBIA UNIVERSITY PRESS, NEW YORK – 1997.

establishing themselves in their adopted countries in the free world. Andrew Handler's untimely death—due to a heart attack a year later—left the task of completing the collection and editing to us. This volume is dedicated to the memory our friend, Andrew Handler, who inspired us to remember and record our experiences.

Brief biographies of the contributors are at the end of the book.

Susan V. Meschel and Peter Tarjan, May 2016

ACKNOWLEDGEMENTS

First, we wish to thank our friends, some who go back to our teenage years and others who appeared later in life, who responded to the call for writing about their transplantation into the Free World.

We also wish to thank our three previewers, who took considerable time from their busy schedules to read our manuscripts and provide helpful comments: Professor Sander I. Marcus, Department of Psychology, Illinois Institute of Technology, Chicago, IL; Professor Julia Mirsky, The Spitzer Department of Social Work, Ben-Gurion University of the Negev, Israel, and Dr. Paul Belloni, Social Service Administration Library, The University of Chicago, Chicago, IL.

We also owe our gratitude to Etta Gold, Librarian of Temple Beth Am Congregation, Coral Gables, Florida and Susanna Moross Tarjan for their careful reading of the manuscripts and recommending numerous corrections. The responsibility for any remaining errors rests on our shoulders, the Editors.

We thank Joshua Tarjan for his patience in coaching the process of formatting this book.

Last, but not least, we thank our spouses George and Susanna for their patience and support during the years while this book **had** taken shape.

Susan V. Meschel and Peter Tarjan

CONTENTS

DEDICATION	v
ACKNOWLEDGEMENTS	vii
TABLE OF CONTENTS	viii
INTRODUCTION by Andrew Handler and Susan V. Meschel	ix
PRELUDE TO IMMIGRATION	1
GENDARMES by Peter Milch	2
RETOUCHING STALIN'S MOUSTACHE by Tom Muhl	12
LOST AND FOUND IN AMERICA by Michael Simon	38
TO ENGINEERING VIA A SLOW NAVY SHIP by Peter Tarjan	66
AN UNSUCCESSFUL ATTEMPT TO EMIGRATE	96
TEMPTATIONS by János Várkonyi	97
HELPING A FRIEND TO IMMIGRATE	112
IN THE NAME OF FRIENDSHIP by Andrew Handler	113
A LIFE-LONG FRIENDSHIP FROM COMMUNISM TO USA by Susan V. Meschel	119
INITIAL STRUGGLES IN ADJUSTMENT TO THE NEW WORLD	132
THE REFUGEE AND THE PRINCESS by George Pick	133
FUN WITH THE LANGUAGE by George Robert Steiner	153
THE FIRST TASTE OF FREEDOM – AN IMMIGRANT EXPERIENCE by Susan V. Meschel	163
HUNGARICAN by Gabor Kalman	178
FIRST STEPS by Marianne Revah	187
CRISS-CROSSING THE ATLANTIC	205
THE STORY OF MY TWO IMMIGRATIONS by Marietta Vig	206
THREE LETTERS FROM ANDREW SZEKELY	217
From Israel, 1971—Easter Sunday, 1982— June, 1994	
A RETURN TRIP	246
RETURN by Risha Schatell	247
EPILOGUE	262
BRIEF BIOGRAPHIES OF THE CONTRIBUTORS	263

INTRODUCTION
By Andrew Handler and Susan V. Meschel

Some History That Binds These Stories Together, by A. Handler

The contributors to this book--the third and concluding volume of personal, youth focused reminiscences--share a common, albeit varied past. All of us are either practicing or professing Jews. In our seventies we still vividly remember the sounds and images of the Second World War and the Holocaust. We had lost parents, relatives and friends. Our recovery was painstakingly slow. We struggled to regain the emotional and intellectual equilibrium and reintegrate ourselves into a society which had rejected us.

After a short lived experiment in democracy in Hungary after WW II, a new threat appeared on the horizon. Life went on, but our fragile faith in the future and the resolve to rebuild the shattered world of normalcy was soon challenged and severely tested. The inevitable spread of Soviet-inspired communism swept away our hopes and expectations. Our childhood had been lost, and now our adolescence also faced the danger of being lost. An all-embracing, unforgiving and uncompromising system evolved around us, creating stifling social economic, intellectual and ideological realities and priorities. Despite confident and optimistic predictions to the contrary, between 1948 and 1956 in Hungary the socioeconomic standards of our secular and religious life eroded. Once, one of the most assimilated communities in Europe, Hungarian Jews faced a new hostile regime. Under the deceptive façade of official tolerance, the communists espoused a relentless campaign of discrimination and contempt.

However, all attempts to brainwash us failed. The sounds and images nurtured by foreign broadcasts, mainly the Voice of America, BBC and Radio Free Europe we listened to in secret, as well as letters from relatives living abroad could not be extinguished. No matter how severely Soviet and Hungarian authorities assailed the Western world and the emerging state of Israel, we retained an equally defiant outlook and did not surrender to the total obedience the communists demanded.

In the fall of 1956 our dream of leading unfettered lives was realized by a dramatic event which temporarily interrupted the rulers' plans to build a lasting socialist future. A protest movement of reform-minded and nationalist politicians, writers and students quickly reached a point of no return and spilled into the streets. The slavish, unquestioning relationship to the Soviet Union was severed by popular resentment.

However, the desperate pleas of help of the new revolutionary government produced no positive response beyond expressions of sympathy and future cooperation. Inevitably, the Hungarian Revolution was crushed by the overwhelming Soviet military power and the communist government was restored to power.

Not all was lost in the events of the heady weeks of the revolution and the subsequent fierce fighting. For a few weeks the border to Austria was unguarded. Without much hesitation over two hundred thousand people, Jews and non-Jews alike, left Hungary escaping into the world of uncertainty. We grabbed the opportunity and held unto promises waiting to be fulfilled. Overnight we became refugees, possessing little more than the clothes we wore during our often frightening crossing into Austria.

We were eager to start new lives wherever fate and good fortune guided us. Our eventual varied destination allowed us to find new ways of living and studying as well as growing new roots in unfamiliar ground. We never wavered or looked back with regret.

We came to stay without submitting to the lure of nostalgia for our former homeland, the often merciless and hostile land of our ancestors. Our decision to break with the past and to fully assimilate to our new homeland was rewarded with a new citizenship and promising opportunities.

This book is a chronicle of our journeys to freedom and fulfillment.

In conclusion, we honor the memory of our elders. We acknowledge the guidance, inspiration and support of our parents, the leaders of the Budapest Jewish community as well as our caring teachers, especially the directors and professors of the Jewish High School of Budapest (now known as the *Scheiber Sándor Gimnázium*) and the National Rabbinical Seminary. We hope that our stories will add yet another chapter to the growing literature of deeply felt and fondly remembered—occasionally funny—personal stories, which mark the sojourn of all immigrants, irrespective of the differences in language, in nationality, in culture and in religion, united in the fervent belief of personal renewal and redemption.

Andrew Handler wrote this introduction in 2012.

The Goals of This Book -- S. V. Meschel

We do not only aim to share our struggles and experiences in adjusting to a new homeland as a way to encourage others in transition, but have a more general purpose. Possibly the greatest mass migration in history is faced at present. Millions of people are forced to leave their homeland on account of wars or political and economic hardships. Particularly young, foreign students--as we were, years ago--are undergoing many facets of stress, due to the challenges of language, culture, social customs and family pressure. Our hope is to inspire those young refugees who had to interrupt their studies. These stories may also aid counselors and educators to understand and empathize with the plight of their charges.

To illustrate the relevance of this topic, I wish to quote "Student Talk Culture Clash," a workshop reported in The Chicago Maroon by Hinani Manglik in the University of Chicago newspaper on 1-28-2014. Rachel Jean-Baptiste, Professor of History opened the workshop urging the study of the psychological effects of immigration. A panel of six immigrant students from Asia, Latin America and Africa discussed their personal experiences, clashes with relatives, relationships with native peers and their attempts to adapt to popular American customs. The panelists experienced similar culture clashes in America.

The essays contradict the general assumption that those who were able to leave the scene of a catastrophe -- such as Europe under the Nazis, or other periods of chaos, are the fortunate ones, who would live happily ever after. The plight of refugees is illustrated by Walter Roth in "Toni and Markus: From Village Life to Urban Stress," Amazon, 2014.

Roth explored the everyday lives of his family in Germany prior to World War II and their immigration to Chicago in the late 1930s. The book focuses on the emotional trauma arising from painful adjustment problems his father and sister faced with tragic consequences. Refugees do need to make difficult adjustments toward becoming fruitful citizens in the new land.

Lastly, I wish to quote from Roger Cohen's essay:[3]

> "The strain of burying the past, losing one's identity and embracing another, can be overwhelming. Home is an indelible place. It is the landscape of unfiltered experience, of things felt rather than thought through, of the world in its beauty absorbed before it is understood, of patterns and sounds that lodge themselves in the psyche and call out across the years. When home is left behind or shattered, an immense struggle often ensues to fill the void."

Our essays have a different tone in the sense that most of us never felt at home in the land we left behind, where we faced constant persecution.

The story of a German Jewish immigrant is included, who returned to his hometown after 50 years to claim his goldsmith certificate that was denied him by the Nazis. His story illuminates survivor guilt–not uncommon among refugees who lost their family–and his awkward encounters with former friends. Returning to the scenes of horrible memories deserves further study.

---

[3] The battle to belong. Depression and an immigrant's struggle to assimilate; The New York Times, January 9, 2015.

We hope our book would help those who struggle to adjust to the new world around them and overcome the demons from traumatic experiences.

During the past few years we have read, heard and watched the news about the westward and northward exodus from troubled and war-torn lands in the Middle East and Africa. Most of the contributors to this collection had enjoyed the aura arising from the 1956 Hungarian Uprising and were aided by a variety of people, organizations and governments welcoming refugees from the Soviet Block. The current situation is strikingly different for the refugees trying to enter Europe and beyond, meeting considerable resistance toward this gigantic human flood. We hope that our stories may provide a modicum of hope for a good life for the fortunate ones who may settle in a free and democratic country. Our best wishes to all!

PRELUDE TO IMMIGRATION

Gendarme with rooster's feathers

Photographer

Young and old Stalin with mustache

Hungarian refugees arriving in New York aboard the U.S. Navy's General LeRoy Eltinge ship, 1957
From the National Archives, Washington, D.C.

GENDARMES
By Peter Milch

In 1953, when I was graduating from high school, I had three strikes against me:

> Strike 1: My father had not been either a laborer, or a share cropper, but a successful businessman.

> Strike 2: I was not willing to atone for the sins of Strike 1 by becoming an avid and conscientious communist.

> Strike 3: On account of Strikes 1 and 2, my high school principal did not give me a recommendation, thus making me ineligible for higher education.

After considerable difficulties, by next fall, I was successful in landing a job in an industrial research institute as a laboratory technician. The Institute was a great place. Most of the professional and some of the support staff was young–and not so young–Jewish men and women. A joke was going around at the Institute that we could get a minyan together–a prayer service requiring ten Jewish adults–on a moment's notice. These were people who, in the past, were denied an education because of their religion, and embraced their new opportunities with gusto. They were smart, talented and eager to prove their worth. They also realized that I was in the same position as they were a decade earlier for different, but just as obnoxious reasons.

One day the word got around the Institute that we were getting a new Personnel Director. We only had a temporary one and he had left months earlier. Everybody was a bit apprehensive. A Personnel Director in those days meant a local spy for the secret police. They were the hatchet-men who made sure that everyone toed the party line. The Institute was not what we now would call politically correct. These were scientists, who cared more about their field than about politics. Even the local secretary of the Communist Party, Lester R., just talked a good game, but his heart was not really in it. If someone made some anti-government comment in front of him, he would turn around and say:

— I didn't hear that!

When the new Personnel Director arrived, everyone was pleasantly surprised. Paul G. was young, friendly, and—according to the women--handsome. He was a chemist like the rest of us, but he readily admitted that his background was in police work.

He invited each of us—one by one—to his office for the purpose of getting to know us. But this wasn't an interrogation, not even questioning, just a pleasant chat about background and family and so on. Later on, when we got to know him a little better, he even told jokes about the government, but made sure that the picture of Stalin above his desk was turned toward the wall. Soon, there was a small group of us who were constant visitors to his office, discussing everything from girls to sports, movies and occasionally even politics. One day, when a bunch of us was sitting together without Paul G., discussing that Paul was really a nice guy, Gabe P. said:

—*You know, Paul is such a nice guy, he might even be Jewish. Let's make him an honorary Jew with the name of Grünwald.*

We marched into his office and told him about our decision. He greeted the news with uproarious laughter. He loved the idea and was actually proud of it.

Of all the people in the Institute, probably I had the best relationship with Paul G. We had a lot in common. We grew up in the same neighborhood, went to the same high school, and had a mutual friend, Johnny F., who was a few years older than me, closer to Paul in age, but I knew him from our temple, and we got along very well. Paul G. claimed that Johnny had been his best friend until Johnny moved out of the neighborhood and they lost contact. I have not seen Johnny since that time either, but every once in a while a neighbor would hear about him and pass it on to me, and of course, I did report it to Paul.

The stories Paul told me about his high school experiences were quite interesting. Paul's father died during the war (I assumed he was in the army), and when the war ended, Paul had to get a job to help support his family. Local governments started to get organized and Paul applied to become a policeman. He received some short training, a uniform, a shotgun, and a regular beat. But shortly after that, school started, and Paul wanted to finish his senior year. He managed to get a new assignment at the police with a 2 to 10 pm shift. That meant that he could go to school in the morning and still go to work—school ended at 1 pm. The only problem was that he didn't have enough time to go home and change. He went to school in his uniform and with his gun, which he always unloaded and put in the corner of his classroom. On a Friday, two weeks after school started, the Principal came to his class and asked Paul to step out. In the hall, he told him that the school custodian had to go to the bank to pick up the bi-weekly payroll. Conditions were such that it was dangerous to walk around with a lot of money, even in the middle of the day. So, Paul, with his gun on his shoulder, accompanied the custodian to the bank and the payroll arrived safely. This was repeated every second Friday. However, by the end of the year, Paul had to take the customary comprehensive exams and was reluctant to go. The Principal assured him that it would be OK, and when Paul returned with the payroll, the Principal informed him that he had just passed all his exams.

With a high school diploma under his belt—a meaningful achievement in Hungary—Paul was promoted to Detective and got a new assignment. In plainclothes, he would walk around in areas where homosexuals were known to congregate. Being young and handsome, he was often propositioned, and his answer was always:

—Wait a minute, Honey; I'll be right with you!

By the time he could recognize about a dozen of them, he blew his whistle, the uniformed police moved in and Paul would point out the guys who propositioned him. The police took them down to the police station and beat them up.

After a few years, he resigned from the police force, enrolled at the university and became a chemist.

My friendship with Paul cooled off a bit after a certain incident. Word got around that Paul had fired Mr. M., an elderly, quiet, benign cleaning man. — I walked into Paul's office and said:

—Paul, are you out of your mind? Whatever possessed you to fire Mr. M.? He is a benign old man, who couldn't hurt a fly.

He was taken aback that a lowly technician, even though a friendly one, would dare to challenge his decision. He pulled himself up to his full height (he was 6'2"), glared down at me and said:

—Not that I owe you an explanation, but maybe you'll change your mind when I tell you that this "benign" old man used to be a gendarme. You should know what that means. Gendarmes were a vicious, fascist police organization that patrolled the countryside in the unincorporated areas, usually on horseback. The main characteristic of their uniform was the plumed hat decorated with black-and-blue tail feathers of a rooster. They were generally referred to as the rooster-feathered-guys.

I walked out of his office, but something just didn't sit right. I went down to the area, where the custodial staff had their lockers, and there was old Mr. M., packing up his belongings. He didn't even look up, just kept packing. I didn't beat around the bush.

—Mr. M, is it true that you were a gendarme?

At that point, he looked up, had a sad smile on his face and said,

—My dear boy, Peter, you are old enough to remember what gendarmes looked like. Have you ever seen one?

—Sure, I have—I answered.

—OK,—he said—what do you remember about them?

—Mainly their rooster feathers–I answered.

—Anything else?—he continued the query.

—Yes,—I said—they were all big guys.

His smile became wider.

—That's right; you had to be at least six feet tall to become a gendarme.—Look at me!—I am 5'5". Do you think they made an exception for me?

—So, where does Paul G. get the idea that you were a gendarme? –I asked.

His smile became sad again.

—Peter, my boy; I am not an educated man like the rest of you here. I've been a cleaning man all my life. From 1937 to 1942 I had a job cleaning gendarme barracks. Those bastards got drunk after every patrol and sometimes even before. I had to clean up their puke and their crap, and if I didn't do it fast enough, I got kicked in the ass. They treated me the same way they would have treated you.

—Thank you for asking—he said, and with his packing finished, he walked out of the building.

I did not have the stomach to go back to Paul's office. I avoided him from then on and shortly thereafter I also left the Institute and joined the Rabbinical Seminary.

A little over a year later, the revolution broke out and I had a chance to leave the country. It was something I had been waiting for seven years, ever since my sister left and went to New York. Back in 1949, when she left, it was a lot more dangerous to leave the country illegally and I was too young to undertake such a risk.

But during the autumn of 1956, it was much easier. My mother and I crossed the border into Austria without any difficulty, and I was confident about being on my way to America.

Our first stop was Vienna. This was my first introduction to western life and freedom. A friend of my sister and her husband were in Vienna at the time, trying to make arrangements for his elderly mother to come out of Hungary as well. We went to see him in his hotel room. It was mid-morning and Mr. B. was waiting for us. We sat down and started chatting about his mother, whom my mother knew well, when there was a knock on the door. It was room service, bringing him his breakfast. It was a simple American breakfast, two eggs sunny-side-up, bacon, toast and coffee. To me it looked like a feast. I have not seen eggs in months. Mr. B must have seen that my eyes practically jumped out of their sockets. He picked up the fork and immediately put it down.

—I don't have time for this now, I'll have breakfast later. Peter, would you do me a favor and eat it?

It took me a few seconds to vacuum up the food on the plate, and to this day I think of Mr. B as the most generous man in the world.

For the first few days I did nothing else, but walk around in Vienna. I found the city fascinating, the selection and opulence of the merchandise in the stores, and—above all—the friendliness of the people. When you walked into a store, all the sales people greeted you as their potential customer. When you left, they said good-by and thanked you for coming in. I wasn't used to this. In Hungary, in the state-owned stores, nobody cared. They were unfriendly and morose, as they were paid the same salary whether they sold anything or not. They couldn't care less.

Of course, the first thing I had to do was to register with the police as a refugee. I got my grey ID card, which entitled me to free transportation on the city's street cars. This almost got me in trouble. I learned to speak German as a very young child. My teacher was a middle-aged lady from Vienna, and so I learned to speak the Viennese dialect. One day, after showing my grey card to the conductor on the street car, I asked him for directions. He found it odd that a refugee spoke German like he did. He stared at me and my card for a while then walked to the other end of the car and started talking to a policeman.—Fortunately, I had to get off at the next stop before they had a chance to come back, but I don't know what would have happened if I had not gotten off.

After a few weeks in Vienna, we were finally on the list to go to America. A train ride to Munich, Germany; an overnight stay in Army barracks, and then we boarded a plane.

This was my first flight ever. After a short stop in Scotland, we got on the plane again for the long leg of the journey. I had a window seat and after we were airborne, I dozed off for a short while. When I woke up, it was pitch dark outside and the flight was so smooth that I thought we were standing still. All of a sudden I got really scared. I was sitting just over the wing with a good view of the engines, and to my chagrin, there were sparks coming out of the engines—this was a propeller plane, not a jet. When a stewardess passed by, I pointed out the sparks to her, and she must have noticed that I was scared out of my wits. She smiled and told me that this was perfectly normal and I should call her when the sparks stop coming, because then we would be in trouble. I went back to sleep and woke up again as we were preparing to land in Newfoundland. This was in December, the snowiest part of the year. I had never seen so much snow in my entire life. They brought buses to the plane and drove us to the terminal building. The bus was running between two snow banks, rising higher than the bus. The next stop was Camp Kilmer, New Jersey.

Again, we were housed in army barracks and they informed us that the only way we could go out if a relative came to get us. But there were no phones to call any relatives. I tried to make friends with various clerks and guards and talk them into letting me use their phone, but had no luck. Fortunately, my English teacher in Hungary stressed conversational English; I could converse, but my powers of persuasion were not good enough. Finally, I wandered into the area where certain relatives gathered to pick up their kin. I talked to a middle-aged man, gave him my aunt's phone number and asked him to call her after he leaves. He must have made the call, because the next day my aunt and uncle showed up, followed shortly by my sister. The reunion with my family, especially with my sister, is indescribable. I hugged her so hard—I almost broke her in half. I was a fourteen year old little boy when she left, and here I was a twenty-one year old giant, compared to her.

Of course, there was a lot of paperwork involved in our release and I tried to facilitate things by running from one office to the other. I had no problem making the clerks understand what I was trying to achieve, but in one office I hit a brick wall. The man in the office had some sort of a regional dialect—probably southern—and while he was trying to be very helpful, I could not understand a word he had said. In my frustration, I ran out of the office, grabbed my aunt by the arm and said:

—*Come in here and help me, this guy doesn't speak English.* —
The whole family got a kick out of this.

The next day I was out of Camp Kilmer and at my sister's house. It was New Year's Eve and champagne never tasted so good. New Year's Day in New York was unforgettable. I knew a lot about New York and the U.S. in general from my sister's letters over the previous seven years, but it is one thing to read about and see pictures of the Empire State Building and another to go up to the top and look around. The rest was beautiful, but for me, not unexpected. The few weeks in Vienna prepared me for the western life style, but—of course—it did not compare to the grandiosity of New York. Although I embraced my new lifestyle easily, the years in communist Hungary did not disappear without a trace. For a long time, if I was walking on the street with someone, having a conversation, I automatically lowered my voice when I saw a policeman. It took me a long time to overcome this acquired habit.

I stayed with my sister for a few weeks, but in January I found a job and shortly after, an apartment of my own, and I started to live like an average American.

One afternoon during that summer, I was walking down Broadway, when I saw a familiar figure approaching from the opposite direction. It was Johnny F., my old friend. I had not seen Johnny for more than ten years, but recognized him immediately. When Johnny was a young boy, he had some sort of thoracic surgery during which they had to remove a rib from one side. Not having the support of the rib, his entire upper body was leaning in one direction and gave him a lopsided appearance. I greeted him by name when we were abreast, but he didn't seem to recognize me. After all, I was about ten or eleven when he last saw me, and I was twenty-two now. When I told him who I was, he was overjoyed and we spent a long time catching up on family and other matters. We exchanged addresses and phone numbers, and were about to part company when I suddenly remembered:

—By the way, Johnny, I used to work with your friend, Paul G.

—Oh my God, Paul G...–I haven't seen him since we left the old neighborhood. He used to be my best friend when we were kids. He was such a nice guy.

—You are absolutely right. He was a wonderful guy. We even made him an honorary Jew.

Johnny burst out laughing. He was laughing so hard that I was afraid he would wet his pants. When he finally calmed down a bit and was able to talk, he looked at me and said:

—*You made Paul G. an honorary Jew? But Paul was Jewish, at least his father was. That's why he was kicked out of the Gendarmes.*

Still chortling to himself, he walked away and left me standing there with my mouth open and mumbling to myself:

…And these people were running the country…

RETOUCHING STALIN'S MUSTACHE
By Tom Muhl

As a young man, the only thing I really wanted more than being a famous jazz pianist or a tennis champion was to be a great painter. In 1956—within a matter of days—my entire world would change and rearrange itself as a result of the bloody and ill-fated revolution in Hungary.

Born into a relatively peaceful era of European history, before the Second World War in Budapest, I had talented and cultured parents. My father was an actor-turned-musician; a member of the string section of the Budapest Philharmonic, and my mother was an artist and musician, content to see herself as a professional housewife.

After the war, we were very poor. My musician father was on the blacklist for having quit the communist party, so no orchestra would hire him. He was working at odd jobs and my mother took in ironing so we would have something to eat.

My family needed the money to live on, so I dropped out of art school at age seventeen, and went to work as a window-dresser and later became a graphic artist for one of the department stores. I also found a part-time job painting large outdoor movie posters at night. I liked that kind of work but couldn't continue because the army wanted me.

It was in 1952 when I first caught sight of Andrea at a dance. She was dark, willowy and sensual; but what impressed me the most about her was that she took me seriously. Much later in our relationship, she expressed the idea that we must have fallen in love out of loneliness. I walked up to her and with my knees quivering led her to the dance floor.

With her, I felt a sense of ease, no longer threatened by the shapeless angst that seemed a permanent part of existence during the years of the Nazi occupation and even beyond.

Andrea and I were married in June 1955, and in late November, I was drafted into the army and wound up in the Army's Studio in Budapest.

After the boot camp, I managed to get myself transferred to the Army's Communication Section in Budapest. That section consisted of mostly civilians, who made use of me as their go-for.

After a few months of being their janitor, they let me set up my own easel in a faraway corner of the studio. To develop flawless technical skills, they suggested I should try to paint copies from reproductions of the paintings of famous Hungarian and Russian masters.

My first project was a well-known oil by a Russian painter; the fateful storming of the Winter Palace by the proletariat during the 1917 Russian revolution. My initial boredom slowly subsided.

— *Major Biró really liked your painting. He wants to hang it in his office. How do you like that?* — said our overseer, a sergeant.

— *Could this mean that they would let me do some really big posters for the anniversary celebration?"*

A few months passed and I was getting restless. I dreamed of being free and a civilian again, able to spend my days with Andrea in the green hills of Buda, across the Danube. Despite my spring fever, during those weeks I did complete several copies of notable paintings. One day, our sergeant made one of his surprise visits to our studio. He motioned to me to stand at ease, reached into his shirt pocket and presented me with a long list of paintings by nineteenth century Hungarian artists. Next to each painting on the list was the name of a high-ranking officer.

— *Congratulations, Private. We're becoming famous, aren't we?"*

I was assigned to create copies of those masterpieces for the brass.

One rainy afternoon, the sergeant reappeared,

— *Listen here, you hidden genius — we're getting very close to the May Day celebrations. You know what that means... Lots of red ornamental placards with pictures of Stalin, Rákosi, etc., and we'll have a very large portrait of Stalin and Lenin at the front entrance of the Officers Club. Major Biró instructed me to give you the order.* — *So, what have you got to say, Michelangelo?"*

I did not know what to say.

— *Thank you Sergeant.* I said stiffly.

— *I'll get to it right away."*

I collected a large assortment of reproductions of pictures of Stalin and Lenin. After dozens of sketches, I was almost ready to start painting, but the large canvas, approximately 10x18 yards, wouldn't fit inside the studio. I painted it on the floor of the studio with the help of a ten-foot ladder and a reducing glass. The project was much more difficult than I had anticipated. The two parts were assembled in front of the building.

When that day arrived I was as nervous and excited as any playwright at his premier. A few days later, the ancient telephone rang in the studio.

— *Leonardo, the Major wants to see you.*

I was surprised, and a little uneasy about it; I quickly put on my cap, buttoned up, brushed my hair, gave my clunky boots a quick polish and fifteen minutes later I was standing at attention in front of the Major.

The Major was on the phone; when finished, he sat down, leaned back in his chair, and looked up at the ceiling for a while. Finally, he stood up again.

— *Private Muhl, do you know why you're here?* — He paused.

— *I need an explanation from you, and I need it good and fast. Your practical joke is going to have far-reaching consequences.*

I started to feel dizzy.

— *Sir...,* I managed to say with great difficulty, and then stopped.

— *I don't know what you're talking about, sir... I'm sorry Major... Sir.*

— *You mean to tell me nobody approved that poster outside our building before it was exhibited? You mean you haven't any idea that if things are not straightened out soon, at best, I could lose my job. Most likely, you and I could both end up in the Gulag, sentenced to a good long time there for subversive activities and making a mockery of our beloved father, Comrade Stalin?*

It all started to make some sense to me. It was that bloody mustache of Stalin. I had a lot of problems with it while painting it. I copied the picture from the official, boring version of Stalin in his fatherly fictional forties or fifties. But I remembered a photograph of him in his early twenties, and repainted his mustache: full-bodied, heavy and black. I thought it was more interesting and it actually made him look younger and more virile. Everybody else in the studio liked it too, so I left it that way and went on to paint Tovarish Lenin.

— *Major, please let me explain to you what happened. I was kind of... exercising my "Artistic License", so to speak.*

He stood up erect and walked over to me.

— *Listen here and listen real good, Private Muhl! I don't give a rat's ass about your artistic self-serving stupidity.* — *Can you fix that bloody mustache by Wednesday?"*

— *Yes, Sir!*

— *Yes Sir, what?*

— *I can do it, sir. But I need some help.*

Transplanted Lives ◆ 15

— *Fine!* – He picked up the phone and snapped,
— *Lieutenant Sipos. I want you to go with private Muhl and make sure he gets all the help he needs to straighten out this friggin' mess about Comrade Stalin's mustache.*

Sipos ordered a cherry-picker and a crew of handymen; the crew lifted me up to the third floor and lined me up with Stalin's profile, exactly at the mustache. To my greatest relief, I finished the work the night before May Day.

Across the street stood a red brick Greek Orthodox Church; occasionally I stopped by that church for a quick prayer when I felt lonely or depressed. It didn't matter to me what denomination it was. My father used to say that any dark and quiet place is good enough to communicate with God. I went inside to relieve my tension…

On a day in October 1956, a group of young men and women began to gather in front of the heavily guarded building of Radio Budapest. Their peaceful demand to broadcast some proposed changes to the government's policies was answered by the Secret Police with tear-gas and bullets. I did not know then that all this was just a prelude to what was to come. Overnight, the revolution broke out on the streets of Budapest. Hungarian flags appeared everywhere with the communist emblem cut out of the middle.

At first, I was elated and agreed fervently with those who wanted changes for the better. In the ensuing chaos, I changed into civilian clothes and joined the demonstrators.

For several days we thought the revolution had succeeded. Andrea and I were among those lucky ones who narrowly escaped the great massacre in front of Parliament in which hundreds of demonstrators were mowed down by the Hungarian Secret Police, the *AVH*.

On November 4 the euphoria ended. The Russian tanks rolled back into the city. Fresh Soviet troops, soldiers of the same army that saved our lives twelve years earlier, were going house to house to restore a brutal order. I wracked my brain for a solution that might keep Andrea from being raped by the marauding soldiers. I came up with the idea to paint ugly, festering sores on her face. With flour, water and oil paint, I completed my greatest creative work, transforming the smooth, young face of my wife to repulse the most bestial of men. And it worked! When the Russian troops barged into our room, they fired a burst from a machine-gun into the ceiling, then stopped short in front of the sickly looking woman who sat in a dark corner, a babushka wrapped around her head.

— *Nagyon beteg,* — I said. Very sick. Shuddering in disgust, the Russians quickly left the house. We felt thankful and greatly relieved. But after that day, we both knew in our hearts, it was time for us to move on and face the unknown—a future whose course we could not predict.

We had no definite plans. We took a packed train to Szombathely, near the border with Austria. I felt the gaze of a railway man across the aisle.

— *I know what you're up to,* — the man said in a low whisper.

— *Maybe I can help...* — After we regained our composure and asked him what he meant, he told us that the end of the line was crawling with Russians and we would have no real chance to pass through unnoticed. We followed his instructions.

The train slowed down near a pine forest. We jumped off and tagged along behind him. We passed the edge of a tiny village where our guide came to a halt. He pointed toward a clearing on the distant horizon:

— *On the other side of those fields it is already Austria.* — This is as far as I can go for now, before they could have my neck for trying to help you. I have a wife and son waiting for me at home, you know. From here on, you're on your own.

— Thank you, sir. We're very grateful. But why are you doing this?" — Andrea asked.

— The answer is simple: I don't like guns. This is one way I can fight the Russians. — He was gone almost instantly, seeming to melt into the trees.

During the next hours, we must have walked several miles, going around in circles in the dark. I was walking at least twenty feet ahead of Andrea at all times, in case we stepped on a land mine, so it might at least be possible for one of us to survive. Suddenly, the black sky was floodlit with phosphorescent flares and we could hear bursts of machine-gun fire that appeared to come from all sides.

At dawn, we slowly crawled along the edge of a canal until we reached the yard around a farmhouse. We walked up to the house, shuddering and terrified, but so exhausted that we didn't care whether the people inside would turn out to be Austrian or Hungarian. — A man came to the door.

— We haven't seen any of you lately, — he said in German. — How did you manage to make it?

The next morning we heard that the Austrian border patrol recovered the bodies of six Hungarians in the swale we had just crossed.

A few weeks later, in December, we landed at London's Gatwick Airport along with a dozen other Hungarian refugees. I did not know what to expect. There was a rush of excitement of course, mixed with fear and uncertainty. I would have to learn how to live in a free society. But I felt some kind of blind faith.

— Oh God, this is so exciting, — Andrea said. — I wonder where they're taking us.

— I'm sure it's not the Ritz Hotel.

I was certainly right about that. After a polite reception at the airport by the local Women's Volunteer Service, and some tea and biscuits, we were whisked away by bus to a remote, abandoned WW 2 army camp at Swindon, in the Midlands.

December in the dilapidated former RAF barracks was wet and cold. The gray mist seemed to have settled inside our rooms as well as in our heads. We moped around all day, feeling sleepy and tired. I tried to practice my broken English on our keepers, people from the nearby charity organization, while Andrea gave Hungarian cooking lessons to the designated English cook. Our roommates and fellow refugees, a young Gypsy family of four, were loud and constantly arguing, so we went for long walks and tried to feeling friendly toward the melancholy green English countryside. We felt increasingly unsettled and restless in this camp. Following our narrow escape through the mine-infested marshes of the Austrian frontier, we were grateful for our safety and security. Then, just before Christmas, a nearby hotel was looking for help. We volunteered.

— *They tell me you are a painter. Is that right?* — asked Mr. Bullock, the manager.

— *Well, yes, but I am still learning,* I said in uncertain English.

— *Brilliant! That's exactly what we need,* said Mr. Bullock with a broad smile. *Come with me, mate!*

— *See that stage over there? Right now it's blue. Right? OK. I want you to paint it red and green for Christmas. Something festive for the holidays, you know. Use your imagination; I leave it up to you.* — Right. — *You'll find all the paint and the brushes you might need in the backstage area over there.*

Mr. Bullock did not exactly have my brand of humor, but even painting walls sounded much better than washing dishes. I threw myself into the project with zeal and finished it in two days. Mr. Bullock was delighted.

— You have to have a sense of humor in this life, my boy, he said in a fatherly way and handed me one of his cigars. Then he went on, admiring my masterpiece of red and green walls, with stylized reindeer and Christmas trees.

In a few months, Andrea was getting restless. One evening while ironing my shirt in our small room she declared:

— I just figured it out. We've saved up enough money for two one-way train tickets to London. What do you think? We can't stay in this dump forever. We'll have to go sooner or later, so, let's do it now. We've done enough for the Raven Hotel, haven't we? Or do you want to be Mr. Bullock's court painter for the rest of your life?"

I had also been concerned about our future, of course, but I had not been able to come to any decision. I wasn't ready for another change after what we had been through.

— OK, I said. — But do we know anybody in London? And what are we going to use for money? Have you thought of that? We need to work. What are you going to put on your resume? You can't just write "female, Hungarian dishwasher, some English spoken..." Why not stay another six months or a year; save up enough money so we do not have to end up in a soup kitchen somewhere in London?

— All right, but listen to me! We can present ourselves at the British Council. They're still helping the Hungarians from '56. We're political refugees. They owe it to us. And they have the money — as she handed me my shirt.

— Who's your source of information about all this, if I may ask?

— Never mind the source. Trust me. I know what I'm talking about. Don't worry about a thing.

Three weeks later we did give notice to Mr. Bullock, and after a foolish and festive farewell party with our friends in the kitchen we took the train to London with one suitcase containing all our earthly belongings.

— *If this doesn't work out, we can always go back to sleep at Paddington Station,* — I said, as we were heading toward the British Council for Refugees at the Carlton Hotel, a one-time luxury institution that was now vacant, except for a group of refugees.

— *I had noticed that the benches were wide and comfortable.*

— *Oh, hush! It'll work, don't worry!*

The Carlton had seen better days; it was dirty and dilapidated. After registration and some other tedious formalities, someone handed each of us an orange and a banana, and ushered us into a crowded area with a notable odor: a mixture of rotten oranges and cigarette smoke. Dozens of refugees were waiting to be processed. We took our seats in a corner and waited. Eventually we were interviewed by Mr. Bromley, the Director of Services, a distant cousin of Lord Bromley, we were told. He was a small man, well into his fifties, very thin and very British. He had volunteered his time and money to help the Hungarian refugees.

— *Thomas Muhl, artist,* he was reading aloud from a thin dossier, — *and his wife, Andrea. Well, well, well! A real Hungarian artist...* looking at us over his glasses.

— *Glad to meet you. You are the first artist among all the refugees I have seen. Yours is a nation of artists, musicians and writers, isn't it? What a shame we have to be meeting like this. But, never mind. Tell me...,* turning to Andrea, *where are you staying at the moment?*

— *We just came to London, this morning.*

Mr. Bromley turned to his secretary:

— *Is there any vacancy somewhere, Mrs. Kane?*

— *No, I'm afraid not, Mr. Bromley. We have filled the last spot an hour ago with a family.*

— Hmm... Awkward situation, I say. But, not to worry! — he said wrinkling his forehead.

— Is there anybody else, waiting outside, Mrs. Kane?

— Two more couples, Mr. Bromley.

— Fine! Here is what we'll do. You and your wife go outside and wait until I call you. It shan't be long. Then I'll take you somewhere.

On our way out Andrea asked Mrs. Kane for two more oranges. We went back to our seats with our empty stomachs and a lingering headache. Mr. Bromley appeared soon enough with a smile, wearing an old raincoat and a well-worn brown hat.

— Are we ready? Okay. Let's go and find a cab.

We obediently followed him.

— Could you tell me, Mr. Bromley, where you're taking us? — I asked, in the taxi.

— Yes, you're going to stay at a very nice place, near Hyde Park, until we find you a vacancy, somewhere else. It's called the Gore Hotel.

— I understand you haven't quite finished your studies in the art school over there — he continued. — Would you like to attend the Royal Academy in London? I can arrange a scholarship for you. Think about it! You don't have to decide now. You both must be tired.

The Gore Hotel was small and had retained a large part of the elegance of a bygone era, but the atmosphere still appeared to be cozy and graceful. We were shown to our room, said goodbye to Mr. Bromley, and after a shower we had a nice supper, courtesy of the British Council, in the well-appointed and delicate looking old dining room.

— Far cry from the Raven Hotel, wouldn't you say? — I said, to Andrea.

— I thought you liked the Raven Hotel.

A few weeks later in the winter of 1957, we were settled into a rent-free flat in the outskirts of London, thanks to Mr. Bromley. I got my scholarship to the Royal Academy and we began to live the life of a regular married couple. Andrea got a job as a waitress at the Hempstead Tennis Club and although she didn't speak much English, her continental charm and sexy good looks compensated for her lack of eloquence. I worked part time as a cartoon film animator at the Halas&Batchelor Studios in Soho Square. Mr. Halas was a Hungarian who had immigrated to England before the war. He and his wife had started and built the largest cartoon film studio in London. Although animating cartoon characters seemed to me the most excruciatingly boring work in the universe, I was happy to have a job, and the people in the studio were considerate and helpful. I learned a lot about the graphic arts business, information that became very useful to me later in my career.

I still had my occasional nightmares. I would wake up in cold sweat in the middle of the night, dreaming about being captured and unable to leave Hungary. But the days were good and I felt relatively happy. Then one day we received a telegram from the British Council letting us know that Andrea's mother had also left Hungary and was staying in a transition camp in Austria. She had located us through a Center for Missing Refugees. She was on her way to America, where she had been offered a job as a psychologist at Children's Hospital in Ann Arbor, Michigan. *"Hopefully you can join me there soon!"* she wrote.

Andrea was so electrified by the news that she was ready to head straight for the US embassy, but I wasn't so sure. I liked England and the people. Admittedly, our situation was far from perfect. The economy was uncomfortably regressive. There were still certain traces of the traditional English xenophobia, but we felt accepted and liked by many people. Andrea saw the situation differently. She became more and more critical of everything

British, starting with the weather, then the food, the snobbishness and even Mr. Bromley.

A few months later we received a letter from Ann Arbor. Everything was just great, her mother wrote. The people, the food, her apartment, the job, everything was fantastic. *"You have to come, kids. Here, you'll have a future!"*

Later she sent us a letter of sponsorship and formal invitation, so that we could get an entry visa in less than six months. After several long and heated arguments, I gave in and we applied for visas to the USA, shortly after we received the immigration affidavit. We got the visas, but I was temporarily rejected, because of a small suspicious spot on my chest X-ray taken at the US embassy. I had to wait until it healed and the spot calcified. That could have been months or even years. After long discussions we finally agreed that Andrea would go ahead without me and I would join her later.

— My mother says there's a much better chance for someone to be admitted to the states if his wife is already there, — she said. I couldn't disagree, but the prospect of us being separated for months or even years, did give me a lot of anxiety.

Toward the end of 1957 my visa to the United States was finally granted; I sent a telegram to Andrea in Michigan, and made reservation for a flight on Pan Am. I spent the remaining three weeks in London, visiting all the sights like a real tourist, and spending my days with friends from school, and at the only properly heated place in London, the British Museum.

On the day of my departure from Heathrow Airport I felt a tiny bubble of hope.

When I got off the bus in Ann Arbor, Andrea was waiting for me at the gate, waving at me with a broad smile. All my doubts about our long awaited reunion evaporated; she appeared lovelier than ever and seemed genuinely happy to see me.

Her mother's house was sunny and spacious. She was hardly ever home. She worked hard, taking care of her patients at the University Children's Hospital. We stayed there alone all day, trying to keep busy by practicing our English on each other or raking up the leaves in front of the house on balmy October afternoons.

— *This country's the greatest. I wouldn't live anywhere else. Especially back there...* Andrea said.

— *You mean back there in Hungary, or England?*

— *They can keep them both.*

Then one day I called my Aunt Charlotte, in Florida.

— *Tommy darling,* — she said in Hungarian with an American accent, — *what do you want in that cold Michigan with those dull Midwesterners? Come and stay with us in Florida!*

Fall was unmistakably coming to a close. In the mornings, I would attend some English classes at the university and take long walks around the campus. Later I would sit and read in the stuffy library, and contemplate my uncertain future in America.

By the end of November, the first snow had fallen. I would frequently sit by the fireplace and watch the dancing flames, thinking about my parents in Hungary. I would anxiously wait for their letters but had to read between the lines. The secret police censored all letters coming from, and going to dissidents.

Andrea and her mother were already in a state of premature Christmas euphoria, roaming the shops and department stores. One day, at the University Library, I had a chat with a friendly clerk. I mentioned to her that I was an artist.

— *Guess what! My brother's also an artist at a large advertising agency in Detroit. You might go and see him.*

The following week, I took the bus to Detroit for an interview with her brother Bob. He asked for a portfolio with samples of my work. I thanked him, bought some art supplies, and, in a week, came up with two layouts I liked. One was for the new car named Edsel and the other one for a beer called Black Label.

They liked my work at the agency. The Art Director paged through my book with a poker face.

— I'll be right back... — He reappeared with three or four men in shirtsleeves. They all shook hands with me and then picked up my portfolio, passed it around, and kept repeating,

— Good stuff, good stuff...

— Fresh stuff. I like it! I like the way you think" Bob said. — How would you like to work for us?

— I'd like that very much.

January was coming to a close. I decided to call the Detroit agency.

— Sorry, Thomas, I've meant to call you, but we got busy. I'd love to have you here, but unfortunately, we're having some budget problems...

Next morning I had a letter from Aunt Charlotte:

— Max and I are driving to Detroit next week to visit his relatives. We would like to stop over in Ann Arbor, to see you. I'd also like you and your wife to join us on our way back to Miami.

I was ready to go, but wasn't so sure about Andrea. My mother used to say during the war that if anything should happen to her, her sister, Charlotte would take care of me.

— *You would never guess that she had spent a year in Theresienstadt, a Nazi concentration camp. She's a real live Pollyanna, a little bit like you,* — I told Andrea.

I had become increasingly unhappy with our financial dependence on her mother, and resented her indirect competition for Andrea's affections. This wasn't anything new. When we were first married, we were also forced to live with her. As a part-time student and poster artist, I did not have a steady income, but then, I was too blinded by my promethean love.

Two weeks later, Uncle Max drove his 1954 blue Rambler into our driveway.

Charlotte and Max were sitting next to each other on the small sofa like two adorable little dolls, both of them short and pudgy. Max, somewhere in his seventies, still had a beautiful mane of white hair and Charlotte wore an almost real looking, yellow-orange wig. They radiated peace and kindliness.

At the end of the visit, Aunt Charlotte affectionately hugged and kissed me and said at the door,

— *We're going back to Florida next Friday; if you decide you want to come, give us a call and we'll come and pick you up on our way back. But darling, please, don't wait until the last minute!*

It wasn't easy to convince Andrea about the trip to Florida. Naturally, Helen wasn't thrilled either. It was supposed to be only for a few weeks, but both women knew if I should find a good job we might stay there indefinitely.

It was hard for us to leave our parents behind in 1956. Looking back now, we were almost children. It almost broke my heart when I had to say goodbye to my mother on a misty November morning, knowing well that I might never see her again. And I'll never forget the tears in the round blue eyes of my nine-year-old sister, holding our father's hand. But we couldn't stay. I deserted the army and had no identity papers. My parents knew that if I had remained there I could end up in prison or worse, in Siberia. They were sad and disconsolate to see us go, but tried not to show it. They didn't want to make our departure more difficult.

Although Helen didn't overtly oppose our hastily planned departure; there were lots of tears, moans and whispers, and predictions of catastrophe, which weighed heavily on Andrea for a long time.

— *Kids, just wait until you meet Aunt Julia!* — Charlotte said somewhere in Ohio. — *She's a darling; almost ninety, but sharp as a blade.*

— *Yeah, I remember she used to send us care packages after the war.* —*What's her story?*

Aunt Julia and her husband David arrived at Ellis Island with only one little suitcase at the turn of the century. In less than two years they had saved up enough to quit their jobs in the garment district and opened an outdoor stand on the Lower East Side selling fashionable hats for women. Aunt Julia designed and fabricated them at night in their little apartment in the Bronx. "Julie's Paradise" turned out to be a great success. Within five years, they sold the store and moved to Florida.

Land on South Beach was sold at bargain prices. Uncle David bought a nice piece of property and in less than two years, they built one of the first hotels on Miami Beach. It turned out to be a long, hot summer, and their success in the hotel business was much delayed. By November, they were nearly broke.

With sheer guts they persevered. The following season the long awaited tourists started to trickle in and later on they swarmed.

Uncle David and Aunt Julia prospered and became known for their lavish parties in their Palm Island home with six-piece gypsy bands flown in from New York in the winter, opera singers from Europe in the spring, trips to their summer home in the Catskills and weekend shopping sprees on Fifth Avenue. All these mild excesses would not have mattered so much, if it weren't for David's love of horses at Saratoga, and Julia's passion for greyhounds on Miami Beach. They both had irresistible passions for gambling, which they considered to be just an innocent hobby.

"Nothing ventured, nothing gained!" was Uncle David's idea of the way to live.

"You can't take it with you!" Aunt Julia would agree. In the end, they were forced to declare bankruptcy.

Uncle David suddenly died of a heart attack and Aunt Julia went into severe depression. Then she met a Polish investor at the dog races, of course, and they became close friends. On Julia's advice, he bought the Flamingo Apartments. He also died of a massive heart attack a few years later and Julia inherited the apartments and enough cash to retire comfortably and avoid gambling as much as she could after that.

— *Well, Aunt Julia sure sounds like a true classic.*

— *If it weren't for her, none of us would be here, darling. She helped many people to come to this country. Even Sam, in New York.*

— *You mean Uncle Sam?* — I asked.

— *Yes, and she also introduced me to Max. Isn't that right, old boy?* — Max nodded.

— *Remember, Tommy, we're a strong family. We stick with each other, no matter what.*

We drove up in front of Charlotte's apartment house nearly at dusk. She showed us into the extra bedroom and promised to have dinner ready in an hour.

We unpacked our bags, and wasting no time, walked to the beach. Only days after wintry Michigan, standing in the lukewarm Atlantic up to our ankles was an experience that I know I will never forget.

We paid Aunt Julia a visit the following day.

— *Welcome to America, darlings! Look at them, girls! — Aren't they a beautiful couple? — Come in, children, have something to eat and drink, don't be shy! Then I'll show you to your room. You'll like it, it's clean and comfortable.*

Aunt Julia's vacant apartment was in her two-story "Art Deco" Flamingo Apartments.

For the next few weeks we loafed around and tried–unsuccessfully–to keep cool. The days were steaming and the nights seemed even hotter with the broken air conditioner in our window.

Thanks to Max's connections, I was able to find a part time job as assistant to a Cuban portrait artist in the lobby of the then popular Carillon hotel. Our studio was on the lower terrace without air-conditioning. I was almost drowning in my own sweat, working on flattering pastel portraits of cheerful tourists, while Maestro Julio merrily chatted away with his friends and collected the money inside the cool lobby. He gave me one third of the price of every portrait and so, for the first time, I was earning my own money in America. Although I liked the luxuriant beauty of the tropics as well as my loving relatives, I soon realized that—at that point in my life—Miami Beach just wasn't for me. I was feeling trapped without any tangible plan for our future.

One morning, I heard Aunt Julia's voice coming from the terrace.

— Tommy darling, are you there? — I just got off the phone with Uncle Sam in New York. He wants to see you. He remembers you as a little boy, from Hungary. He says he's got a job for you!

— Listen to your Aunt Julia. New York is the only place for a smart boy like you. Uncle Sam also said you could stay with him until you find your own place. I'll help you to pay for the tickets and you can pay me back when you'll have the money.

I found Andrea stretched out in the sand, roasting herself in the fierce morning sun. When I sat down next to her and told her about Uncle Sam, and the prospect of moving to New York, she gave me an incredulous look.

— The whole idea is unrealistic... – she laughed a bit and turned over. But I didn't see it that way. To me New York represented growth and success in the future. I was determined to have a rewarding career in the advertising field. The provinciality I had experienced in Michigan and Florida led me to believe that I belonged in the big city. I felt the need for a fast paced tempo and interactions with bright, progressive people. I was wondering why Andrea couldn't understand that. But then I remembered her mother's emotional grasp on her.

— *I don't think it's such a bad idea,* — I said — *we should talk about it.*

In the afternoon Andrea went shopping with Aunt Charlotte while I was trying to figure out what to do. Andrea had grown up virtually without a father. Her parents had divorced when she was eight, and from that moment on she was the only object of her mother's love and attention. A strong and overprotective relationship had developed between mother and daughter. I realize now that such things are commonplace with single parents. But when we first met, I was too young to understand, or care. I'll have to have a talk with her when she comes home.

— *Did you find something you liked?* — I asked, when she returned from her shopping expedition, flushed and weary.

— *No, but I'll never go shopping with Charlotte, again.*

— *Why not?*

— *For one thing she's cheap; cheaper than you! With all that jangling jewelry and expensive clothes on her, she took me to all the bargain basements in Miami, where you have to grope your way through mountains of merchandise and be pushed around by all those nice old ladies... just to save a few dollars.* — She was genuinely upset.

— *Just because I haven't got the money doesn't mean I haven't got any taste.*

— *Well, don't worry about it. When I get that job in New York, I'll buy you anything you want.*

— *What job in New York?*

— I think we should sit down when you're more relaxed, and talk about it.

Andrea disappeared into the walk-in closet and a minute later returned in her T-shirt and Bermuda shorts. She fixed herself a drink and sat down on the rattan sofa, stretching her legs with a big sigh. At last she turned to me.

— Look, I'm not sure what I want, but I'd like to know what you want. Simply put: Would you like to go to New York?

— Would you? — she asked.

— Yes!

— I don't know what to say... I want what's best for you and best for both of us. If you really think we should go, then we ought to go. Why don't we sleep on it? You can give Aunt Julia an answer tomorrow. She's not going anywhere.

Not for the first time in my marriage, I was surprised by her sudden change of mind, but I trusted her good intuition.

The following Sunday we were lying next to each other in the soft sand. It was very early and except for the seagulls and a few joggers, the beach was peaceful and virtually deserted. Andrea was lying on her back with her eyes closed, my arm wrapped around her waist.

— Do you remember the Raven Hotel... — I said. — ...the one in Droitwich in England?

— Oh, God! Do I remember?

— Well, it seems as if that was the last time we were really together; just you and me, only for each other. Ever since then we have been losing and finding each other. I just hope that we would never have to lose each other again.

We arrived in New York at the invitation of a man who had been married to another of my mother's sisters, Aunt Caroline, who died during the war. The first time I ever saw Uncle Sam was in the early spring of 1945 in Budapest at the end of the war. Our family–like everyone else in the city–was starving. The whole city was in shambles. We managed to move back into the kitchen of our former apartment, replaced the broken windows with cardboard to keep out the snow and wind, and chopped up much of the furniture for fuel in the kitchen stove. One of the coldest winters of the century, it also seemed the longest. Our apartment was on the third floor. One morning we heard a high-pitched voice calling my mother's name from the courtyard.

— *Elsie . . . Elsie!* — the voice shrieked. My mother asked me to go outside and take a look.

— *It's a strange looking man, Ma,* — I reported. — *He says his name is Shamu, or something like that.*

— *Oh, my God! It's your uncle Shamu, my sister Carolina's husband. I thought he died in the camps,* — my mother said, wrapping her scarf around her head, and running outside.

He had been on the road for several weeks. He was among the fortunate few survivors of Bergen-Belsen. He stayed for only a day or two but left us with enough head and body lice to last for months.

Now, a dozen years later, I was standing with Andrea in front of my Uncle Sam's apartment on East 49th Street, hoping to find a job and a place to live.

Sitting across from Uncle Sam, I began to remember some of the stories my mother told me on the long winter nights after the war. Uncle Sam was born at the turn of the century in a small town near Krakow; he never stayed in one place long enough to make friends. He had been charged with petty theft, burglary and fraud, and his name was on the list of the police in several countries in Central Europe. At some point, his path crossed Hungary and happened to meet my mother's younger sister, Caroline.

The real truth came out several months later, but by then it was too late. Caroline and Sam, as he wanted to be called, were married and honeymooned in Paris. They seemed unsuited for each other, even physically. Aunt Caroline was a tall and big woman, next to her Uncle Sam seemed even smaller and more comical than he actually was. His questionable reputation and the shady characters with whom he had been seen were even more disturbing.

According to my mother,

"One day, they showed up at our door again. They were a sorry sight, they looked sick and hungry. I invited them to come inside and asked no questions at all. After all, she was my sister... Your father almost killed me when he came home and found out. — They were running away from the French police."

One night there was a knock on the door. It was the police. My parents reassured the policemen that they had some relatives visiting from out of town. After that incident, Uncle Sam and Caroline disappeared without saying goodbye.

"That was the last time I ever saw my sister. Those were terrible days. The Germans were marching on Poland and every day there were anti-Jewish demonstrations in Budapest. The war was approaching dangerously... Then, as you may remember, after the war your Uncle Sam paid us a visit again, right after his return from the death camps. Years later, he sent us a letter from New York, with a photograph, showing him in front of a television set, wearing an overcoat and with a hat on his head. He looked very prosperous."

— *Listen kids, I want you both to feel at home!* — said Uncle Sam. — *I'm sure you'll be comfortable here. The extra bedroom is all yours. Tomorrow we'll go see a client of mine. He owns an ad agency and his brother is his partner.*

Next morning we went to see his friend, Bernie Brummel, at the Brummel & Brummel Ad Agency in the Pan Am building.

— Bernie, I'd like you to meet Tommy, my nephew from Hungary. He's a talented artist and would like to work in advertising. I want you to see his work. He could be a great asset to your agency.

— Take him to see my brother, Lee. He's the creative guy.

We left Bernie and Uncle Sam said,

— Let's go have lunch at Manny's! They got the best matzo ball soup in New York City.

— Uncle Sam, would you mind if I asked you a question? — I said, after we found a table, and settled down with our plates of soup.

— Of course not. We're family. Ask away!

— What I want to know Uncle Sam, — I began slowly, — ...what exactly do you do? I mean work?

— Oy! Manny forgot the salt, again...

— I would like you to know that I have worked hard all my life. When I was young, I dug dirt and tended to the horses on my parents' farm in Poland. Later, when I was older, I went to work in the local barbershop as a novice. I became a professional barber at age twenty. As I recall, I was working in Vienna for this anti-Semitic Austrian scumbag for a few weeks, until one day he made a snide remark about the Jews. We got into an argument and I was just about ready to slash his goddamned Nazi throat with my razor, when, thank God, a customer showed up; so I just packed my bag and left. — Well, about a week later, I got on a train for Budapest. I loved the city and the people, especially after those cold and snobbish Austrians. That's where I met your Aunt Caroline. One day–as I was relaxing in the steam room at my favorite Turkish bath–I overheard two fellows sitting next to me talking in Polish. I said hello to them in Polish and they asked me what I was doing; what was I making a week; would I like to make more money; and so on and so forth. They asked me to meet with them the next day at the Café Metropolis, and asked me if I'd like to join in with them. I said sure, and the next day, after we ordered some drinks, I wanted to know what we would be doing. So the older guy said to me, it was very simple. They had some merchandise they wanted to sell. All I would have to do is find customers. With everything I'd sell, I would get a generous commission from these two, all in cash, no paperwork, and no headaches. The more I'd sell the more money I'd make. It would be all up to me.

— So I guess you asked where the merchandise would be coming from. — I asked Uncle Sam.

— Sure I did. The two Poles looked at each other for a split second then the younger one said it was the surplus from their big warehouse in Poland. Stuff the big stores couldn't sell. I wouldn't have to worry about that part of it. All I would have to concern myself was to find customers and Sell, Sell, and Sell! They even told me that one of their associates made enough money in two years to retire.

—Did you ask whether he retired to jail, or if not, where else?

— Of course, but they just laughed at me and at our next meeting I agreed to give it a try. After making sure I wouldn't be involved in any hanky-panky, I went on to hustle their crap: cosmetics, sundries, wigs, hairpieces, orthopedics, rubber gloves, and thermal underwear, almost anything you could name. They sold real cheap, for next to nothing. So I had a pretty good idea they weren't legit, but I didn't care. I was making more money selling their cheap junk in one day, than I could make in a week working as a barber.

He told me about his adventures in the demi-monde and said,

— I made myself a promise at Bergen-Belsen. After almost a year of watching people dying around me–knowing it was just a matter of time for my number to come up–I swore, if I ever come out of it alive, I'll never starve again. I'll live life to its fullest, one day *at a time. — It was a jungle at Bergen-Belsen and it's a jungle out here.*

His prediction about me turned out to be true. I did get the job with Brummel & Brummel, Inc. and began my work in the advertising world. I began to grow new roots in this still unfamiliar soil.

When does a newcomer settle down, if ever? When does an immigrant begin to feel safe and comfortable, if ever? Tom Muhl did land a job and soon became an important contributor to the advertising firm as a creative artist. Later, he moved to the San Francisco area continuing his work as a commercial artist. Tom and Andrea were divorced. Tom returned to England, where he received an assignment to join a British advertising firm's office in Budapest, where he spent a few years after the fall of communism. Tom retired from commercial work, returned to Miami and began to paint as a vocation. His unique style has attracted much attention. Many of his paintings are illustrations of his personal experiences and some deal powerfully with the horrors of the Hungarian holocaust that he had experienced first-hand as a child.

This text was derived—with the author's permission—from Tom Muhl's autobiographical work, **"Retouching Stalin's Moustache: Arrivals and Departures, Destination Unknown,"** *Xlibris Corporation, 2002, by his friend, Peter Tarjan.*

LOST AND FOUND IN AMERICA
By Michael Simon

Preamble to the Revolution

I applied to the Technical University in Budapest in 1954. My father—who disappeared as a slave laborer in the Soviet Union during World War II—had been gone for twelve years, but several of his former colleagues had connections to someone on the faculty. So I got in! This was far from an automatic process as admission did not depend as much on one's grades as it did on the social preferences of the political system. I was lucky to be considered the son of a left-leaning engineer rather than the grandson of a bourgeois businessman.

As soon as classes began, I realized I was in the wrong box. But Hungary did not offer either a box for me to flower or an opportunity to change my field.

My third year was rough going. The professors were remarkable. I still remember my excitement with quantum mechanics. I found the classes fascinating, but my talent for mathematics and the ability to concentrate were insufficient. With stronger commitment, I should have been able to surmount the difficulties. Gradually I became convinced that engineering was not for me. But how to find an alternative? Fortunately the Revolution came to my aid.

The Revolution

The weather on October 23—the day the Revolution began—was sunny and pleasant. I was up early as my mother was going to Vienna by train to visit her cousin in Graz. In 1955, Austria became a free, neutral nation. My mother had long wanted to see her cousin, but until this time one could not get a passport to go west. To improve her chances, she applied for her passport while I was in the

Hungarian Army during the summer. Having me in uniform, I served as a hostage for the government to assure her return. She did receive her passport and that morning, before anyone could guess it was to be a historical day, she took the train to Vienna.

As the train pulled out I waved her good-bye and went home. Later, I crossed the bridge to the campus on the Buda side without the slightest notion that in a few hours there would be a revolution and Soviet tanks would clank down our street.

As I arrived, the students were debating whether to march or not to march. Soon, we were walking north along the Danube to the monument of General Bem, a Polish hero, who led Hungarian troops against the Habsburgs and their allies, the Russians, during the 1848-49 Revolution. At last, we stood up to oppose the oppression we all hated.

From there, the crowd walked to the Parliament Building and called for Prime Minister Imre Nagy, whose name has since become synonymous with the Revolution.

It is fascinating to contemplate how small, unrelated events determine history!

Had that day been cold and damp, as autumn days often are in Budapest, the crowds probably would have melted away and the day would have become a tiny tick in history. Had it rained, most of the marchers would have gone home. But it was more like a spring day. It was a truly spontaneous outpouring of public sentiment. Nearly everyone despised Communism, the Soviet Army, and the puppets who served the interests of Soviet Union.

After Imre Nagy spoke, I met a classmate and friend, who told me about shooting at the Radio Building. I had enough excitement for the day and went home.

Next morning I looked down from my fifth-floor window and saw Soviet tanks roaring down the street in the morning fog.

Over the next few days I walked around town a lot, but did not witness any fighting. The revolution seemed to erupt on its own, much like a volcano.

Nationalism has been central to life in Hungary. Hungarians, as many other nations in Europe, unify around feelings of victimhood.

A week later the Soviet tanks and armored cars were gone. The Red Army had withdrawn. In fact, the Kremlin withdrew its Russian-speaking troops to replace them, on November 4, with soldiers from the Soviet Far East, who did not speak Russian and could not be influenced by Russian-speaking Hungarians. — Kirgiz and Uzbek units were unlikely to defect.

But between the two Soviet attacks there was peace! Most people, including me, believed that the Soviets would leave for good because we wanted to believe it, and Hungary could become a neutral country, much like Austria. So when on October 30 the radio called for university students to join the newly formed National Guard to replace the police, I signed up.

My mother sent a letter asking me to follow her to Austria as she heard the border was open. I answered: For the first and only time I felt Hungarian and saw hope for a better life in Budapest; I planned to stay. This experience shed light on the difficulty of leaving one's birthplace and made me understand my grandfather and my father, who refused to leave the country in the late thirties when black clouds of Fascism appeared.

The National Guard assigned me to lead a squad of about ten students to guard an arsenal on the outskirts of the city. We were armed with Soviet submachine guns from WW II, left behind by our liberators from the fascists in 1945.

When our guard duty ended, we returned to the campus by truck and I went home.

My childhood friend and fellow student at the university, Péter, stayed for night duty at the news center on November 3. At dawn when they heard the rattle of the approaching tanks, he and another student left, instead of preparing to resist. They crossed the nearby bridge over the Danube under fire. The two guys appeared breathlessly and asked whether they might sleep over. My mother's bed was empty, so I said, yes.

The night before the 4th was quiet, but in the wee hours of the morning a large Soviet artillery shell hit a room two windows down in the next building. I remember listening to the rubble falling out of the fifth floor and hearing my own heart beat so loudly that I wondered whether it was Péter's from across the room. Years later I asked him about that night, but he did not remember anything. He had been so tired that he slept through it all.

Over the following weeks I became convinced that emigration was my only reasonable choice. Although some people still had hope for the revolution to succeed, pessimism enveloped most of us. The city stood still! The University was closed and there was little to do around the apartment.

One day, passing the headquarters of the Communist Party, a sailor held me up with a gun and ordered me inside. Yes, Hungary has a tiny navy of gun-boats on the Danube and for some reason the sailors remained true to the Communist government.

They ordered me to put my hands up against the wall and patted me down for weapons. I remember laughing. They found nothing dangerous and let me go. Next time I chose a different route. If that was a prediction of life in Hungary, I wanted no part of it!

The Revolution was the most inspiring event of my life, but it was over as indicated by the omnipresence of Soviet troops. The next three weeks were depressing. Slowly, I made up my mind about leaving.

I asked myself:

— *What should happen if I left?*

I answered:

— If I did not like what I found in other lands, I could always return to Hungary. If I returned, the Commies should love me!

Then I asked the same question in reverse:

— What would happen if I stayed?

— Well, the answer was that I should hate myself for the rest of my life for this missed opportunity. I made the decision! The remaining question was:

— How?

Exit Hungary

I don't remember what gave me the idea to contact Otto but I did, and we were going to leave together. Otto was older than me, a doctor, past his residency with the Ambulance Service. Our mothers were friends and worked together. Otto was jaunty and self-assured, he earned the nickname *Tigger* in his family — they all had nicknames from *Winnie the Pooh*. He was just the kind of person one would want as a partner in an adventure!

We thought of a cover story in case we were caught. By mid-November Soviet troops were trying to stop the westward flood of people. At first, many people simply rode a bus to the border and walked across to Austria.

A family friend obtained a pass for me, asserting in Hungarian and Russian that I was going to the border area to buy lard. The alibi was thin, but better than none. He also gave me some Hungarian money. I packed a leather briefcase with an extra pair of underpants, a toothbrush and, I can't explain the reason, a tie. I bought three bottles of imitation rum. The alcohol was real!

I spent the night before our departure with Otto and his wife, Klári. Their neighbor had a fancy record player and as we were leaving, he put on Mozart's Requiem. If we got into serious trouble, a requiem would be performed for our souls.

In the morning we took a train west to the last stop at the border, Mosonmagyaróvár, where Hungary, Austria, and Slovakia meet. The train was full of people, all intent to cross into Austria. Soviet soldiers were checking everyone's papers. At Otto's urging we turned away from the first checkpoint and found an unguarded side door to leave the station. At the bus stops across from the station we found a bus going west toward some small villages. A former maid for Klári's family was living in the area. We got off the bus and trudged to her house over a muddy road in the dark.

With the help of our overnight hosts, we hired a peasant with a horse-drawn wagon to take us close enough to the border to walk across easily. They also knew a man who, for a fee, would walk us over to Austria. I don't have a photograph from that day as I left my camera behind for fear of endangering my cover-story.

Our driver was a typical Hungarian peasant, quiet and serious. He drove his horse at a walking pace. As there was a drizzle and the air was cool, Otto took out a large bottle of very strong fruit brandy. Klári took a sip and so did I. Our coachman grabbed the opportunity and swallowed about a pint. — Soon he was drunk, not just tipsy, but totally inebriated. Fortunately, I knew how to drive the horse and Otto knew about drunks from having served with the Ambulance Service. The peasant started shouting,

— I have to piss!

Otto and I lifted him off the wagon, but he was unable to stand. We held him up, but he still could not relieve himself. We lifted him back on the wagon and he continued to scream. A Soviet jeep came by with Kalashnikovs between the soldiers' knees. They must have seen many a drunk and laughed at Otto and me struggling with the screaming peasant. They did not stop, they just laughed. We continued at his pace toward our appointed guide in the village near the border.

When I opened my briefcase, one of the three bottles of rum was broken. I gave one to our guide as he greeted us. Fortunately, Otto knew how to handle drunks. Before our peasant descended into his alcoholic stupor, Otto had learned the name and the location of our guide for crossing the border. In retrospect, Otto might have planned to get our peasant drunk, but I doubt it.

At the house of our guide our drunk driver sobered up enough to ask for his money. Otto kidded him that he should pay us as we had brought him so far but, of course, we paid him. As soon as it was dark, we followed our guide across a muddy corn field. Otto was talking to him while I was helping Klári and carrying someone's child. My briefcase was light; helping others was not an imposition, although the muddy field was difficult. To our right, we saw lights. According to our guide those were headlights of Soviet tanks.

A man in our group was carrying a heavy load of his professional books. It was fascinating what he considered essential for the start of a new life. In retrospect, I compared his heavy, probably useless books with my old tie in my bag.

Stumbling through the mud, we came upon a ditch; it marked the border. After we climbed up on the Austrian side, I took the last bottle of rum, passed it around and, as a good conservationist I threw the bottle back across the border for someone to collect the deposit for it.

Welcome to Austria

Soon a man appeared in a green Austrian uniform. I still remember his smile, something no Hungarian border guard of the period would have allowed himself. We were in the town of Andau, and he directed us to a school building where they served us hot chocolate. Perspicacious Otto was talking to a Hungarian from North America. Otto's new acquaintance had sent someone to rescue a relative. He came in a small station wagon to collect his relative, who had not yet arrived that night. This man offered us a ride to Vienna. I sat in the back on a spare tire and my bottom was sore by the time we arrived near Schönbrunn, the Hapsburg's answer to Versailles.

Otto came to our rescue again! He convinced the owner of a restaurant — everyone was excited about Hungarian refugees — to feed us dinner. We called my mother in Graz and the restaurateur directed us to a small hotel, where we promised that in the morning my mother would come with Austrian money and pay our bill. We all bedded down in one room.

During the night Otto was shouting in his dream. He dreamed that he returned to Hungary on his own volition and could not leave again. For the coming year I had a similar dream nearly every night and heard from others that the dream of returning was par for the course. But that night I did sleep well. I woke at dawn from a dream about tanks rumbling down the street. When I looked out the window, delivery trucks were bringing fresh bread and other goods to the city.

My mother arrived and we went to register as refugees with the local authorities. Fortunately my mother spoke German fluently. We also had to sign up with a country that would accept us as immigrants.

We stayed in Vienna for several days. A day or two later my step-father arrived. After telling my mother that I would not go where he was going, he and my mother parted. He was mighty sore at me for having ended his marriage, but his anger did not much matter to me.

After a few days in Vienna, while Vice President Nixon was inspecting the flood of Hungarian refugees at of President Eisenhower's request, my mother and I boarded the train to Graz. — Eisenhower had already tripled the immigration quota for Hungarians.

The train took us through the Semmering Pass and the country appeared wealthy, compared to Hungary, and peaceful.

Although the Soviet occupation only ended recently, Vienna and the countryside both appeared prosperous. Everything was clean! But memories of the Austrians' love for Hitler did enter my mind. While I had no interest in settling there, Austria was a perfect place for me as a freshly released prisoner.

We spent some time with our relatives in Andritz, a village just outside Graz. It felt like a dream. The place radiated peace. My mother's cousin, Tante Irene, was wonderful to me and Onkel Fritz was an ideal host.

The weeks swept by and we had to think of our future. Mother and I returned to Vienna and tried our luck with the US Embassy.

My mother's clarity about where to emigrate was remarkable:

— *From the US we can go anywhere; from anywhere else we could not go to the US! Let's go to the US!*

Brazil was our second choice as my mother had a cousin in Saõ Paolo. I also considered England as I had always dreamed about that country. An English-speaking country would offer much more hope.

A few days later, we boarded a bus to a camp for refugees destined for the US. The bus was heading east from Vienna and we were all tense traveling toward the Hungarian border. Not one of us wished to go back to Hungary!

In the camp matters quickly deteriorated. Jews became the target for old-fashioned anti-Semitism. Hitler did succeed to amplify the ancient tradition of antagonism toward Jews, but under Communism overt anti-Semitism was silenced by the government. The preponderance of Jews in the Communist leadership exacerbated anti-Semitic feelings. Once outside Pax Sovietica, the old hatred exploded. And we became its targets! Some of the refugees celebrated their new-found freedom with Jew-baiting.

As a solution, the Jewish refugees were moved to WW II barracks near Salzburg. It was Christmas Eve as our bus was heading west on the new Autobahn. Snow was falling. In a way our trip was a journey through a magic land; in another sense, it was a long trip into the unknown.

Our new camp looked out on the Austrian Alps. It was beautiful! Despite this, I caught "camp sickness." I did not feel like getting out of bed, while others were playing soccer in brilliant sunlight. On top of this, the office lost our papers. For two or three days, it felt like an eternity, we waited to hear about our journey across the ocean, but there was only silence. My mother rose to the occasion and went on a sit-down-strike. She said,

— *I will sit here until you find our papers!* And she did!

Off to the USA

Right after the New Year we were on our way to Munich in brilliant sunshine surrounded by a snowy landscape. At the airport we boarded our plane, a DC-4 or DC-6, and took off in the evening. We flew over London after dark. I had never seen a city so large and with so many lights! The grid of streetlights seemed endless. In the wee hours of the morning we landed at Shannon, Ireland.

The planes in those days needed two or three refueling stops to cross the ocean. It was a bumpy ride, especially over the Atlantic. A fellow traveler used several bags to relieve her motion-sickness. I told her that we did not have to pay for our ticket, only for the bags. She was too far gone to respond.

From Shannon we flew to Iceland and then to Gander in Newfoundland, Canada.

In the fading light of the evening of January 4, our plane was passing over the Statue of Liberty in New York harbor, an inspiring sight! We landed at McGuire Air Force Base in New Jersey.

At customs all fruit was confiscated. Most of us had not seen an orange for a decade and we saved up the precious fruit the Red Cross ladies had passed out in Munich. This was a hard blow, but we were too tired to be overly upset. We were bussed to Camp Kilmer, a WW II staging area for G.I.s bound for the European theater. The camp was reactivated for Hungarian refugees in 1956.

As our bus traveled on a New Jersey highway, I marveled at the large trucks with so many lights that they appeared to be rolling Christmas trees. Some houses still wore their Christmas decorations, the likes of which I had never seen; a real contrast to dark, gray, dismal Budapest.

At Camp Kilmer I found the Army food wonderful, although some Americans expressed their sympathy for my having had to eat it. All the scrambled eggs one could wish! Those Americans had no idea what a blessing such abundance was to me! In Hungary, eggs were expensive and hard to come by.

We were all excited about the beginning of the rest of our lives, but had no idea how they would unfold.

Mother's cousin, Eva, and her husband, Alex, came to see us from New York. Their visit implied care and attention I had not expected, and also stories for the next half century about how they missed a dinner invitation in Brooklyn that night.

Back to School

A few days later, my mother and I were informed that Pennsylvania State University provided several scholarships for students who had attended a university in Hungary. The town of State College, as we learned later, collected money for us refugees, and a group of citizens drove their cars to Camp Kilmer to take us to their town.

It was a memorable trip to State College on January 12. The line of cars rolled along US 22, now an Interstate highway. The air was crisp, the land covered by snow. We stopped at a road-side restaurant. The surprise course was a salad: half a canned pear on a bed of cottage cheese, with paprika sprinkled on top. Having come from a land where paprika was a basic staple, this was novel, but I ate it with relish.

When I arrived to this country I was furious with John Foster Dulles, Eisenhower's Secretary of State, for having encouraged Hungarians to rise up against the Soviet occupation and then abandoning them to the tanks of the Red Army. For years I felt betrayed by the Dulles-run State Department until I realized that had the US or NATO come to aid the Hungarian Revolution, a world war might have followed and none of us would be here to enjoy the good life. But, as a provincial idealist, I expected perfection.

Among my cohorts, I was not the only one to leave Hungary in 1956. Péter, Andrew, and one other friend left, but we weren't the only ones. Of my high school class of sixteen, one went to Canada, two to Israel, three to England and three to the US. At our 50th reunion, in 2004, this was an important topic of conversation.

At State College I was deposited in the home of a family, who received $10 a week for my room and board. I had my own room on the lower floor and the hosts were good company. Charley and Gladys had three children. Sharon was the oldest at six, Lynn in the middle, and David, approaching two. They, along with their television set, taught me English. They also taught me how to be an American. One day David was crying, his nose running and he seemed to be miserable. I asked him,

— How are you David?

He said,

— Fine!

That taught me that while Hungarians pride themselves on some clever answer in response to such a question, in America I was to be "Fine!"

On the black-and-white television set we watched Arthur Godfrey, Ed Sullivan; *The Mickey Mouse Club* and *I Love Lucy* were also important.

The cereal boxes taught me much about spelling and punctuation. Back then, nutritional information did not take up space on cereal boxes; there was only "important" stuff to read, such as games and recipes!

Those were complex and exciting days! I remember more clearly my walks with David on my shoulder than any of my classes. In Hungary, brilliant scientists taught us fascinating subjects such as quantum mechanics and filled me with excitement even though I could not do the homework. At Penn State a tired, middle-aged man read the textbook to us about brushes with and without pigtails employed in electric motors. I could not fathom his "lectures" and, most definitely, could not remember any of it.

Gladys told me years later that I shouted in my sleep every night. I had the same response to emigration as Otto in that hotel room in Vienna. In my nightmares I was back in Hungary on my own volition and could not get out of the country again, although I did want to. Even in my dreams, Hungary felt like a jail-cell, a trap.

With all the heart-ache and emotional difficulties that confront a new immigrant, especially one as confused and troubled as I was, the thought of returning to Hungary never occurred to me. As hard as those first years in America had been for me, they were infinitely better than gray Budapest and life in our unhappy apartment.

Charley, who ran the Meteorology Department of Penn State, employed me as a work-study student. I was to tabulate air temperature data over Point Barrow, Alaska at 10,000, 20,000, and 30,000 feet. The data came from weather balloons. Since there were no computers for tabulation, I served as such. It was a mindless job that allowed my daydreaming.

One day I was walking on the sidewalk along grassy front yards when a policeman pulled up in his cruiser, got out and walked through the grass to a house. He did not notice me, but my response was typically Hungarian! I still remember it after all these years. In Hungary, a policeman walking toward me was scary and would put me on the defensive. In the States, one is innocent until proven guilty. In Hungary I was guilty in the eyes of authority, until I proved my innocence. We carry our emotional baggage as snails carry their shells.

Shopping was a spectacular experience after poverty-stricken Budapest. Many items in the supermarket were totally new to me! In Hungary, we had a piece of bread for breakfast, if lucky, topped with butter and jam. At *Wise Markets* or at *A&P* the variety of boxed cereals seemed endless. Meat, eggs, and all the things we could barely get back in Budapest stared at us from shelves and coolers! Gladys pointed out that on average, a large paper-bag full of groceries at the supermarket cost $2.50!

My mother was taken in by a Jewish family, and that made her relax; they were *"Members of the Tribe"* and less threatening than outsiders.

My mother often quoted that when someone asked her about her religion, she said,

— *I am a Jew.*

The response in America in 1957, — *That is much better than if you were a Catholic!*

— John F. Kennedy became President three years later.

During my first summer I was working at the University. My mother and I shared a small apartment with a few pieces of worn furniture loaned to us, where I listened to my favorite music on a borrowed record-player — Mozart's Don Giovanni, Bruch's violin concerto — over and over again. It was a dreary time. I was separated from everything I had known and was in need of a father more than ever. Perhaps I also missed the family that had given me emotional support. Charley, Gladys, and their children were wonderful, but as much as I liked them, they were not family. They did not understand my background and they could not. Bright as they were, they had lived their lives in a world different from mine. Despite of all this, I pulled through, although it did not seem likely at the time.

That summer my mother moved to New York. Her cousin, Eva, was ready to help her. Mother was hoping to find a job and start a new life. Mother found an apartment in Queens and shared the rent with Otto's younger sister.

Around Thanksgiving I talked Laci, a young Hungarian guy, into driving his car, loaded with my mother's stuff, to Queens. Laci knew how to drive, but only had a learner's permit as he did not speak English well enough to take the test. Panni, another Hungarian refugee student, did have a license, but she did not feel ready for the two-hundred-mile trip to New York City and back. I was the navigator, quite a crew!

We drove to Battery Park to look at the Statue of Liberty and we also went to the Metropolitan Opera to hear *Lucia di Lammermoor*.

By then a fraternity took me in. The guys of *Sigma Alpha Mu* were helpful, supportive, and liberal with their gift of feeding and housing me, but I was in no state to be helped. Other Hungarian students at Penn State were able to concentrate on their studies, while I stared at my books and after a few minutes I was either lost in my own thoughts or asleep.

I felt horrible for letting down the University, the fraternity, and all the good people who made an effort to help me.

It was clear that engineering was the wrong line of work for me, but I was also in need of serious psychological help. Several years later I found the solutions.

First, I found photography as a profession. Making photographs made me define what I liked to see and to describe and through the process of visual description I learned about myself.

Second, I met Carol.

Third, I found a good therapist.

Of course, I did not quickly snap into normalcy! Even now, when I am past seventy-nine, I still carry many unresolved burdens from the past. But I found something to do that was more than a way of making a living. I found a vehicle, a non-verbal one, to focus my thoughts, my ideas, and my imagination.

Carol and I, both troubled souls, were like two one-legged cripples who learned to lean against each other and walk. But more about that later...

My self-image was confused except when I was in the darkroom of the University's Photo Club. As my first purchase from my work-study earnings, I bought a camera and that became my closest friend.

During the spring of 1958, my grades remained low, much too low. The straw that broke the camel's back was a lab class. I wrote my lab notes in a spiral notebook, as I had no idea how to type. The teaching assistant would not accept it unless it was typed. First I was angry, but later I thought he might have realized that I was not meant to be an engineer, not even an engineering student.

At the end of the semester they put me on academic probation and I left Penn State for good. That was the lowest point in my saga as an immigrant. Life was hard, but the worst of it was that I failed those who had helped me. This added guilt to my state of confusion.

New York City

By this time my mother had an apartment in Manhattan and I moved in with her. For the summer I found a job north of the City in a factory producing transistor radios. It was my last attempt at engineering.

We lived on West 82nd Street from where I took the subway around five in the morning to the last stop. From there, I had to walk quite a few blocks to the factory. This job was truly the last stop of my engineering career! The production curves of the other workers went up as they sat by the tables where the radios came along to be assembled. Mine was high at the beginning and then it fell. The foreman put me to repair those sets that did not meet the specifications of the final test. My performance was again high at the beginning and then it fell. The message, as I realized later:

Find a profession that would hold your interest; one that did not lose its thrill as soon as you learned it.

During the summer of 1958 my mother and I took a bus to visit her friends from Pécs, who emigrated right after the war, arriving straight from a concentration camp and settled in Virginia.

Our bus stopped in Arlington, where the waiting rooms, the toilets, and the drinking fountains were all segregated. It was a shock! Our hosts, who married in a Displaced Persons (DP) camp, spoke the language of red-neck Southern segregationists. He told stories about blacks with venom. Another shock!

The difficulties in the new country herded immigrants into little ghettos in the nineteenth and early twentieth centuries. These enclaves provided emotional support. When in the late 1950s my mother moved to the Upper East Side in Manhattan, a local resident could get by with very few words of English. One could buy food, clothing, furniture or jewelry by asking for a salesman in German or Hungarian. On East 86th Street they sold German sausages by their original names, and paprika and *"mák"* (poppy seeds for pastry) in Hungarian.

Becoming a Photographer

In the autumn of 1958, I signed up at a photography trade school after I figured out that the cost of the course was not much higher than the fee of an employment agency, and the school offered free placement service for its graduates. For the first time in my life I was learning something I truly enjoyed and did well. The school was far from demanding, but I made photographs I liked and made new friends.

My photographs at this trade school foretold my approach years and decades later. I photographed situations in which there was little movement; places and people in contemplation. And that remained my interest.

After finishing the course, I worked for a photographer who started his career working with Edward Steichen in the Pacific, documenting WW II from the US Navy's point of view. I saw how people made money and the commitment and concentration the process required. We photographed food, cars, bowling equipment, and anything else that came along.

For a while my mother and I shared a nice apartment; the previous tenant left behind the furniture. He also left the roaches and there were plenty!

At Curlee's studio we did interesting jobs and some traveling. In the spring of 1959 Curlee and his crew got a job to photograph a full-page magazine ad for *White Horse* whiskey to appear in LIFE and LOOK magazines. The agency wanted the use of a certain horse whose owner had retired to Florida. I remember the warm air, the sunshine, and old people. Back then they seemed very old to me, living in small cement-block buildings on fingers jutting into the Gulf. They appeared late in the morning to sit outside for much of the day and moved inside as the sun was setting.

I did not only learn about photography and what went with it, but also about the English language. I remember everyone in the studio laughing at me when I used the plural with the word *popcorn*. This brought a laugh as did my spoonerism, when I called the boss's cigarettes, "Henson & Bedges."

Curlee was renting out his small upstairs studio. The first tenant made a deep impression on me. James Abbe was the son of a photographer by the same name. His father was mentioned in photographic publications from the previous decades. Mr. Abbe was the first to note that I was a troubled young man in need of human contact. He did care. His attention to me was what mattered. As I had grown up without a father, with uncles and other male relatives who saw me as a failure, I had no male role model to follow.

I worked at Curlee's studio for more than a half a year. I quit because another interesting job became available.

Mr. Abbe had contacts in the world of photography and sent me to a friend whose beloved assistant had just left. Ervin Blumenfeld was a small chubby guy with a remarkable ego. After nearly thirty years in the US, his accent was stronger than mine. We did not communicate well. He was a Dutch Jew who escaped the invading Germans in 1940 to be locked up as an enemy alien in France, but he escaped and came to the US to become a fashion photographer.

I was an immigrant, also Jewish, and with an accent. I was also highly neurotic, another similarity. He should have understood my predicament, but after a few months he fired me. He needed an assistant, not a psych-patient. Parting ways was not a bad thing, nevertheless, upsetting.

After Blumenfeld, I had several jobs, but I planned to be an independent advertising photographer one day.

My sanity was saved after I joined a hiking club. The group went on walks in the hills north and west of the city. We went by bus or train nearly every weekend.

Finally, I had friends in America! George influenced me the most. He had been a policeman in England. He moved to New York with his family due to the acute post-war housing shortage. Here he became a plasterer, doing precision work to house huge IBM mainframes of the era. His matter-of-fact directness impressed me. George's example taught me that with a goal and a will, one could lead a life of one's choice and define one's freedom.

When I last saw him in the 1970s, he had just received his PhD in history or political science.

This was important for me as for disrupting my studies following high school, my future looked rather bleak. All my Hungarian contemporaries had completed their studies on time and had jobs appropriate for their education. I did not have the education and I felt — I did not know, just felt — that the rough and tumble world of advertising was no more my business than engineering. Realizing this took the better part of a decade.

I continued to make photographs and went on hikes. My life was full! And, better late than never, women began to interest me. When I had friends, my mother's jealousy came between us. A few years later, with a therapist, I finally started to understand what was going on.

My therapist was a woman, about my mother's age, who had worked with Jewish refugees in Europe after World War II. She had learned the patterns of her patients and led me to understand the incestuous relationship between a mother and her son when the father was gone. When this became clear to me, I set up a joint appointment for us. I felt this was the only way we could communicate and understand each other. At the last minute my mother canceled the appointment. This was in the mid-sixties. Decades later I am still saddened by her unwillingness to make the effort. I realized later that conflict resolution between a mother and her son does not require a war or death, divorce is sufficient and the outcome is nearly identical.

Fortunately, my life on the weekends was mine. I started seeing young women whom I met through hiking trips.

"Greetings" from the U.S. Army

In June, 1960, I received summons from Uncle Sam:

"Greetings...!" I was drafted! I was to appear at the US Army's Induction Center in lower Manhattan at 6 am on a specified morning. I arrived on time and walked in line with naked young men, each holding a paper cup labeled *"Urine."* I gave my sample, had my blood pressure taken, my sensory organs examined, and as we were lined up to load the bus to Fort Dix, a clerk asked,

— *Have any of you ever worked for a foreign government?* I asked,

— *Does an ROTC program in Hungary count?*

The clerk said, — *Yes! If you swore allegiance...*

So I stepped out of the line to the great envy of a young man who was close to tears from not wanting to be a soldier. I had to fill out some forms. One of the sheets asked for my addresses since 1938, the year I was two years old! So I filled out the forms the best I could while the clerks munched on their sandwiches. They took my papers and told me to go home. It was a hot July day and I was exhausted. Walking up on Broadway, I stopped at every beer-joint. By the time I reached Canal Street, I was quite relaxed.

The next day I went back to work, feeling free.

Enters Carol

As usual in my trade, I often changed jobs, met interesting people, continued to earn low wages, but life was good. I enjoyed Sundays in the forest and the people I met. Then, in July 1960, I met Carol.

We communicated well from the beginning and what was less than perfect in our relationship, we have continued to try to resolve. Now, more than fifty years later, we are still working on it!

On the Sunday after my visit to the Induction Center, the hiking group had planned a trip. At the start, a young woman was having trouble with her sack on her back. It was not made for backpacking, and I offered my help. After the day's hike a few of the guys went out to eat with her, but I was the one who got her phone number! Since then, we have been inseparable.

As the oldest girl in a large family, Carol missed much of the pleasures of childhood. We related well, talked all the time, and still continue to do so. We both had trouble with college; we both wanted to understand the world around us and we both had battles to fight with our personal pasts.

Carol and I spent much time together We often met for lunch, hiked on weekends, although, as I found out later, Carol did not enjoy walking nearly as much as riding her bike, but someone stole it from the basement of the YWCA, where she was living. Fortunately for me, she decided that walking was better than spending Sundays in the city.

In January, 1961, I was summoned by the US Army's Counter-Intelligence Service to ascertain whether I was sufficiently trustworthy to defend my new homeland. Carol responded to the news with,

— *Let's get married!*

— So we went to City Hall with a high school friend from Hungary and my mother as witnesses. Afterward, Carol and I went out to have a hot dog at *Neddick's*. That was the amount of formalities we could tolerate. We sent a letter by Special Delivery to Carol's parents, not realizing that the Post Office did not offer that service in the village of Shirland, Illinois.

My interview with the Counter Intelligence guys was hilarious. I do not think they thought so, but I was well entertained. I wanted to talk so much that they would judge me unfit for trust. They tape-recorded their interviews as they stood there in civilian clothes with pistols in holsters under their jackets. They looked funny and I kept on talking. They ran out of tape and I still kept on talking. Still, they would not consider me unacceptable and a few months later I received another *"Greetings..."* by mail.

So there we were, married, with very little money, but with hope for our relationship and our future. I continued to work for other photographers and together we contemplated our future. Carol was twenty-one, I was twenty-four. We had a long time ahead of us and we were looking forward to spending it together. We moved into a small apartment on the ground floor of a brownstone on East 89th Street. We had little furniture, a few plates and very few other dishes, but we were young and none of those details mattered. The view from our window was a stretch of concrete where stray cats raised their young.

About then, my old ulcerative colitis acted up again and I contacted a doctor who knew his stuff. Soon after, the Counter-Intelligence guys must have digested my chatter and decided that the Army could use me without endangering national security, but due to my colitis, I was rejected on medical grounds.

In another job with a photographer about my father's age, he said one day,

— *If I had the money, I would put you through college!*

Someone told me about Dr. Freed's class at the Educational Alliance on West Broadway. In Dr. Freed's monologues and the ensuing discussions I discovered a world I had always sought, although I had not known it existed. We spoke of the meaning, philosophical and psychological, a photographic image may and often does carry. The process is much too rapid for the photographer to meditate on such issues in the process of making a picture. Afterward, examining the resulting image the viewer may discover significant points of view.

We sat in a classroom with prints on display, Dr. Freed commenting, the students discussing. Decades later, the same was happening in my classes in Beloit, in Aspen and on Martha's Vineyard. I never saw Dr. Freed again, but I wish I had; I owe him a lot.

I have no recollection how we came in contact with a real estate agent, who sold us a house on West 20th Street for $22,500. It was a good buy but it would have tied us down for many years. Carol's response was immediate and desperate. She said,

— Then we cannot go to Europe!

We sold this property at a loss, but decided there were more important things in life than money and a run-down rooming-house in Chelsea.

After a few steady jobs, I started to freelance, which I did not really like. It was nice not to have a regular schedule, but I needed a more dependable paycheck. I wanted to be free to go to Europe with Carol. My citizenship paper arrived and I could get a passport. Carol spoke of traveling for a few weeks, maybe a month. I was certain that such a short time should be little more than a teaser, not a satisfying experience. So I aimed for a limit set by money rather than time.

Near the end of the summer in 1963 we parked our possessions at our friends and gave up our apartment. We bought plane tickets on Icelandic Airlines, the least expensive way to cross the ocean. We planned to spend a week or ten days in Iceland and then go on to our destination in Scotland. From there we planned to hitchhike as long as our money would last; we had little idea how long that would take. Our resources included a bunch of my relatives around the Continent; many of them I had never met before.

Carol was working for a company that produced paper-making machinery, owned buildings and operated paper mills. Carol walked into the boss's office with an idea:

— I know you have factories in Europe. My husband is a photographer. It may be advantageous for both of us if he might photograph your plants.

As a result, I had three days of work that would pay for a good part of our travels. In August, we boarded a four-engine prop-jet; our luggage consisted of two rucksacks on frames. We planned to travel as simply as we could.

Our "Grand Tour of Europe" took us all over the Continent and the details do not belong in here, but with help from my extended family in Europe, we spent on average, $2.50 a day for both of us. At that time people took along *"Europe on Five Dollars a Day."* We outdid them four times over!

Return to Reality

Upon our return to New York, my job became a turning point in my life. George, my employer, was six-foot-six, while I am five-foot-six. We had spirited arguments. It was hard to argue with a giant, but George turned out to be as close to a father as I ever had. He was not necessarily nice to me, but he learned to respect me and this was mutual. Over the years, I created a composite dad. Having a real one, should have been much simpler and would have saved me much heartache, but the few people who did help me, did change my life for the better, very much better!

I worked for George for two years, from 1964 to 1966, when it was time to see whether I should be a commercial photographer on my own. I did all right! I made more money, adjusted for inflation, than ever after, but the work did not please me. I liked photographs and I liked people. Making advertisements felt like producing tomorrow's trash. But those years were busy and exciting. I learned much about photography, people, and myself.

I wanted to go into business with as little overhead as possible. Our apartment had a 3 by 5-foot closet next to the bathroom, which I turned into a reasonably efficient darkroom with a sink and a small table. I ran in the water through a rubber hose and the waste-water into the toilet through another hose. Later, with another guy, I rented the main floor of the house for a studio. The arrangement of living and working in the same building cut down on commuting costs and time.

A medical doctor once told me the most important factor for good health was to choose one's ancestors with care. I did not do well as I inherited my bad teeth and my less than perfect posture from my mother; my tense nervous system and my stomach problems from an unknown ancestor. I suppose, the war and its aftermath also had some influence. According to a colleague of my age, also from Hungary, our generation in the old country was three inches shorter on average than either the previous one or the one that followed us. We were also cursed with bad teeth and above average kidney and eye troubles. So much for the choice of my date of birth...

On October 14, 1966, Amy, our first child was born. In the morning I delivered a job to a magazine; in the evening I was in the maternity ward to see our baby; my buttons were popping! It is a heady experience to see one's first child for the first time.

When Amy was born we lived on Lexington Avenue. One must have substantial means to raise a child in the City. We started to contemplate a move out of the City.

Freelancing was difficult and I did not like it. In 1967, a friend told me of a job in Philadelphia, but commercial and advertising work had no appeal to me. Several years earlier Dr. Freed got me interested in looking for meaning in photographs.

The eleven-month stint in Philadelphia did not only provide time to save some money but I met another person engulfed by a dilemma similar to mine. This designer had graduated from an art school and when he thought of becoming a teacher he worried little about finding a job. His professional credits were widely known.

My prospects were much less bright. I had never taken an art course and lacked a college degree. But good luck and support from Carol's parents landed me at a small liberal arts college where I had a highly rewarding thirty-year tenure.

Becoming a Teacher

My search for a way to photography as art received a boost in 1968 when, following Carol's research, I signed up for a photography workshop in Aspen. *The Center of the Eye* turned out to be the first truly successful summer-school in photography and I was there during its second year to learn much about the subject, about myself, and about a world I found fascinating. The next summer, I returned to Aspen as a teacher. By that time I was on the way to teach at Beloit College in Wisconsin, where I had had an introduction.

Some years earlier, Frank, the Chairman of the Department of Art & Art History of Beloit College, attended the Toronto World's Fair and saw great promise in multiple projections of slides accompanied by sound as a new medium. Although he was in his fifties, he had a young and fresh mind and thought of bringing the excitement of the new art form to his students. Through Carol's mother I found an introduction to Frank.

I walked in the door and had the technical knowledge, or at least certain aspects of it, to turn Frank's idea into reality. Frank and I set up shop in the attic of an old building on campus where we worked with a group of students, several Carousel slide projectors, and a punch-paper-tape programmer that could be triggered by signals on an audio tape. By today's standards it was like building a nuclear bomb with a stone axe, but our students worked hard. We also worked hard and put on a major performance in the College's Field House in the spring of 1969, after nearly a half a year of preparations.

My new work, teaching photography and working in academia, was like coming home! I understood what I did not know and, understanding that, I could fill in the voids in my knowledge.

We moved to Illinois when Amy was a year and a half. Nicholas arrived just as my students put on the multi-media show in the Field House.

My classes were full, I loved what I was doing and with my interest not only in photography, but also in the minds of budding photographers, I had a great time. Decades later, many of my students continue to tell me that they did love it as well. Some have been earning their living by making photographs, but even those who work in other fields speak of the inspiration the camera brought to their lives.

Conclusion

It appears that after a hard start in America, a decade later I found a haven of peace and fulfillment as a teacher. Looking back over the nearly six decades as an immigrant, my best decisions were:
* leaving Hungary in 1956;
* choosing photography as a profession;
* marrying Carol; and
* becoming a teacher.

This manuscript was extracted from Michael Simon's so-far-unpublished autobiography with his permission by Peter Tarjan.

TO ENGINEERING VIA A SLOW NAVY SHIP TO AMERICA
By Peter Tarjan

PRELUDE—1954
Our last year in high school was very tense in our all-boys school in Pécs in 1953-54. Our teachers were constantly stressing us about our upcoming "Maturation" exams, an ordeal following our final year; three long written tests followed by five oral exams in one day. The teachers convinced us that failing—or even doing poorly on those tests—would mark us for life as failures. This was not true, because admission to universities was not based on merit alone, but how the applicant's family fit into the socialist system. This weighed more than grades and recommendations. The favorites of the "System" were the children of factory workers, landless farmers, salaried white-collar workers without property, in that order. "Class Aliens," or worse, "Enemies of the Working Class" had no chance. For boys, the alternative to higher education was three miserable years as foot-soldiers, a most unattractive option. So… we all tried to behave very well despite being seventeen, with raging testosterone levels.

    Math and the sciences were easy for me. My best buddies were applying to medical school in our town, but I wanted to get away from home, from my paternal aunt's grasp, a survivor of Auschwitz and a widow, who tried to hold on to me like a lioness to her cub. The *Műegyetem*[4] was one of the most selective institutions in the country; 8 hours by regular train from Pécs. Secretly, I wanted a transportable profession. Physicians need to be re-licensed in a foreign land, but—I thought—engineers can find work anywhere. I was hoping to get out of my homeland in the future, from where my parents, my maternal grandparents and most of our relatives

---
[4] Polytechnic University of Budapest or *Budapesti Műszaki Egyetem*, in Hungarian.

were sent to their death by the Nazis and their Hungarian henchmen, and where communism offered neither hope nor opportunities for a free and meaningful life. I applied to the Electrical Engineering faculty of the *Műegyetem.*

My idea to leave Hungary was not new; I tried to leave with a Zionist group for Israel in 1949, but when I announced to my aunt the call to join a group, she responded: *"Over my dead body."* And that was that...

Following my Maturation exams—with excellent grades—I took the train to Budapest for the entrance examination. Hundreds of applicants were boasting about their technical achievements, bragging about their radios and electronic gizmos built from scraps. They scared the hell out of me, as I had no experience as a hobbyist and felt rather hopeless and intimidated. However, I must have done well on the written tests, because those subjects didn't come up when a panel of three dudes interviewed me. It was a grotesque setup: three men on a podium sitting behind a table, while I sat below on a bare chair. They were only interested in my parents' occupations. My father had spent his short life working for a single company. He became an apprentice tanner as he was kept out of law school on account of the *Numerus Clausus* law of 1920 that limited the admission of Jews (and other minorities) into universities. He earned a law degree by "correspondence," while working as a tanner and then he was appointed to manage the firm's office in Budapest. — My mother was a self-employed piano and voice teacher. But in 1954, although I had been an orphan for nearly a decade, those guys kept asking me about my father's possible role as an exploiter of the proletariat. After a long interrogation they let me go. – About a month later I received a letter of acceptance.

- Wow!

Engineering School

There were few survivors in my immediate family. My Uncle Kornel had lived in Zagreb since the early 1920s. He, his wife and two children spent the early '40s in Italian concentration camps, followed by two years with Tito's partisans and six years as "Displaced Persons" in Italy. They settled around Boston in 1950. — Luckily, his name did not come up during the interview! — Ágnes, my mother's sister, was living in Budapest and Böske, my father's sister, in Pécs; they were very different people and disliked each other. Böske objected to my living with Ágnes, hence I joined nine guys in a room with five double bunks in an old mansion in a suburb; a long tram ride to our classes in Pest, and even longer to the main campus in Buda. The mansion only had toilets and sinks; hence we received a weekly pass to the nearby Turkish bath. These were the conditions in the socialist state for its future professionals. But hardly anyone had to pay for tuition and most of us received a small stipend from the government to cover room and board, books, school supplies, tram tickets, etc. —I don't know how we managed to get by, but we were all struggling.

Our first day of "Orientation" produced a memorable episode. Our "Study Circle," about 30 freshmen, was welcomed by the secretary of the Communist Party of the Electrical Faculty; a thin man in his thirties, wrapped in a leather overcoat, accompanied by a silent young woman whose eyes scanned us non-stop. Comrade Secretary was babbling on when a guy—assuming anonymity—made a smart-ass comment. Comrade Secretary turned toward the voice, stared at him and said:

— *Be careful what you say Comrade So-and-so!*

Everyone was in a shock as we realized that this man had memorized our photos and names from our applications and had the power to destroy any of us. Fear was planted in everyone's heart; we never discussed our feelings toward the regime after this episode.

After some time, we moved into a former ministry building on Castle Hill with a large common shower. If my roommates hadn't already known, it became clear that I was a circumcised Jewish boy, which leads to an anecdote characteristic of the atmosphere. Our food in the mess was miserable, but on Good Friday, the entrée was a very good piece of steak to challenge the faith of each Christian. I was sitting with three of my roommates and happily began to eat my steak, while the others paused. One guy quietly asked me whether I'd like to have his steak. I gladly accepted and then the other two followed suit. I had the best meal in years, while my buddies were watching me. This was living proof that their outward support of communism combined with atheism was not even skin deep.

The Uprising
Fast forward to the fall of 1956! — Stalin had been dead for three years; Moscow's control over every aspect of our lives began to loosen up. Hungarian intellectuals began to criticize the official policies in newly formed literary circles. By October, student groups were whispering about the mandatory study of Russian, the history of the Bolshevik Party and Marxist Economics. Our university—and especially our dormitory for about a thousand engineering students—was gradually coming to a boil. A big meeting at the university's library on the evening of October 22 was followed by another huge meeting in our mess hall on Castle Hill led by Lieutenant Marián—from the equivalent of the ROTC program. A list of demands was formulated and a peaceful demonstration planned for the next day, Tuesday. We went to our classes next morning, but every place was abuzz: *Are we going or not?* — Official edicts were issued about allowing the march, and then reneged, but

finally, thousands of us, engineering students, began our march, walking arm-in-arm along the Danube to the statue of General Bem, a Polish hero of the 1848 Uprising against the Hapsburgs. Red-white-green flags were hanging from the windows along our path, but a hole replaced the emblem of the socialist regime. The speakers could hardly be heard by the enormous crowd. The rest is history…

By nightfall, overworked and underpaid workers from the suburbs came to town, broke into an arsenal and seemed ready for anything. I went to the national radio building on the Pest side, where a crowd gathered to have our demands read and heard across the country. Ernő Gerő, chief of the Communist Party, denounced the "counter-revolutionary mob" on the air and requested help from the Soviets, whose forces were permanently stationed in the country. A Hungarian tank was parked at the corner, but the crew told everyone they had no ammunition.

Later that evening I walked to Ágnes's apartment as it seemed unwise to cross the bridge to return to the dorm. Russian tanks were already rolling into the city and the next 12 days were very exciting. The events of those heady days may never be sorted out completely. After a few days of fighting, the Soviet forces withdrew and left chaos behind. Imre Nagy, a moderate communist, became Prime Minister again; new parties cropped up like weed, newspapers of every political orientation began to appear. Cardinal Mindszenthy and other political prisoners were released from jail. I joined the new National Guard at our university and recall two assignments: adventures in driving a truck loaded with hitchhikers—without having a license, and producing newsletters based on foreign radio broadcasts.

I served at the "Nerve Center" on campus. A group of students monitored the news from abroad using all sorts of military radios. As I knew a little English, I was to listen to broadcasts from the

West. Whatever we could decipher, we contributed to a newsletter that was reproduced on a mimeograph machine and then passed out around the city.

It appeared that the former communist officials accepted the change in the political system, but secretly they appealed to the Soviets to save the country from falling out of their sphere of influence. I was on duty in the newsroom at four in the morning on Sunday, November 4, when we heard tanks rolling back into the city. The newsroom belonged to the "Defense of the Homeland" faculty and an officer was nominally in charge, although it seemed a free-for-all to mess with the radios, typewriters, mimeograph machines and to come and go.

Some of our ragtag group wanted to go out to stop the tanks with our rifles, but the officer advised us that if we confronted the tanks, we'd almost certainly get killed and, more importantly, the campus would be shot into smithereens. He told us to shut down the equipment and leave one by one, or in pairs. A fellow student and I left together. As the tanks were approaching, we decided to cross the bridge to Pest to find a safe haven. The only other person on the bridge was a Hungarian soldier. We left our rifles behind, but he kept firing toward Pest despite our protests. Fire was returned and bullets were bouncing off the pavement. The soldier was shouting that his life was over but he wanted to kill as many Russians as possible. At last, we reached the Pest side alive and went to the nearby home of my childhood friend and classmate, Michael, who was home with his stepfather. Amazingly, his mother was visiting relatives in Austria—it took a miracle to get a passport. Michael offered us some food and a couch to get some sleep. We slept for twelve hours; then it was time to leave.

It was obvious that the Soviets were in charge again and rumors circulated about an exodus toward Austria. This was my opportunity to leave, but there were two things to consider:

— Did I have the right to leave my aunts, who took turns in raising me after I became an orphan in 1945?

— And whether I should stay to finish my studies — risking that I would not be charged by the new regime with "counter-revolutionary" activities--and then hope for another chance to leave with an engineering diploma?

I sought advice from Miklós, Ágnes's ex-husband, whom I had respected and loved as far back as I could remember. Miklós was an architect, but as a Jew, was unable to find work after graduating around 1923 until after WW II. During the war Miklós was active in the anti-Fascist underground, forging identity papers for people threatened by the fascist regime and the Nazi occupiers. Miklós listened to my dilemma and declared:

— *I would rather be a truck driver in the West than an architect in Hungary,* — but he considered himself too old to take off for the West on foot. He also assured me that my life belonged to me, not to my aunts. My adult life was just beginning and my aunts had had many good years along very bad ones.

Exit Hungary

I tried to team up with my cousin Juli, her boyfriend and their pals to leave together, but they hesitated. I went to say goodbye to Juli's family. Her brother, Gyuri—a brilliant young engineer—said he'd rather be a professor in Hungary under the regime that he nominally served than a dishwasher in Chicago. And his forecast almost came true for both of us: he did become a professor and a few months later I was washing dishes in a fraternity not far from Chicago. Ironically, I also became a professor three decades later. But I am getting ahead of my story.

The morning of November 21, I left Ágnes's little apartment in my hand-me-down clothes from my Uncle Kornel and a thin briefcase. I said good-bye to Ágnes, telling her that I might be back that evening or might not for a long time. I don't know what thoughts were passing through her head as she considered me her own child, but she did hide her emotions like a champion.

Budapest was in terrible shape, the streetcars weren't operating, and the tanks damaged the rails. I walked to a dairy plant on the outskirts of Buda as I heard rumors about the possibility of hitching a ride out of the city from there. While waiting all day with lots of strangers in front of the plant, I became chummy with three teenagers, a boy, his sister and his pal, who hoped to get to their relatives in Trieste. After dark, trucks began to leave the plant. Some stopped and allowed people to climb aboard. The four of us got on a tarp-covered truck heading toward Lake Balaton. We got past some Hungarian guards; they shone their flashlights under the tarp, but they didn't bother us.

The truck dropped us off at Siófok's railway station; we bought tickets to Keszthely, the last stop for this train, and settled in a cabin. The conductor checked our tickets and he seemed to know that the majority, if not all his passengers, were trying to escape to Austria. We gave him some money, and he promised to pass on any news. Shortly before Keszthely, the conductor advised us to get off at the next to last stop as each passenger would have to prove the reason for being in Keszthely. To sneak across the border was definitely not an acceptable excuse...

Some 40 people, mostly strangers to one another, got off the train at a railroad crossing in the dark around 6 in the morning. We walked westward all day and slept for a few hours in the hay loft of a farmer. The second day, a local man volunteered to lead our group that had swollen to nearly 200, but when he collected his money before dark, he assured us that we were near the border and we should walk straight to reach it. Many hours later, after two long days of walking through muddy fields, often in cold rain, hungry, and fearful of being caught, our group arrived in a village around 10 at night. We didn't know whether we had already crossed into Austria, but it was clear that our guide lied. Some folks asked for shelter, but were rudely turned away for fear of getting into trouble with the Hungarian or Russian patrols.

To our surprise, four Hungarian Border Patrolmen emerged from the dark and offered to take no more than 40 of us to the border with the condition that we would march in formation, surrounded by the four of them. In case we ran into a Russian patrol, they would tell them that we were their prisoners and they were taking us to the proper authorities. The three kids and I decided to take a chance and joined the formation. We marched in the night for a long time and then the patrolmen told us to wait for them by some hay stacks.

It was getting very cold and we kept pinching each other to stay awake and literally not freeze to death. After a long wait the patrolmen returned and led us to the plowed border where they bade us farewell. We gave them whatever valuables we still possessed and began our trek of another 5 kilometers toward the nearby village. The girl's knees began to buckle, and we took turns in dragging her along. Soon we saw the powerful flashlights of the Austrian patrol. They led us into a village, already set up for this emergency. They offered us coffee and bread and then directed us to the local tavern turned into a shelter for the arriving refugees. It was already filled way beyond its capacity. People were asleep on top and under the tables. I found a spot on the floor near the door to the one and only unisex toilet; sat down next to another fellow and immediately fell asleep. When we awoke next morning, the folks around us were really surprised as they thought we were both dead. All night people marched in and out of the toilet, stepping on us, but we never moved.

Refugee Life

The next five weeks were filled with new experiences. We were bussed to a station and then by train to Steyr, a lovely old town, where we were housed in a prison. I was in a large cell with about 20 people. By chance, my cellmates included my cousin Gyuri's three friends and bridge partners, and two of their lady friends. They had cards and as the ladies did not play bridge, they invited me to be their fourth partner. A few days later the Red Cross gave each of us 10 schillings, about 90 US cents at that time. Driven by curiosity, my first purchase was a banana. While strolling through the town, I noticed a basket of green bananas in front of a *Meinl* delicatessen. When I was a child, there was a Meinl shop around the corner from our building and the smells brought back memories. A clerk asked politely what I wanted. – Banana—I said. – How many kilos? — Nur eine banane. – I replied in my miserable German. He politely gestured to pick one out. He weighed it and asked for 2 schillings. — My curiosity backfired. I expected a wonderful experience and it tasted like mush. Oh, well…

My next adventure in the free world was at the cinema. I had studied English, but never from native speakers. English language films were inaccessible during communism. I hoped to see an American film and luckily, the marquee showed one. My ticket cost 5 schillings and I waited with excitement for the film, but it was dubbed in German… What a disappointment… but I stayed to the end in fascination and awe. The story was about a group of teenagers living in luxurious houses, driving big cars and mingling with beautiful girls. There was trouble brewing between two guys over a lovely brunette and the movie ended with the boys racing their cars toward a chasm ending in disaster. – A year later I described my synopsis to an American student, who told me that Jimmy Dean and Natalie Wood were the stars in *"Rebel without a Cause."* The film had made such a strong impression on me that I had serious doubts whether I should apply to immigrate to America where there are such crazy and wasteful people.

Officials from various governmental and private agencies began to visit our camp to discuss immigration to their lands. New Zealand appealed to me the most. I remembered a wartime joke from my childhood. — Kohn tells his friend Grün that he is leaving for good. — Where to? – To New Zealand. – Why so far? – Kohn says: — So far from what?

When I told my wiser bridge partners about exotic New Zealand, they advised me that if I went there and didn't like it, it would be very difficult to immigrate to the US, but from America — if I found it as crazy as it was in that film — it should be easy to leave for New Zealand.

I knew little about my Uncle Kornel, only that he was a mechanical engineer, who had lived in Zagreb, spent time in Italy after the war and his family was living in the Boston area. My Aunt Böske corresponded with Kornel, who sent packages of second-hand clothes to her, and my wardrobe came almost exclusively from those packages. But I didn't have his address and had no way to find it in an Austrian refugee camp. I heeded the advice of my friends and applied to immigrate to the United States.

We had an exciting adventure in Steyr. After several days of playing bridge in the prison-turned-refugee camp, our band of bridge players got scrubbed clean and led by Goncsi—a former military officer, fluent in both German and English—we went to town to an elegant coffee house where the bridge club held its weekly session. I still had 3 schillings and we possessed some strategic information, namely that an espresso cost 2.80. Our group of four guys and the two ladies marched into the establishment, sat down at a table, ordered a "simple" espresso for each and asked for cards. By the time we finished our espressos, we had played a rubber or two, when the waitress came to our table with pastries and more coffee. We were stunned as we couldn't possibly pay for all those goodies. When Goncsi told her it was a mistake, the waitress pointed to another table with four ladies playing. One of the ladies decided to treat us. We thanked them with big smiles. But then they asked us to switch partners. We couldn't refuse, so two of our partners moved to their table and we were joined by two Austrian ladies. We were lucky, as we won the first rubber, at which point the ladies reached into their purses and put some money on the table for the winners. It was small stakes for them, but seemed to be a fortune for us. We tried to refuse their money, but there was no way; those were the rules of the local bridge club! We had to continue. Never in my life had I played as carefully as that afternoon and we ended up winning a few schillings. Goncsi was a superb bridge player, he and his partner also won without breaking a sweat. But it was like walking a tightrope!

There was a very good looking teenage boy in our cell. One afternoon the two of us went to town to explore. Two school girls were examining a store display and we stopped by them. We were obviously refugees in our still scruffy outfits, but the girls smiled and I struck up the conversation by

— *Do you speak English?* — The brunette happily replied, but the pretty blond remained quiet. We walked around with them; the brunette and I were trying to communicate in English, while the other two were mostly smiling at each other. The girls had to go home, but we made a date for another day. We scrubbed ourselves as clean as we could for our young ladies. The brunette wanted to practice her English, so we talked about whatever our limited vocabulary permitted, while my pal disappeared with the other girl, and as if life were an old silent film, made out with her in a doorway. We had been advised that the next day we would be transported to another, bigger refugee camp near Salzburg, so we said goodbye to our *frauleins* and the little brunette gave me a tiny passport size photo of herself as a souvenir to remember her in America. Although I lost her picture and forgot her name, the sweet memory of chatting with her in English is still alive after nearly six decades.

Our next stop was a refugee camp near Salzburg, built by the Nazis and then inherited by the Allies. Everyone was busy with paperwork, wanting to get out of the camp and start a new life somewhere. Based on an agreement among the Soviets and the three western occupiers—the US, Great Britain and France—Austria's four post-war occupied zones were integrated into a neutral country between East and West in 1955. Due to this neutrality, US Air Force planes could not land in Austria.

Refugees heading for the US were transported to Munich and then flown, about 60 per plane, across the Atlantic. President Eisenhower permitted about 30,000 Hungarian refugees to enter the US above the existing quota. But this process was too slow and inefficient, so they took some ancient troop transport ships out of "mothball" and each ship carried about 2000 refugees to America. Austria being both neutral and land-locked, I was to cross the Atlantic from the US Navy Base in Bremerhaven, Germany.

There were problems in our new camp: overt antisemitic activities arose and even ended in fights. The other problem was food: there was very little and almost inedible; noodles with lots of black pepper for flavor. By the time we boarded our sealed train for Germany, we were really hungry. In Munich, Red Cross ladies handed up sandwiches through the windows, as we were not allowed to leave the train without visas. After gorging on those sandwiches, we had enough left for the next day, but at each stop the good ladies brought more food. At the US Navy's pier an Air Force band greeted us with wonderful jazz. Leaving the train, walking up the plank onto the ship I first set my eyes on a sea. It was not quite what I expected: dark brown water, strewn with trash. The crew motioned us to descend into the bowels of the ship and claim a bunk; those were stacked floor to ceiling four high.

Soon we were on our way toward the Atlantic Ocean. It was late December and the ocean was rough. I don't even want to describe my first experience with *mal de mer;* it was awful! Most of the day I sat on the top deck of the wildly swaying boat, close enough to the rail just in case… There was plenty to eat, but most of us ate nothing but oranges and ice cream. We were amazed when the kitchen crew dumped enormous amounts of untouched food into the ocean and we watched the creatures of the ocean follow the ship for their unexpected lunch.

During our crossing, officials of the government conducted interviews. Most spoke Hungarian and were screening for communists, potential spies and other undesirables, as well as trying to find out how we might fit into America.

There was a second-generation Hungarian-American from the Labor Department, who gathered a bunch of young men in a stairway after his day's work to chat about life in America. I joined one of these events when a lad asked him about the Ku Klux Klan which we had heard about in anti-American propaganda. He admitted that the KKK did exist and they were going after Negroes and Jews. My young compatriots nodded understandingly. — Of course… — Then our man added that they also hated Roman Catholics… — *Roman Catholics? How can that be?* — They seemed rather surprised and scared, while I cherished the moment with *schadenfreude* – as they say in German.

Christmas day was quiet and the American staff consumed all the booze they had smuggled aboard the officially dry Navy ship. They all seemed hung over the next day. — The ship was to arrive in New York a few days before the year was over, but due to the rough seas we only arrived on New Year's Eve. Our ship needed a tow to enter the port, but all the tugboat pilots were out celebrating the New Year, and our ship was anchored in the harbor for the night. At the first light on New Year's Day everyone was on the top deck watching the Statue of Liberty at a distance, and the non-stop traffic along the shore. We thought it was only a show, a demonstration of the wealth of America, as none of us had ever imagined so many cars trailing one another. We concluded the cars were going around a loop just to impress us. The short segment along the shore was the Brooklyn Esplanade.

Good Morning, America!
By ten in the morning, our ship was tied up at the Brooklyn Navy Yard, where once again, a military band welcomed us. We traveled by bus from Brooklyn to Camp Kilmer in New Jersey, where an old Army camp was set up to accommodate the Hungarian refugees.

Two soldiers were in charge of our one-room prefab with about 50 cots: an older African-American sergeant and a young private. I could not understand the sergeant, just as I was unable to understand the black sailors on the ship. But the private—a rather unhappy soul—was willing to chat and told me he was studying chemistry when he got drafted. Out of boredom, the sergeant was listening to our conversation and after he had studied my dark curls which hadn't seen a barber for at least a couple of months, he said something like, — *Don't he look Jewish?* - I am sure I did.

There was little to do at Camp Kilmer except for watching color TV showing experimental broadcasts from the nearby RCA labs in Princeton. Color TV seemed like a miracle in 1957, especially to us. In Hungary I had only seen a ghostlike experimental black and white image on a 4-inch screen in a store window. It was indeed a miracle!

A lady from HIAS[5] interviewed me. I told her about my uncle, an engineer in the Boston area and, she was confident in locating him. The next day she asked whether my uncle was a rabbi, rather than an engineer, as she was able to locate Mr. Kornel Tarjan at a synagogue. This gentleman was indeed my father's older brother, who after several periods of alternating employment and lay-offs, took a job as the superintendent of Temple Beth El in Belmont, where his compensation included an apartment. The lady talked to him and the next day, on a Saturday, a tall, well-dressed gentleman walked into our prefab asking in Hungarian for Peter Tarjan. I rushed to greet him and he looked at me skeptically. He expected his nephew to be over six feet, like my father, his own son and even his beautiful daughter. Instead he was looking at a 5-8 shrimp. Whether it was in my genes, or due to severe malnutrition—that was all the height I ever reached. After a few questions, he did accept me as his kin, and then checked me out of the camp. Soon, we were flying from Newark to Boston. The lovely stewardess offered us refreshments, which I turned down for fear of causing my uncle unnecessary expense. All the while my uncle was asking me innumerable questions about his sister, my experiences, and lots of other topics, interspersed with his dry comments about America. From Logan Airport, we took the subway and at the transfer to the Harvard line my uncle bought the Sunday paper that weighed at least five pounds while muttering about this crazy country. By the time the bus took us to Belmont, it was late into the night and we went to sleep. – The next day, Sunday, we met my uncle's wife, Aunt Jolan. They separated after 35 years of marriage, because—among other reasons—Jolan refused to move into the temple. — After a few transfers, we arrived in Sharon, a suburb, where my cousin Lucy, known as Medi in the family, was living with her husband, Nello, and their two little boys, Ronnie, about 3 and

---

[5] Hebrew Immigrant Aid Society

Gary, a year younger. Melinda was born a few months later. Suddenly my family re-expanded beyond my wildest expectations!

One of the congregants of Beth El was an MIT professor, Dr. Lion, a former refugee from Germany. Within days, through his connections, I was granted an interview in MIT's metallurgy department for a position as an X-ray technician. I had to admit that I knew little about X-rays and not much about metallurgy, having completed a year-long course in material science, where the most important item was to memorize the famous "Iron-Carbon" or Fe-C diagram. It was considered so important that when the professor's staff took attendance, each student had to sign a card and draw the diagram on its back. Without an acceptable diagram, one would not be counted as "present."

My interviewer at MIT was sufficiently impressed by my "Fe-C" diagram – but more likely as an anti-Communist freedom-fighter — I was offered a job at the hourly rate of $1.55. About eight days after my arrival in the New World, I was gainfully employed!

My uncle gave me a few dollars for a haircut, bus fare and lunch money; and I became the proud owner of a crisp little Social Security card. My supervisors included two young faculty members and a technician. The more senior professor sat me down the first day and gave me a lecture on metallurgy. I listened very carefully and had a vague idea what he was talking about, but there was one word that I couldn't figure out. He seemed to be talking about Adam. — Adam... who could that be? When he asked me if I had any questions, I asked him about this Adam. I can't describe his expression. He must have thought he was dealing with a complete moron, and repeated something about "Adam," the smallest part of matter. I suddenly realized that he had been discussing atoms in his—to me—strange accent. When I said ATOM, he seemed somewhat relieved and passed me on to his colleague, Roy Kaplow, who turned out to be a wonderful mentor and teacher. – Roy placed me under the supervision of their technician, who taught me how to make tiny sintered bricks from various metal powders, which were fired in an oven and then subjected to X-ray studies.

I was introduced to an undergraduate, a fraternity boy, who spoke a little Hungarian, who tried to orient me about college life. He attempted to explain the difference between dormitories and fraternities, but I could not understand the concept of being "brothers" with a bunch of guys just because they slept under the same roof, while others could not be brothers because they lived in a bigger building, a dorm. Strange country...

Hail Purdue!
Meanwhile, Van—Kornel's son, née Ivan in Zagreb—was a sophomore in mechanical engineering at Purdue, studying on the G.I. Bill after his service during the Korean War. Van was raised tri-lingual: the family spoke Hungarian, their nanny spoke German and everyone else spoke Croatian. When he was about eleven, their troubles began. They were interned by the Italian occupiers on an Adriatic island. When the Germans took over, the Italians let them escape and join Tito's partisans. Van was a little patrolman at the age of 12. After a couple of years, the Jewish followers of the partisans were sent across the Adriatic to Southern Italy, already liberated by the Allies. During the next few years Van learned Italian while he was an apprentice typewriter mechanic at the famous Olivetti firm. They immigrated to the US in 1950. Van learned English quickly and began to sell vacuum cleaners door-to-door. He realized it was a dead end and joined the US Army during the Korean War. He spent 33 months in Korea was discharged as a Master-Sergeant. He enrolled in a high school equivalency program, followed by Purdue.

When Van learned about his younger cousin in Boston, he called, and called again—always "collect"—and convinced me to visit him as soon as I had enough money for airfare.

By the end of January I had my first paycheck and asked Roy to let me take a few days off to meet Van. Roy graciously agreed and with $50 borrowed from my uncle for my return, I flew to Chicago, where I had to purchase a second ticket to West Lafayette. I boarded the DC-3 with my cardboard suitcase. We landed in 20 minutes and to my surprise the stewardess announced:

— *West Lafayette, the seat of Purdue University.* — I thought the first stop was at Gary. I took my suitcase and headed toward the exit, while a guy entered the plane, grabbed my suitcase and we both descended from the plane. To my great surprise, there was a crowd of about a hundred people standing around the stairs and there stood Van in his green Army overcoat, whom I instantly recognized from his photographs. We hugged while a camera was flashing, and Van whispered to me to give a press conference about my experiences as a freedom fighter. I had no idea what to say, so we all walked into the building, where Van delivered a speech, in English, of course, which I hardly could follow. The crowd included Rabbi Engel, the director of Hillel, and representatives of various student organizations and fraternities. How Van organized this, I'll never know, but his roommate was a photographer, who took numerous pictures, developed them that night and somehow forwarded them to the Chicago, Indianapolis and Lafayette papers. Their Sunday editions carried our photo and the story about *"The arrival of the first Hungarian freedom fighter at Purdue."*

I don't remember how we spent the next day, Sunday, but Monday morning Van led me to the impressive Administration Building, where we were recognized from our photo in the Purdue Exponent, the school's paper, and then received by the Dean of Foreign Students. Within fifteen minutes I became the recipient of two scholarships to cover my $300 tuition for the first semester. I was admitted as an "unclassified" student and was sent for advising and start classes immediately.

Van was absolutely wonderful! He shared his room with me and introduced me to everyone he knew, and he seemed to know everyone. Rabbi Engel arranged a $150 grant for me and someone took me shopping for my textbooks, supplies, a slide-rule at the campus bookstore and for a small new wardrobe, as I was wearing a much-too-big suit, donated by the Red Cross in Steyr. The clothes in which I began my journey were far gone, especially for an undergrad at an American university.

Rabbi Engel arranged invitations for me to the three Jewish fraternities; all willing to accept me as a guest with the condition that I'd be working in their kitchen and dining room for room and board. I was to choose a "house" to live in. I was also invited to have dinner in one of the girls' dormitories with a group of Jewish girls.

Once or twice a week the dorm residents were to dress up for dinner, so I sat with seven elegant and glamorous young ladies, looking like movie stars to me, but I was hardly able to converse with them.

After the formal dinners, I chose to join the Sigma Alpha Mu fraternity, but I don't remember why. I shared a tiny room with a sophomore, a formal young gentleman with an impressive collection of shirts, pants and jackets in our closet, where my wardrobe took up only a few inches.

Classes had already started and I was enrolled in three EE courses and in English for Foreign Students. Despite the classes being small, I didn't connect with any of my classmates; I was studying alone with quite a bit of difficulty understanding the technical jargon.

Meanwhile, I had to write to Dr. Roy Kaplow and explain why I abandoned the job they so generously offered me at MIT. He sent back a very nice note along with my last paycheck and his best wishes. Many years later I came across his name as a developer of a thrombus filter for the vena cava using Nitinol, a "shape-memory" alloy. I tried to reach him and learned that he died of a heart attack in 1982.

For the summer—with Van's help—I got a job at Teletype Corporation in Chicago, where he had established himself as an ace designer during the previous summer. We drove to Chicago in Van's big old Dodge and shared an attic room in an old brownstone building at Lincoln Park. We spent virtually all our time together at work and after, and we took evening classes at the Illinois Institute of Technology. After I registered for Freshman English and bought my textbook, I browsed around in the bookstore before my first class. At the opposite end of an aisle, I recognized Peter Dallos, whom I last saw in our English class in Budapest. He was also enrolled in the same English course while working at Zenith Corporation. He is a Professor Emeritus at Northwestern University; an international authority on the physiology of hearing, who became an accomplished sculptor in his retirement.

Teletype hired a few summer interns and assigned each one to study a novel printing method to accelerate the output of machines. I was assigned to study electrical discharge techniques. Not knowing about the Xerox process, I managed to develop reasonably legible electrostatic dry printing, but the process was already patented by Chester Carlson in 1938, although the first Xerox copier appeared only in 1960. My weekly salary was $90—I felt rich. One of Van's girlfriends "fixed me up" with her girlfriend and I felt confident enough to ask her for a date, my first date in America.

Back at Purdue… Rabbi Engel needed caretakers at the Hillel building and offered the job to Gene Pergament and me. Gene was a doctoral student in plant genetics. Saturday afternoons we went shopping in his old Chevrolet when all perishable items were reduced by half before the store closed for Sunday. Neither of us was much of a cook, but we managed to get by. Gene was a fan of T-bone steaks, which he smeared with mustard and baked in the oven. I could not understand why he cherished those overdone, sour-tasting steaks. – The parents of one of Van's buddies sent him a stack of frozen steaks from Montana. He invited Van and me for a feast and for the first time ever I had a rare steak. It was an awakening!

During the first weekend of the new semester Hillel held a mixer; there were five guys for each gal in the undergraduate body and this was a great opportunity for the guys to check out the new crop of girls. There was a cute little freshman with bright and shiny eyes, very dark bangs and an outgoing personality, and—to everyone's amazement—she wanted to be an engineer. In those days the majority of the women either studied Education or Home Economics, a field that has remained a mystery to me. I'll never know why, but Andy took an interest in me and this evolved into a wonderful companionship. She corrected my papers for grammar, but she was too smart to need my help with her math and physics classes. Although we spent lots of time together during that year, at the end of her freshman year she went home for good and I felt very lonely for the rest of my stay at Purdue.

Gene and I shared all sorts of chores at Hillel for our rent-free apartment. My scholarship no longer covered full tuition, so in addition to my savings from the summer job, I also earned a few dollars setting up the furniture for Sunday school and working at the Computing Center as a data plotter for a buck an hour. The Burroughs 205 computer calculated the coordinates of boxes representing the components of an aircraft in various projections, and we sat at a long worktable plotting those points on a sheet of graph paper. Whenever I had an hour, I went there to earn a dollar.

After a while they offered me a job to babysit with the computer once a week from midnight to 8 am, when I had to go to a class. As I arrived in class—always a few minutes late—I promptly fell asleep. Despite this, I did well enough to graduate "with distinction" two years after my arrival.

The job required me to stay awake and watch a bank of red lights on a console. When a specific one lit up, it was a prompt to feed a punched paper tape into the tape reader and then continue watching the lights. When an emergency light came on, it was time to phone the technician on call. I often had to call this poor guy around 3 am to come and fix the machine. He was my classmate, but as an ex-G.I. he had gained considerable experience with electronics during his service. He tottered into the huge lab half asleep—grouchy as could be—and ordered me to turn off the overhead lights. Then he opened the door of each cabinet until he found the culprit, a vacuum tube that did not glow in the dark. He quickly replaced it and was on his way back to the sack while I continued babysitting. The tubes had a "Mean-Time-Between-Failures" of about 1000 hours, so with thousands of tubes, these events were far from infrequent.

After my first semester as an "unclassified" student, the university granted me credits without proof for all the preliminary courses in physics, math and chemistry and even for 12 credits of Russian. Yet, I still needed to earn a lot more credits to compensate for the mandatory ROTC for my native-born classmates and other non-technical subjects. With very heavy loads, I graduated in January 1959 with the BS in Electrical Engineering. I applied to a few schools to work on my master's degree as long as their application fee was not above $10. Purdue offered me an assistantship and when I received a similar offer from MIT, the Dean—a former MIT professor—advised me to go to Cambridge, instead of staying.

Back to MIT

In January, 1959, I was back in the Boston area. Reflecting upon my worldly goods: I left Budapest with a briefcase; arrived in the US with an additional shopping bag; left Boston with a cardboard suitcase, and when I moved back to Boston, I had to spend about $200 of my life savings on Railway Express to ship my stuff. This left enough money to pay for my room at the Graduate House and about a dollar a night for dinner for the first month. A few times during that first term I went to visit either my uncle in Belmont, or his wife in Brookline, who regaled me with lots of stories about the family, along with a solid meal. Jolan was a very good cook and she loved to have my company. Although she had lived almost all her adult life away from her homeland, she enjoyed our chats in the only language in which she was conversant, Hungarian.

After a year at MIT I had to report my income to the IRS. One of my buddies discovered an accountant who had the idea to claim our tuition payments as a business expense for maintaining employment as research assistants. The IRS did not object and we got our refunds; mine was about $200. At the age of 24, I was dreaming of having wheels, like a typical American teenager. My girlfriend was studying at Brandeis and I was tired of taking the bus there and hitchhiking back after midnight. There were two options: either an old scooter for about $150 and $50 for insurance, or about $50 for a car and the rest for insurance. She was afraid of riding a scooter in Boston weather, so I bought a beat up 1949 Ford from a post-doc from Poland, who wanted a "little more dependable" car to tour the country before returning home. The car was a "one-door" model, because the passenger door was permanently locked in a collision. – Imagine the expression on the face of the cop during my road test for my driver's license when I told him that he had to get in from the driver's side and slide across. No surprise, he flunked me!

Before my second attempt, a friend took me to Watertown to practice stopping on an infamous steep hill and then moving forward without rolling back, or else I'd flunk the test again. The old Ford had a start button directly over the handbrake, which could no longer be locked; it had to be held with considerable force. Sure enough, the cop ordered me to climb that hill and stop along the way. I pulled on the handbrake and as I pressed the gas pedal, the engine stalled. I was in a real pickle: pulling on the brake handle with my left hand and trying to reach the starter button with my thumb seemed impossible, but while twisting the ignition key, the engine did start and we began to move. I could feel the officer's cold sneer. — As we stopped at the Police Station, I was certain to have failed again, but as the cop was sliding across the front seat, he hissed:

— *Come inside to get your license!* — Hallelujah! — I became a driver! Free and independent!

Vagabonds become land owners

By August, 1960, I finished my thesis and had a job offer from General Electric in Syracuse, NY. I plowed all my earthly belongings into my ancient Ford and five hours later arrived in Syracuse, my home for the next seven and half cold and miserable years.

At GE I met another engineer, originally from Bratislava, Czechoslovakia. Peter Stark and his buddy, George Jarny had escaped from the Eastern Block during a stop in Berlin in 1959 while traveling with a tour group to the East German coast. "Stark" and "Jarny" were wannabe globe-trotters and the three of us met in Miami for a two-week vacation in Jamaica and Haiti in August, 1961. We were all stateless, without passports. Permits from the

INS allowed us to re-enter the US and we headed for the Haitian Consulate for visas. Surprise! The consul suspected us of trying to settle in Haiti. — No visas!

The Jamaican consul was very nice and wished us a pleasant stay on his beautiful island. That night we stayed in a small hotel without air conditioning on the "wrong" side of Collins Avenue on South Beach. It was too hot to go to sleep, so we went out to explore Lincoln Mall. Unlike today, it was a deserted area with little to do, but, we passed a store front with pictures of astronauts and palm trees in the window that aroused our curiosity. A bored man was leaning against the entrance. As I was more fluent than my pals, I asked the man about those pictures.

— *Come inside, boys!* – he replied and we complied. In ten minutes we left as partners in a one-acre lot somewhere "near" Cape Canaveral, with the not-too-convincing promise of orange trees on our land. It was ours in exchange for a $10 American Express "Traveler's Check" and 10 bucks a month for about 10 years. To our credit, we paid it off, but never set eyes on the property. Many years later I was driving north for a family vacation and asked a gas station attendant along the Interstate highway how to get to Canaveral Groves. He scratched his head and then said:

— *There is no way to get there!*

But many years later we received an offer and sold it for about six times what we paid for it, but in real purchasing value, it was probably a wash at best.

Jamaica was beautiful, but driving on the left side almost ended in disaster several times. We rented a Jeep in Ocho Rios and drove through a lush jungle with villages fit for an adventure movie. The Haitian consul in Kingston welcomed us and issued our visas to his country. All was well; we could use our prepaid tickets. Unlike Jamaica, Haiti was very poor and terribly depressing in the days of Papa Doc's dictatorship. We stayed in an old, run-down hotel where a taxi driver befriended us. He offered to drive us around in his big Chevy for a fixed fee per day. He took us up in the mountains to a place that appeared to be either an inactive school or a motel, where he informed us in a mixture of broken French and English that we could obtain some sort of protection there. The owner, a Voodoo doctor or *Houngan* had a good racket: Before a client would go abroad, the doctor gave him a talisman. If the client did well, he'd send money to the doc. If he had problems, the doc would send another talisman. – The Houngan treated us to some scotch and then tried to hypnotize us silently in his bizarre chapel. It didn't seem to work, so he asked in Creole that only one of us should stay with him. We all chickened out and left without his "protection." But who knows what was in that bottle of Johnny Walker.

Settling down…
From Syracuse, I commuted to Boston every couple of weeks to visit my girlfriend. To share the expense and have company, I met Marty, a history student at Syracuse and a Brandeis alumnus who wanted to visit Marsha, his fiancée, in Waltham. We became good buddies and after a long ride Marsha invited me for dinner at the apartment she shared with Susanna. On the way back, Marsha was having a major meltdown over Marty's departure. Susanna and I were waiting uneasily in the living room until the crisis ended.

In 1962 I became a US citizen; Marty was one of my witnesses. That summer I got my very first passport and took off on a five-week trip to Western Europe with my buddies from Bratislava. For the first time in six years I was able to talk to my aunts by telephone.

A few months later Marsha and Marty were married and living in Syracuse. Susanna was back with her parents in Manhattan and she often borrowed their car to visit "M&M." I often joined them and we had a good time. To make a long story short, Susanna and I were married the day after Christmas, 1964, more than 50 years ago. Earlier, I quit my job that I hated at GE and also became a PhD student at Syracuse University. Susanna decided to work on a master's degree in Social Work. We were both on fellowships and lived the reasonably care-free life of graduate students.

My pleasant memories of graduate school are tied to our friends, fellow sufferers. At the end of February, 1968, I presented my dissertation. Two days later we left Syracuse and haven't been back since. By then "Freddy Fetus"—of unknown sex—was growing inside Susanna's womb. I also had a job lined up in Miami and we decided to blow our life savings, which wasn't much, on one long trip. We parked our rusty VW in New Rochelle with Susanna's aunt and uncle, and flew to London to see Panni, whom I hadn't seen since 1946. Panni was my mother's closest friend, who protected me during the tail end of the Fascist period in Hungary. We stopped in Brussels, Amsterdam, Paris and Vienna, then took a short, but very tense flight to Budapest. Poor Susanna was a wreck as she wasn't sure which moment some Hungarian goon might steal me away for good. After all, I did take part in the Uprising, left the country illegally, and they considered me a deserter. When I did not show up at the university in '57, the army sent me an induction notice to my Aunt Böske's address. The poor old lady showed up in lieu of me and gave them my address in West Lafayette. The army then sent me a postcard via sea mail (if anyone remembers that...) to report about a month before the card arrived, or else...

Those two weeks were tense in Budapest and Pécs, visiting my aunts, a few more distant relatives and friends, but at last we were back on a plane to Vienna, then to Istanbul and to Israel, where we were blown away by everything and even considered looking for a job at the Technion. But we did return via Athens, Rome and Florence to New York in early May. By then Susanna had grown a substantial belly and was tired of her maternity outfits that she had already worn for 11 weeks. The VW did start up and I drove to Miami to begin work at Cordis Corporation, a medical device manufacturer. A few days later Susanna arrived by plane, we found an apartment and waited patiently for Joshua's birth.

We planned to stay a year or two in Miami, but we have lived here for more than 47 years. We have lots of friends, mostly transplants from various parts of the world, and we gather for Thanksgiving, Seders, birthdays and other occasions. This is our family now.

Aaron arrived three years after Joshua. By then we had a little house on a canal where the boys and I could swim and raft on a huge inner-tube.

My job had its ups and downs, but it let me see much of the world as I became a technical ambassador for the company around the globe. Meanwhile, poor Susanna had to cope with our boys and crazy dogs. — There was no Skype in those days.

After 19 years at Cordis, I was invited to apply for the chairperson's vacant job in the Department of Biomedical Engineering at the University of Miami. The timing was good. In my third career I became a teacher and administrator of a small, but rapidly growing department.

After 22 years at the University, I retired. Looking back over more than five decades, it's been a pretty good run. We have enjoyed a comfortable life and a carefree retirement. The joy of having grandchildren is great; we have three winners. But I need to confess that despite all these years, connections, friends, ties, I have never really felt totally at home in America. Although I am aware of my accent, I cringe when people ask me from where I came from. — Politics is part of one's life. I have sympathized with progressive ideals all my life, yet when I enter into a political argument with a right-wing, native-born person, I am always on guard the person might say something like,

— *If you don't like it here, why don't you go back where you came from?*

No way… My home is here, my heart is here and I hope this country will grow closer to what I consider a just, prosperous, hate-free and peace-loving ideal. These are dark times all around the world, but one must remain optimistic that the sun will shine on all of us again.

AN UNSUCCESSFUL ATTEMPT TO EMIGRATE

A scene in Budapest, ca. November, 1956

https://www.google.com/search?q=budapest+1956&biw=1024
&bih=520&tbm=isch&imgil=NPc09Z8I3IpAUM%253A%253B0K
U_Zx2A2xkoWM%253Bhttp%25253A%25252F%25252Fwww.a
mericanhungarianfederation.org%25252F1956%25252Fphotos.
htm&source=iu&pf=m&fir=NPc09Z8I3IpAUM%253A%252C0KU
Zx2A2xkoWM%252C&usg=__9At1Vt3GZM7f2SwdLt5YNaKvI
Ow%3D&ved=0ahUKEwjcgvP2noLMAhXFbB4KHcQyBVEQyjcIM
Q&ei=b1EJV5yPI8XZecTlIlgF#imgrc=NPc09Z8I3IpAUM%3A

TEMPTATIONS
By János Várkonyi

The First Temptation

To begin this story, on January 18, 1945, the Red Army liberated the Budapest Ghetto. At that point, I was almost certain that my father became a victim of the fascists.

Following our liberation, there was a tremendous food shortage in the city, and we took trips to the countryside for food, usually riding on the roof of the train.

— Why on the roof? — one might ask.

Due to the great food shortage in Budapest, many people traveled to the country on not-too-frequently and irregularly run trains, which were so crowded that there was room only on the roofs of the wagons. City people took their valuables and excess clothing to exchange those for food.

I finished fourth grade with good results, partly because the teachers felt guilty about the events of '44. I spent the summer, from July to September, with a well-to-do farming family in Nyirmegyes, arranged by the National Help Movement. Upon my return I became an extra burden on my mother; so… at the beginning of October, 1945, she decided to request my placement in the Jewish Orphanage. This—of course—was coupled with lots of arguments, but at the end, parental will prevailed. Her main motivation: she felt that she could not provide for me properly. The food situation in the Orphanage wasn't much better, but it did improve considerably after April, 1946.

Dr. Mór Lederer was the director of the Orphanage, whom I had known since my early childhood. He was living in the same building as my grandmother, and he frequently played hide-and-seek with me when I was about four or five. He was one of three people whose behavior, integrity and humanity became my role models throughout my life. The other two were Dr. Fülöp Grünwald, the Principal of the Jewish Boy's High School, and Dr. János Strasser, my home-room teacher in the same institution.

At the end of August, 1948, while I was in the Orphanage's summer camp, I heard that 30 kids were invited by a Swiss Jewish organization for a 3-month long physical improvement program starting in September. The age limits were 4 to 12, but even though I was already 13, they included me in the group.

Sure enough, early in September we set out. The trains in Austria were still in bad condition. We had to cross three occupation zones, each time with severe security checks. On the third day, I found myself in the main railroad terminal of Zurich, with a little tag hanging from my neck with my personal information. The younger children were taken to an institution, and three of us were placed with Jewish families in Zurich. I was sent to the Sussmann family; they were Orthodox and they had six grown children. The house had four stories with a flat roof. On the street level, Mr. Sussmann had a tablecloth factory with 6 or 7 workers. On the first floor, the two oldest Sussmann boys operated a textile wholesale business. The couple lived on the second floor with one of their daughters, Rachel, a university student. There was also a room for prayer, which served as their synagogue; they did not belong to a temple. Mr. Sussmann was very happy when he found out that I already had my Bar Mitzvah, thus I became a permanent member of the minyan.

Jona, a tailor of about fifty, lived on the third floor along with Sosa, a university student from Prague. Both were distant relatives of the Sussmanns. Another son was living in Israel, and the youngest boy was studying at the university in Cambridge. Zsuzsa, the older girl, was living in Lugano with her husband, where they owned a shoe store.

Services in the little prayer room usually included 20-25 people, some of them of Hungarian origin. Only Mr. Sussmann, who was from Ujpest, and the girl from Prague, spoke Hungarian. Although I didn't speak German or any other foreign language, I had no problems understanding the people. I picked up a little bit of "Switzer Deutsch" and generally, from the tone of the conversation, I could extract enough to understand what was discussed. This must be some sort of a special talent I have. Later in life, whenever I was among people who did not speak Hungarian, I could make myself understood with the little bit of English and Russian that I knew. For example, in 1998, my wife and I went on vacation to Mallorca. Before the trip, I learned about a hundred Spanish words, and by using those, the waiter in the hotel did not believe that I could not speak Spanish.

— What did I do in Zurich? — may be the next question.

First of all, I was an important part of the daily minyan. I also helped mailing the factory's packages from a nearby post office. Mr. Sussmann was his own salesman; he traveled a lot and sometimes took me with him. This way, I had a chance to see Bern, Basel, Lugano and Winterthur. In my free time, I got together with the other two boys, and Sosa got me some Hungarian books, which I read voraciously. Often, I visited Marianne, the wife of the oldest Sussmann boy, who was from Budapest and was about 19 or 20.

I never felt homesick, because I liked my surroundings, and I knew that the situation was temporary.

One day Mr. Sussmann told me that on the next trip I should take along a bathing suit. He finished his business fast and we went to a pool. After splashing around a while, we settled down for a long conversation. He asked about my family, about the Holocaust, and finally popped the question:

— *Would you like to stay with us permanently?*

He said that after raising six children, a seventh would not be a problem. He also suggested that after a few years my mother could join me.

It was a difficult decision. On one hand, my mother's letters left the decision to me, although she did emphasize her love for me. She knew that my life would be much better in Switzerland. On the other hand, no other member of the Sussmann family encouraged me to stay. — Finally, I decided to return to Hungary as I missed my mother, the rest of my family, and my buddies from the Orphanage. I also wished to live in our old surroundings, and the memory of my father also was drawing me back.

I left for Hungary in the middle of December and arrived a few days before Christmas. I was well fed and well dressed. I thought I made the correct decision, but my future life contradicted this. Mr. Sussmann handed me a very nice farewell letter with a request, not to read it until I got home. I wrote several letters to my Swiss family, but never got an answer. I assume the main reason was the government's censorship in Hungary.

My story is proof that maturity arising from the experience of life lags behind by years of physical maturation. Although I had lived through hard times by the age of 13, I was very naïve. In reflection, I realize that sentences starting with

— What if…, don't make much sense.

Mr. Sussman's Letter—Dated Zürich, December 7, 1948

My dear János,

On the occasion of your return home, I'll write a few lines as a souvenir. Simply stated, as I have told you before, the most essential feature in the life of a Jewish person is to strive toward self-improvement toward becoming a real person. The best and easiest way to achieve this is by trying to live by all of our holy laws along every path, under all circumstances. It is not enough to pray every morning or evening, although this is an important requirement, but the main item is to be accommodating toward everyone. Never forget that not only now, while you are a child, should you stand by and love your dear mother, but when you become and independent person, always remember your late father and your obligation to your dear mother. Always follow your teachers and don't forget that there is a limit to mischief.

I am convinced that you have the foundation that regardless of what profession you choose, you will become competent and productive. Speaking to your heart, your plans will only reach fruition if you accept my recommendation that you make a promise to yourself never to forget your Jewishness throughout your life.

Mrs. Sussmann wishes you much luck in your life, and asked that you should always wear the "tzitzit.", Believe me, it is not to be ashamed of, and in your adult life you'll be proud of it.

I hope you'll make this promise and will not forget it.

Throughout you entire life our home will remain open to you. You don't even need to ring the doorbell, you return as our son and we will all welcome you as we all learned to like you very much, especially our dear daughter, Schoscha and the entire minyan.,

We are sorry that you had to leave this beautiful country, but I trust the time will come when we meet again.

Although I do not know her, I send my respects to your dear mother and your teachers; and please deliver those small items to my brother which we had sent with you along with the letter and with our regards as soon as possible.

In summary, I wish you all the best and hope you arrive home in good health and continue your studies with enthusiasm. We also wish that you should be able to become a good engineer and be able to move to our holy land, Israel.

Write to us about your life and I promise to reply, although without perfect idiomatic Hungarian, but you will understand it.

We all send our love to you,
        your parents for your vacation,
           Mr. and Mrs. Sussmann

The Second Temptation

In the early days of June, 1953, I must have been the happiest man in Budapest. I had completed my comprehensive final exams with good results; perhaps because I did well, or because the judges overvalued my performance. Unfortunately, I had no one else to evaluate realistically my strengths and opportunities. I decided to become a mechanical engineer, a very popular line of work in those days, for which I had absolutely no talent. But, I had to discover that shortcoming on my own.

At that point, I had already lost all my contacts with the Orphanage, with my high school, and was in a new—to me foreign—environment. Twice, in 1953 and in 1954, I started my studies in mechanical engineering at the Technical University, but for a variety of reasons, I never got as far as the second semester.

My home situation wasn't very good either. My mother remarried in 1951, and my relationship with her second husband was not good.

I held various jobs: a machinist's helper in the baking industry, a pipe-fitter for ovens, an administrator in a shipping office, and a laborer in a warehouse. I finished this phase of my life in the shipping department of a pharmaceutical company; my job was to assemble shipments. I worked with very pleasant people and my boss was a nice guy.

In November, 1955, I was drafted into the army. They sent me to the aeronautical officers' candidate school, where after six weeks of basic training, I received an education in the electrical systems of airplanes. The theoretical part of the training was excellent, but its practical side was poor. In September, 1956, I was sent as a Private First Class to the air force regiment in Kiskunlacháza, where I was not even allowed to touch the radio equipment in the MIG 15 fighter planes.

The political life of the country was becoming unstable. The majority of the people wanted changes and expected those to lead into a more liberal and democratic direction. The conditions at the regiment were somewhat loose and chaotic. For instance, one Saturday, when I was the officer on duty, I tried to assemble a list of names for roll call. No matter how many ways I tried, I was missing seven people. I asked my sergeant what to do, and he answered:

— *Just mark them off as being on furlough.*

After that, my adventures came fast and furious, and I will continue my story in diary fashion.

Sunday, October 21, 1956
I was in a unit of 12 people under the command of an officer. There was a possibility that this unit would have military police responsibilities within a given area. At 10 am, we got a radio

message that in a nearby apple orchard American leaflets were dropped from balloons. My buddy advised me that in case we are attacked, I should fire at the enemy. I had a Russian-made machine gun with an ammunition drum containing 144 rounds.

We did not find any balloons, or leaflets. Apparently, somebody beat us to the scene. But we did collect a lot of apples and took them back to the guys in the barracks.

Tuesday, October 23, 1956
The entire world knows what happened in Hungary on this day… There are numerous books and movies about the events of this day and what followed. — But what happened to me?

October 24-25, 1956
At the regiment, the mood was peaceful, but worried, because most of the personnel were from Budapest and its environs, the center of the revolution, and we were concerned about our families and friends.

October 26-27, 1956
A sizeable portion of the personnel asked the commanding officer for the transfer of the regiment to Budapest, to participate in re-establishing order. No one could respond to this demand, because by this time the leadership of the armed forces, as well as our regiment, had fallen apart.

October 28, 1956
Due to the passivity of the commanders, roughly sixty percent of the regiment deserted. They left on foot, by car and some by trucks. A few naval officers—with guns in hand—tried to stop the deserters, but they failed. The deserters broke through the fence by the runways and set out toward Budapest. I did not go with them.

— I tend to be faithful, but in those days this was more of an instinct than logic.

October 29-30, 1956
Those who stayed behind tried to follow the events through the radio. The service branch of the commanders changed from day to day, but without any effect.

October 31-November 4, 1956
On the 31st, under the command of a captain, four of us were ordered to guard duty at the gate. We had no idea how long this normally 24-hour duty would last. The captain was an older officer, perhaps past 40; a decent guy, who let us take turns to rest on the cot in the guards' room during the day.

After two days, he requested a change of the guards, but the commanders dragged their feet. We followed the events of the revolution as much as we could through the radio. In the meantime, a plane with Hungarian tail markings was dropping leaflets on which a "General Szilágyi" called on the Soviet forces to leave Hungary, or else be bombed by the Hungarian Air Force. The general, apparently, wasn't quite aware of the true situation. There were plenty of aircraft, but no one to fly them.

In the early morning of November 4 we became familiar with the "Soviet Sandwich." I was standing guard in front of the gate, when I heard some loud noise, as if tractors were approaching. It was dawning and I could see the highway where a tank was followed by an anti-aircraft gun, then another tank and another anti-aircraft gun, and so on in a long line. The noise was followed by eerie quiet. A little later we got the word that the Soviets had completely surrounded the 21 fighter planes and 3 bombers standing on the runways. Not even a bird could take off from there.

November 4, 1956
After four days of guard duty, we were relieved.

My friends and I decided to get some sleep, took four cots into the library and locked the door. Early next morning, we heard some noise and words in Russian. They were knocking on our door, but we remained silent. One of us looked out a peep hole: the Soviets were capturing Hungarian soldiers and herding them into another building. Once our building was empty, we hid our guns under the mattresses and joined those already captured. We were in a large dormitory room; it was strange and uncomfortable.

In the meantime, the remaining commanders were holding a discussion with the Soviets. In the end, we were taken to another dormitory with beds. The Soviets took responsibility for our feeding, and we were ordered not to leave the room. The Hungarian commanders were to inform us about the next steps.

November 6, 1956
A T-34 tank and its four-man crew were guarding about 80 to 100 Hungarian soldiers. The guards and the guarded became friendly, which was manifested mainly by the exchange of goods.

November 7, 1956
Some of the soldiers in our group decided to escape through the side, where there were no tanks. With two of my friends, István and Karcsi, I chose the same route and we left around 2 pm, after lunch. By darkness, we arrived in Dunavarsány and we got some food and lodging in the municipal office building; I slept on a desk.

November 9, 1956
Our aim was to reach Soroksár, István's home town. This journey was a little more exciting as we often heard gunfire. We saw a low flying plane with Soviet tail-markings shot down.

István arranged lodging for Karcsi and me with a family, and he went home to his parents. Our hosts were very kind: they placed a huge pot of beef stew with beans and small dumplings in front of us, followed by a big plate of plum dumplings. They apologized that they could only give us one bed, but since we were slim, we would fit. This was the first and only time in my life that I slept in the same bed with a man.

November 10, 1956
Our hosts at Soroksár provided us with a map of Budapest. Contemplating our circumstances, we decided to go to Karcsi's uncle in Zugló by avoiding Ferihegy, the main airport. As we were walking, a military jeep pulled up next to us. The driver was a youngish man, around 30, dressed in a variety of clothing. He looked like an officer; and he asked,
— Where are you guys going?
We told him and as he was going in the same direction, he offered to take us only if we were unarmed, because we had to cross an area where Soviet artillery was dug in. Since we had no weapons, we got in and set off. The area with the Soviet artillery was no problem. They let us through, once we told them that we were unarmed. Our officer was getting fuel from the Soviets, but we never found out what he bartered for it. He dropped us off about a kilometer from our goal; we thanked him and parted company. The last 500 meters, however, were not without excitement. We were already on the street of our destination, when we passed a Soviet tank. We heard something that sounded like a shot and it probably came from the church steeple at the end of the street. The tank backed up a little and then destroyed the steeple.

We went to a house with a front yard and a 7-foot tall concrete fence. The gate was locked. Karcsi was sure that his relatives were home. We yelled, but there was no answer. I boosted Karcsi over the fence and then climbed over myself. We knocked on the door and a man looked out the window. He recognized Karcsi and let us in. A few minutes later we were sitting in the apartment of Karcsi's uncle. He was a man in his fifties, a firefighter, and he brought us up to date on the situation. He also introduced us to the rest of the occupants of the building, who were mainly railroad workers, firemen, or low level government employees. They spent their days mostly in the basement due to frequent gun fire, but they definitely spent the nights down there. They slept on mattresses and blankets spread over the firewood and coal. They combined whatever food they had and the women did the cooking. The men tried to go out to get supplies and also guarded the house. They made room for us in the basement and exempted us from guard duty. I tried, but was unable to sleep. The two guards on duty were checking on the kids and I heard one of them say to the other:

— *Look at those boys, they sleep like logs.*

The next morning, Karcsi's uncle looked over my attire, only my boots were of military origin, the rest of my outfit looked like a collage of a firefighter and a boiler repairman. — I said goodbye to the people and to Karcsi. I got to like this high school educated country boy, but—unfortunately—I have never met him again.

I began the last few kilometers of my trip to Budapest.

Everything went smoothly until I reached City Park. There, I tried to stay in the shadows of trees, because I saw a lot of unsavory characters. I saw a fresh grave, where Queen Elizabeth Avenue and Mexico Avenue cross, in front of a restaurant called Vadászkürt—Hunting Horn. "Jenö Herzfeld" was the name on the grave. From the name and the date of his birth, it became obvious that one of the boys from the Orphanage was resting there. — I walked along Damjanich Street and turned onto Rottenbiller Street, where I noticed a bunch of teenagers with submachine guns. I tried to avoid them and got to the corner of Munkás Street. My father's older sister, Mária Verebély—to whom the family referred to as Mariska Weisz—lived in that building. She was an old maid, 59-years of age, and I wanted to see her. Plus, she had a telephone. From there, I called one of the tenants in my mother's building and asked her to tell my mother that if everything goes well, I would be home by dark. Sure enough, I was home by 4:15 without any problems.

November 11-22, 1956
In those days, it was said that I took a "vacation" from the Army. For reasons I can't recall quite clearly, contact with my mother had been somewhat sparse ever since I joined the Army. When I got home, I found out that my mother and her second husband had separated.

I visited some of my relatives and my great love, Vera Spitzer, who was the younger daughter of the kosher butcher in the neighborhood. I had some money saved up and consolidated the household's funds. I also spent a lot of time standing in line in front of food shops.

In the middle of November, Dr. Ferenc Münnich—the head of the Armed Forces and second in command to the new Prime Minister, Kádár— called upon all soldiers, who had left their posts, to register at designated centers and resume their duties. I thought this over, and while I would have liked to have more "vacation," our funds were running low. If I returned to the military, my mother could manage a bit longer on the remaining money.

November 23- December 4, 1956
On November 22, I reported at the officer's school. They reorganized the guard battalion, promoted me to corporal and assigned me to command a light-machinegun unit, even though I

had never seen this weapon from close range. We were to guard the Ministry of Defense and other important military sites. Four of us, a farm boy from Gyula, a power station technician from Tata, Gyula Trebits, an agronomist from Ujpest, and I shared a room in the Ministry.

One day, while I was alone with Trebits, he asked me whether we were from the same village. My answer was:

— *If you are also Jewish, then we are.*

This was the beginning of a great friendship. We had similar stories: his father was also killed in the Holocaust and he also acquired a step-father with a difference; his stepfather was also Jewish, but they weren't the best of friends. He also had two step-sisters.

Thirty-one years later we became relatives: his nephew married my daughter. Sadly, we lost him early; two days after his sixty-second birthday, he died of a fast-spreading colon cancer.

In the Ministry of Defense, life was tolerable. We were on 24-hour guard duty every other day. In between, I had a chance to see my mother, relatives and friends. During those days, I thought a lot about emigrating, and my new friend, Trebits, had a similar idea.

The offices of the Ministry were rather shabby, but strangely enough, the telephones were working in every room. I called Lilli, my father's sister-in-law. Her daughter, Éva, answered the phone; my only female cousin on my father's side, who was married to a talented architect. She told me that she, her husband and her brother-in-law had decided to leave the country. I was welcome to join them, but in that case, I should be in front of their house at 8 am the next day as they would not wait. This conversation took place at 5 pm. I had only a few hours to make a decision, not a lot of time...

I weighed the possibilities:

If I try and succeed, I am going into uncertainty, without any language skills. If I stay, I am still looking at uncertainty.

I also analyzed the situation in a selfish manner, not thinking about my mother's needs.

Then I was wondering about how the border patrols might behave. In October, when the armed forces fell apart, the border guards remained intact. In the first few days, they did not try to close the border; they left that duty for the Soviet troops. Once Kádár came to power, this was no longer feasible. However, their instructions weren't quite clear. Once anyone was caught at the border, the captive's fate depended strictly on the patrol's commander. I had no civilian ID. It would not have been a problem to obtain civilian clothing, but if I were caught, it would become obvious that I was a run-away soldier and would be treated as a deserter.

In early December, it seemed I was more likely to be caught than to escape and I wasn't about to take such a chance. I did not go to the meeting, and by 9 am on December 4, I knew that I would spend the rest of my life in Hungary. Here ends the story of my Second Temptation and I never got another chance.

HELPING A FRIEND

IN THE NAME OF FRIENDSHIP
By Andrew Handler[6]

Ever since I became fully conscious of my abridged childhood—thanks to the Nazis and their hapless and sometimes reluctant cohorts, as well as the communists who in the name of communal cooperation robbed me of privacy, space and independence—I relentlessly prepared to leave the land of my birth for greener pastures. The destination of my dreams was red-white-and-blue. I learned English, became a life-long devotee of jazz, and an ardent admirer of the Harlem Globetrotters as well as professional football and heavyweight boxing. I also frequented the American Embassy—an admittedly risky undertaking frowned upon by the Hungarian Secret Police. No less dangerous was my plan to experience America by smell. Virtually a daily routine was walking by the nearby garage of the American Embassy at a turtle's speed—the constant source of exhaust fumes coming from a fleet of Studebakers and Cadillac's, which I inhaled with delight.

My world of pretense collapsed under the weight of reality. In the fall of 1956 a group of reform minded intellectuals brought down the much maligned communist regime. For a short time the gates of our confinement flung open and my family and I sprang into action without hesitation. We locked the door of our home—a place of respectable, middle class existence – dressed only as if we were going to work—and took a prearranged departure by truck and motorcycles to the Austrian-Hungarian border, which we

---

[6] Andrew Handler died unexpectedly from a heart attack in 2012, after he had requested manuscripts from his friends and former schoolmates at his Jewish High School in Budapest for this volume. He left behind this hand-written manuscript, which was extended by the personal recollections of Susan Meschel and Peter Tarjan.

crossed under cover of darkness. We managed to reach Vienna and never looked back.

After spending two months in Vienna, we were transported to Bremerhaven for a twelve-day long crossing of the Atlantic in the cramped quarters of a US troop carrier, the General LeRoy Eltinge.

The ship passed the Statue of Liberty and our first stop in the US was Camp Kilmer. From there my father's cousin, a doctor who had left Hungary in 1939, and who had become our official sponsor, took us to his apartment in the Bronx. With that the pieces of my American dream fell into place.

In quick succession the stages of reaching that dream gave no hint of anything but smooth transitions and a gratifying conclusion. With the help of generous scholarships, I completed my undergraduate studies at the University of California, Berkeley, where I was also "adopted" by the Pi Lambda Phi Fraternity and subsequently received a PhD at Columbia University. I was fortunate to secure a position as a historian at the University of Miami, Florida, where I stayed for thirty-two years before retiring in 1997. I married in Florida.

Only once was my blissful academic existence interrupted by a potentially ruinous sequence of a seemingly innocent undertaking. In 1972 I received a sabbatical leave and decided to tour Europe with my wife and parents. As the latter still had relatives and friends in Budapest we agreed to take a side trip to a still communist, albeit somewhat mellowed Hungary. So far, so good...

Andrew Handler died suddenly in 2012 and was not able to complete this essay. However, as a former schoolmate and friend for many years, I felt compelled to gather as many tidbits as possible from our joint friends to jot down the gist of the adventure the title indicates. Andrew and Peter Weinberger, nicknamed Pedro, had been good friends throughout their teen years. Pedro was a great athlete and he shared many of his interests with Andrew, who was an excellent soccer player and a tennis youth champion. Pedro was not able to escape from Hungary in 1956.

When Andrew returned for a visit to Hungary in 1972, he decided to help Pedro escape. This could not be done legally. The Hungarian borders were closed toward the West and a special permit for travel to the West was only possible if the traveler's family ties guaranteed the person's return.

Andrew—in possession of a US passport—managed to get a ride with a diplomatic car from Budapest to Vienna to accompany some confidential documents. He hid Pedro in the trunk. A talented author could write an entire novel about this venture. I can imagine the danger, the stress and excitement of that ride to Vienna. Unfortunately, we do not know the details of this escapade. Andrew succeeded in getting his friend out of Hungary and to Vienna. According to my sources, Pedro settled in Israel for some years.[7]

What was surprising and amazing to most of us, who knew Andrew quite well, that he would even think about participating in such a risky venture. He was a very cautious, logical individual, perhaps somewhat intimidated by travel. Certainly, he was never an adventurer, but in this case he rose to the occasion to save his friend and provide him with a chance of freedom.

Susan V. Meschel

After 19 years of working for Cordis, a medical device firm in Miami, I joined the engineering faculty of the University of Miami in 1987. Shortly after, a Jewish organization held a dinner to honor Raoul Wallenberg, and I was invited along with other survivors, who

---

[7] Pedro was known as Peter Weinberger in Hungary. It is not known what he had done in Israel, but after several years he returned to Hungary, possibly to be with his widowed mother. The last news about Pedro was about his suicide in Budapest. – All those who knew more about Pedro are gone.

benefited from the rescue work of this brave Swedish diplomat. Several survivors at this dinner were interviewed by a reporter from The Miami Herald. When Andrew Handler saw the article, he invited me to contribute my story of survival in Budapest for the collection of stories he was preparing for publication with Susan V. Meschel with the title, "Young People Speak…"

This was the first time anyone asked me to write about my recollections and once I began to write, it became a flood. I delivered the long manuscript and Andrew cut it back to just a few pages. It was intended for teenage readers with short attentions spans—he consoled me. — Andrew was a very efficient and severe editor.

A few years later, he asked me again to write about my experiences after World War 2 in Communist Hungary, which appeared in "Red Star, Blue Star."

Finally, he asked for one more manuscript during the fall of 2011 for a third collection of stories about what happened to me once I escaped from Communist Hungary. My manuscript reached him by e-mail around February, 2012, but he had a heart attack around that time and I learned that he died of another heart attack a few months later.

Despite being on the faculty of the same university, we probably would never have met, had it not been for his initiative to "adopt" me as a fellow alumnus of the Jewish High School in Budapest. There was another "adoptee," Éva Székely, an Olympic gold medalist swimmer and multiple world record-holder who remained in Hungary. In fact, she was at the Melbourne Olympic Games during the Uprising and returned to Budapest, probably because she had to leave behind her baby daughter whose mom and dad were sent to the evil capitalist world to harvest medals for their untrusting native land.

It was around 1992 that Andrew asked me to visit and deliver a $20 note to Éva during my visit to Budapest. They had corresponded extensively as Andrew was very interested in sports, especially in the achievements of Jewish athletes from Hungary.

When in Budapest, I called Eva and asked whether I could visit her. She graciously agreed and I soon showed up at her small apartment on the Buda side of the Danube with some flowers for her. One of her rooms was filled with her trophies and medals from her amazing career and it left me—a former high school swimmer—in awe. When I tried to give her the 20 dollar note, she did not want to accept it and asked me why Andrew sent it. I had no answer. Shortly before leaving, her similarly distinguished daughter, Andrea arrived, who was also an international swimming star and record holder. Her father was the captain of the Hungarian Olympic gold medal-winning water-polo team. Genes do matter…, along with incredible devotion, discipline and perseverance to the sport.

Éva Székely also asked me about Andrew and after many years of correspondence, she was as much in the dark about Andrew's private life as I was.

Andrew's interest in sports was multi-faceted. He was an avid tennis player, but I have no idea who his partners might have been. He also rode his bike long distance, but people seldom saw him on his bike as he rode at the crack of dawn.

Andrew wrote a book about Jewish athletes in Hungary and—according to his former classmates—he was a fine soccer player.

His academic life was also quite private. Andrew had a tiny office in the History Department, where he spent as little time as possible. A few times I was able to talk to him there during one of his mandatory office hours.

After Andrew's untimely death, Susan Meschel asked me to get in touch with Debbie, Andrew's widow, whom neither of us had ever met. I did not even know her name until then. My task was to

Transplanted Lives ◆ 117

retrieve any manuscripts from his home computer for this book. Debbie graciously allowed me to come to her home near the university's Coral Gables Campus and led me to Andrew's den, a combination of his office, his art studio, library, exercise room and private museum. I was able to turn on his ancient IBM computer and found less than a dozen files. His paintings and exercise equipment densely filled the den and there were hundreds of books and a collection of curios.

Andrew Handler was a prolific academic author. There are 11 of his books in the catalog of the University's Richter Library with subjects ranging over Jewish history, sports, legends, a monograph about Wallenberg, the two anthologies of the recollection of his fellow high school students and a few others.

Susan Meschel and I do hope that Andris would approve the way this volume turned out a few years after his death.

Peter Tarjan

A LIFE-LONG FRIENDSHIP FROM COMMUNISM TO USA
By Susan V. Meschel

Recently, in my book club the members talked about how they do not even remember the names of their high school friends. This conversation set me thinking about how different my experience had been. Some of my friendships lasted a lifetime. The conversation motivated me to write about my long lasting relationship with our Triumvirate, Judy, Marie and myself, from 1948 to 2011 and in my heart even beyond that time. Our relationship survived life hardships, Communist repression, illegal escape, immigration and survival in the New World.

Judy and I met in seventh grade at the Jewish grade school in Wesselényi Street in 1948. In a large class of about 45 girls, we picked each other out soon after the beginning of the school year. We talked a lot about many different things, discussed books and shared those. Judy invited me to their home in Buda. I met her mother, who made a deep impression on me. She had on a high neck, long sleeve, dark housedress and her hair was covered with a kerchief. Instantly I knew she was a very observant Jewish lady. She did not look like women in Budapest, but rather as an orthodox Jewish woman from rural Hungary. Those communities were destroyed by the Fascist terror in 1944. Mrs. Borit appeared to be a survivor from a Chasidic Northern Hungarian town, such as Szatmár. She seemed to be a very strong and courageous person. Mrs. Borit mentioned that she asked the Rabbi's permission to use bacon to feed her children during the Nazi occupation of Budapest. I could certainly empathize with such a request for my own parents asked the Chief Rabbi's permission to use hormone supplements for my mother since those were extracted from swine. I learned from Judy that her mother was ill at the time. I did not meet Judy's father until many years later, for he was not home when I visited. In

1949 Mrs. Borit passed away. I never knew what her illness was and as I understood the children did not know either. Mr. Borit kept it a secret and did not allow an autopsy.

That same year the new Communist government nationalized the schools. Our Jewish grade school was disbanded and the students were required to attend the closest neighborhood school, which for us was at Dohány utca 32. Judy and I found each other again in the same class of about 42 girls. I tried to comfort her, for she never fully recovered from losing her mother, but she did not want to talk. Many years later she expressed her professional opinion, *"It was very bad timing to lose my mother at that age."* I argued, *"Is there ever a good time?"*

Our last year in the elementary school was most difficult for both of us. Judy was struggling with the loss of her mother and later her father's second marriage.

My father was a CPA, head of the Finance Department for the Jewish Community Service in Budapest. He wanted to be a lawyer, but could not enroll at a university on account of the Numerus Clausus law of 1920.[8] He attended many law court sessions for fun and took me along. He had interesting hobbies; he resoled all the shoes for our family and he grafted fruit trees. He once bought a tiny tree in Sorrento, Italy, which is still alive. It is huge by now and bears fruit. This is quite miraculous in the climate of Hungary.

My father had served in the forced labor units in Hungary since 1941. Occasionally he could bribe a Hungarian officer with a thousand cigarettes to let him come home on a furlough. My mother and I spent many evenings making those cigarettes with tissue paper and a special tool. In one of his last postcards he asked for kosher shaving cream and instructed my mother to hire a tutor

---

[8] The Numerus Clausus limited the percentage of Jewish students—and members of other minorities—to the percentage of each minority in the general population.

for me so I would not lose a school year on account of the bombing attacks. My father visited us for the last time in early November in 1944; we were already in a house marked with a yellow star. He promised me that he would come back and asked me to take care of my mother. I complained that his chin felt prickly when I kissed him and he promised to shave after the war. That never happened.

We received a postcard dated November 29, 1944 that his unit would be taken out of Hungary. We never heard from him again. I never completely accepted his disappearance and searched many camps and archives for documentary evidence. After several decades of search in 2006 I found out through the Bad Arolsen Archive in Germany that my father was taken to Ohrdruf, a sub camp of Buchenwald. His group was in a forced march to Bergen-Belsen. He was still alive on February 27, 1945.

In 1947 the Rabbinical Council in Budapest declared all who had not returned until then as dead. My mother married her brother-in-law, Miklós Patai. He was my aunt Lenke's husband, who lost his wife and three children in Auschwitz. My stepfather was a loving, affectionate person from a small village in Northern Hungary. As much as we had a very good relationship, I never could call him Dad.

My mother helped my stepfather's work in a small village in the north of Hungary. Their business was buying grapes and other fruit from the local farmers and exporting those to Western Europe. The grapes in that area ripened late and they were able to ship fresh grapes at Christmas time to England where those were in great demand. I stayed with them during the summer months and helped with shipping and bookkeeping, but they had to make arrangements for me to remain in Budapest during the school year. Part of the problem was that I did not want to attend school in a small town, and partly my parents did not want to take a chance of losing our half of our apartment in Budapest and our city residency permit. The government assigned so many square meters a family could occupy and we had to share our apartment with another family.

Around this time Judy and I had many problems to share. She had a stepmother, while I had a stepfather. We treated kids with disdain who had both parents alive, as if they were spoiled brats. We both were very lonely. While trying to cope with the loss of my father, my cousin Ági left illegally with one on of the last Zionist groups to make *aliyah*[9] in 1949. Ági was the cousin I felt to be closest. She was four years older and very maternal. She acted as a sister and substitute mother for me. She also instilled in me the Zionist principles and ethnic pride with stories of Jewish history, military heroes, scientists and other famous people who kept their pride in their heritage. I wanted to join her group for aliyah, but the leaders would not take kids under 16. My mother also vetoed it. Perhaps I was seeking another sister in my friendships.

Mr. Borit's new wife did not wish to take responsibility for the three children. The older brother, Adam, was living in the Rabbinical Seminary, while the younger boy, Gabor, stayed with distant relatives. Judy was given a small sublet room for herself. We visited each other frequently either in her room or in our apartment; we read books which were banned by the regime and baked potatoes in the fireplace.

Our eighth grade, the final year in elementary school, was a very bad experience socially as well as intellectually. The Principal was an ex-Nazi and several teachers were anti-Semitic and committed communists. Typical of the inferior academic level was an essay assignment, "What do you want to be when you grow up?" The title of the prize winning essay was, "I want to be Stalin's stable boy."

---

[9] Aliyah means the return of the Jewish people from the Diaspora to the Land of Israel.

The Principal had the authority to direct the graduating 8th graders either toward high school or industrial apprenticeships. Judy already knew that she wanted to be a physician, while I was very interested in mathematics and science, but had not yet focused on a particular career. We were both excellent students. It came as an unpleasant surprise that the Principal directed both of us to a two-year secretarial school rather than to a classical gymnasium, the path to a university education. As a protest against the regime, I registered in the Anna Frank Gymnasium, the only Jewish high school allowed behind the Iron Curtain. My parents were very upset and wanted me to withdraw my application. Being labeled bourgeois and "white collar reactionary" could cut off one's chances for a university education. My uncle and aunt helped me win my argument. On the first day of school I saw that Judy had made the same decision and once again we were classmates.

During the summer we spent three weeks in a children's camp supported by the JOINT.[10] Judy and I were in neighboring bunks. She developed a crush on a distant cousin who was training to be a pilot. Every evening before lights out I had to sing her a Russian pop song about pilots.

In the Anna Frank Gymnasium, we received four wonderful years of excellent education amidst warm-hearted teachers and trustworthy classmates. It was our second home on a small rational island in a sea of anti-Semitism, communist ideology and people spying on one another. During this time Mr. Borit and Adam attempted to escape from Hungary, but were caught and imprisoned for different periods of time. Judy spent every weekend visiting her father and brother in separate prisons.

Judy and I were joined by a third friend, Marie, and soon we were called the Triumvirate. Marie and I visited Judy every week in

---

[10] The American Jewish Joint Distribution Committee, also known as the Joint, is a Jewish relief organization.

her lonely little room. But Judy and I also visited Marie many times as Judy said "to observe family life," as we both were lonely. Marie's parents and sister were very welcoming to their family celebrations. We all enjoyed helping with a surprise wedding anniversary celebration for them. It was very therapeutic for both of us to feel part of Marie's family. Judy was visiting "her prisoners" every week while living alone. My parents were working in the village in the fruit and wine business nine months out of the year. They paid the relatives who shared our apartment to provide me with dinner. Judy and I usually ate lunch in the cafeteria at the Rabbinical Seminary where she could later meet Adam once he was freed. For a long period of time Judy wore a surgical tape across her mouth in class. We never found out its purpose. When we met in 2006 I asked her about it. She explained that she probably did not want to talk to anybody. We studied together, hiked in the Buda hills and discussed every teenage issue which came along. Marie usually gave advice on social behavior, how to dance and talk with boys. We could not trade clothes because we were quite different in size. I was the smallest of the three of us. However, we rinsed our hair with red onion juice to create a highlight. Of course we smelled pretty awful. Marie and I distilled alcohol from potato peels and turned it into chocolate liquor with artificial essence. We sold the bottles to relatives at Chanukah. The bottles were labeled Ferric Thiocyanate to avoid checking by the authorities.

By order of the government Russian became a mandatory subject. Judy would have liked to learn Latin as preparation for medical school, but this language was considered reactionary and banned. I studied Modern Hebrew which was altogether illegal as Israel was considered an imperialist country, friendly with the USA. However, the study of Biblical Hebrew was permitted. Judy and I were the only non-orthodox girls participating in the Bible translation contest organized by the Rabbinical Seminary.

The annual Purim ball was the big social event in our High School.[11] Many students had worked on their costumes for weeks. In our junior year I dressed up as Madame Butterfly in my mother's Japanese silk robe. Neighbors and friends helped fix my hair and makeup. Marie dressed up as Carmen. Judy did not want to put on a costume, but she did help us. We synchronized our grand entrance to maximize the drama. Marie also participated in the entertainment. She recited and acted a story of an elderly Jewish man traveling on a train, who logically figures out who is the person sitting next to him in the compartment. We rehearsed this story every day and critiqued every gesture and intonation until her performance was perfect. She deserved the roaring applause from the audience.

All three of us graduated with straight A's. Despite our grades, we anxiously waited for responses from the universities where we applied. Our worries had nothing to do with our results, but rather we were fully cognizant of not being part of the proletariat or the peasant class, and on top, we attended a Jewish High School. All these were negative factors toward admission. Judy did not get into the medical school in Budapest, but she went to the University in Szeged, a large town in the South East of Hungary. Marie and I were accepted in the Chemical Engineering program at the Technical University in Budapest. As we had no access to telephones, we could only meet when Judy came to Budapest to visit her family. As a rule only high ranking Party members and some physicians had private telephones.

In October of 1956 the Hungarian uprising took place. After a few heady days of optimism for a better life, the atmosphere changed to despair and hopelessness when the Russian Army rolled in for the second time in 12 days and took power on November 4th.

---

[11] Purim is a Jewish holiday in the spring when it is customary to dress up in costumes and perform skits about the story in the Bible.

The Russian authorities were particularly eager to catch and penalize students who participated in the uprising. My family decided to escape. Judy came to Budapest to be with her family. We had a coded telephone conversation from a neighbor's apartment. I was concerned that arriving suddenly from Szeged she might not have enough warm clothing and offered to leave her a package of shirts and sweaters when we'd leave. All this was expressed in metaphors using flowers and puppies instead of the real objects, because the telephone might have been bugged. When we reunited in USA she told me that the sweaters came in handy during their escape in December when she crossed the border to Austria with Gabor.

On December 6, 1956, Judy and Gabor took the train toward the border, where Soviet soldiers were catching a lot of people and turning them over to the Hungarian Border Patrols. Judy and Gabor did manage to reach the border. With the help of a local smuggler they walked through wooded areas and mined fields while trying to be invisible to the Soviet soldiers in the watchtowers. Judy bravely led the group, although she never had a good sense of direction. As they ran toward Austria they finally saw a sign *"Rauchen Verboten!"* –Smoking is Forbidden!" which clearly indicated that they had left behind the Iron Curtain. This was one of her happiest moments. My sign of freedom was *"Trink Coca Cola,"* the first billboard I saw in Austria.

After I found my first job in Chicago in 1957, I requested the Red Cross to search for Judy's name among the Hungarian refugees. In a few weeks I received a letter with her address in Boston. We also found out that Marie married her boyfriend, Tom Feiner, and was attending the Sorbonne in Paris. From then on we wrote 15-20 page letters to one another and discussed all our problems of adjustment, parents, health, jobs, educational opportunities and social issues.

Judy received her MD at Boston University in 1963 and decided to specialize in psychiatry. She started her training in child psychiatry, however she became too attached to her patients and her supervisor recommended that she change her specialty to adult psychiatry. Later in her career she also studied geriatric psychiatry. She once mentioned that perhaps she was trying to understand her father's behavior.

For many years as devoted she was to psychiatry, she was always concerned that Adam did not approve her choice of profession. Adam did not think of psychiatry as a science, and his opinion was always very important to her.

Marie became a chemical engineer in Paris and moved to Rouen. I earned a PhD in chemistry and married my boyfriend of several years, George Meschel. Judy was my maid of honor at my wedding. I did not realize until many years later how difficult it was and what a huge sacrifice it must have been for her to travel to Chicago. She lived on small stipend and donated blood for cash to help her brothers financially. I felt guilty for many years for having accepted her wedding present.

Marie was the first among us to have a baby, Jean Philippe. I have two daughters, Judith and Eva. Judy was not lucky in love. She had two serious relationships, but neither led to marriage. This was so ironic, for when we were teenagers Marie and I wowed not to marry until our fifties, but focus on a career. Judy was the one who wanted to be a wife and a mother. She felt that her social issues were related to losing her mother as a teenager.

A few years later tragedy struck Marie. She gave birth to a beautiful little girl, who was diagnosed with Tay-Sachs disease. Little Juliet lived only for five awful years. When she died, Marie spent six months in Sydney, Australia, visiting her parents and sister to recover. I volunteered at the University of Chicago Hospital as a guinea pig for the research on the development of the genetic test for Tay-Sachs to help other people avoid this horrible heartache. Judy and I visited Marie separately in Rouen and later in Paris. As I worked in academic research, sometimes I had the opportunity to attend international scientific meetings. I managed to be sent to Nancy, Marseille and Grenoble, and each time I made a stopover to visit Marie. It was heavenly to walk around Paris with her, sitting in the Luxemburg Gardens munching on chestnut crepes, and listening to Byzantine church music in the Old Russian Cathedral. Marie and Tom took me to Giverny. While Tom sat in a restaurant, Marie and I walked through Monet's house and garden where he painted his magnificent works.

Judy came to Chicago to visit us many times. She spent a week with us in a small resort on the shore of Lake Michigan to recover from the emotional loss of an unsuccessful relationship. She has undergone years of psychoanalysis which made her very interested in the delayed effects of the Holocaust. Judy was active in survivors' support groups and wished that I would also participate in similar activities. To her regret I did not have either the interest or the time. My time was needed for my work and my children.

My visits to Boston were fraught with difficult situations. My mother was ill for sixteen years. When the doctors gave up on her case in Chicago, my parents sought help in the Peter Bent Brigham Hospital in Boston. She was in the Critical Care unit when I visited. Judy tried her best to help me emotionally and she discussed her case with the doctors when I was in Chicago. At that time, I had a chance to visit Judy's parents. By then Mr. Borit was a frail old man. His wife was just as pretentious and selfish as I remembered her from Hungary.

Many years later we arranged to meet in Boston at winter time. We took part of the New Year's Eve celebration in Boston; we had tea at the Isabelle Gardner Museum, and Judy took me cross country skiing in the park. She also cooked lobster for our dinner.

That was the first time I ever had lobster and it was a shock for me. The poor lobster screamed in the pot. Judy recalled that I helped cook dinner for Gabor's in-laws who were visiting Adam. In despair, Adam called for help to make dinner. It was very important for him to make the right impression. I already began to cook chicken soup and matzo balls, when Adam called again. He discussed it with Judy that this was inappropriate. Judy sheepishly told me that they thought it would be too ethnic... I said, OK, we will make it into pea soup with spätzle. I felt somewhat hurt in my ethnic pride, but understood that the in-laws were an old American family and Judy and Adam wanted to fit in. I felt sorry that Judy and Adam felt so uncomfortable with their heritage in the presence of the in-laws.

Adam became a well-known neuropathologist. His research was esteemed in many countries, in the USA as well as in Israel and Europe. Adam visited us several times and once even babysat for us in San Francisco. He enjoyed running around with our children. Gabor became an esteemed historian; he specialized in Lincoln and his period which resulted in numerous books. The brothers collaborated on a manuscript about the controversy whether or not Abraham Lincoln was afflicted by Marfan Syndrome. Their joint work made Judy very happy.

One of the most memorable of Judy's visits was at my daughter Judith's Bat Mitzvah. Judy wanted to be part of a Jewish ceremony which she and I could not have. In Hungary only boys celebrated this coming-of-age ceremony. Our generation of girls was blessed in a crowd of 42. I did envy the boys for their festivities with their families. Judy also commented that she was particularly pleased to see this ceremony for she would not have an opportunity for such a ritual in her own family.

I received a long letter from Marie which deeply shocked me. She had developed leukemia and was undergoing treatment in a hospital. She felt confident about the doctor and was hoping the treatment would help her. Immediately I began my search for another conference to enable me to see her. For several months she was improving and I was hopeful for a remission. We talked on the phone a few times. Then her sister called from Sydney that Marie's condition took a nosedive and she was going to Paris. I called a week later and Marie was not able to talk. Her son, Jean Philippe, read me the notes she scribbled on a piece of paper. She requested that I should sing her a Hebrew lullaby. It took all my strength to sing it without bursting into tears. She died the next day. Two weeks later I traveled to the conference and visited their apartment. It was one of the worst days of my life. I could not believe that Marie was gone. We sat with Tom and Jean Philippe and all the time I thought this was a bad joke and she would come out of the other room, smile and say hello. I maintained contact with her husband, her son and her sister, Susan. She wrote to me that corresponding with me seemed as if a small piece of Marie were still with her.

Judy developed melanoma and had undergone three rounds of chemotherapy. Even while she was ill she continued her professional work and made many great trips. She visited another classmate from our high school in Jerusalem and many nature sites in Israel. Judy also visited the Galapagos Islands and archaeological sites in South America. She took her nephews, Gabor's boys, on many ski trips, and to nature sites. They had a wonderful, affectionate relationship.

I prayed for her recovery in the synagogue every week. I needed to find out her mother's Hebrew name as this is the custom for praying for healing. Her mother's name was Reizel. So, Judy's proper Hebrew name for me was Jehudit bat Reizel. The illness spread to her lungs. When we met for a small reunion in Baltimore in 2006, she was already quite ill. It was a wonderful reunion of four old girls, classmates from the Jewish High School in

Budapest, Vera Kestenberg, Vera Bollag from Switzerland, Judy and me. Judy and I had a long conversation; for many years we had not talked due to a serious quarrel. She said that I hurt her feelings, because I did not tell her that Marie was ill. Judy believed that it was my duty to tell her. It took me a long time to explain that Marie made me swear on my life that I would not tell anyone. I could not break my word. I told her all about my last phone call with Marie and about the visit three weeks after she passed away. I asked for her forgiveness and suggested that we should share our grief and make peace. By 2 in the morning we reconciled. I am glad for this since not long after the reunion Judy passed away and so did Vera Bollag.

I said the Kaddish[12] prayer for a month for Judy as one would for a close relative, for she had no Jewish relatives to do so as Adam passed away years earlier.

Now I am the only one left of the Triumvirate. I am blessed with the memory of the wonderful friendship with Judy and Marie.

---

[12] Kaddish is the Hebrew prayer for the dead.

INITIAL STRUGGLES
IN ADJUSTMENT TO THE NEW WORLD

A princess and a Mau

Photo by liz west from Boxborough, MA - Egyptian Mau, CC BY 2.0, https://commons.wikimedia.org/w/index.php?curid=8241906

Susan and her mentor in Chicago, 1957

C118 airplane to carry refugees to Canada

THE REFUGEE AND THE PRINCESS
By George Pick

The huge plane broke through the clouds and the runway became visible as a narrow grayish-ribbon. Inside, the 150 Hungarian Jewish refugees were exhausted after a 30-hour-flight from Munich, with stops at Glasgow, Scotland, Keflavik in Iceland and the unbelievably cold airport in Labrador, where the temperature was -40°F, and the wind hitting our faces felt as painful as if someone were scraping our skin with sandpaper.

The last two airports were NATO military bases. We were allowed to go to the Quonset huts, where uniformed American pilots sat around eating their sandwiches. There was a long, stainless steel food-container in the middle of the hut and we were instructed to help ourselves to sandwiches. I selected a ham and cheese sandwich embedded in two pieces of white bread with the consistency and taste of cotton. The ham and cheese were terribly salty and the can of Coca-Cola only partially quenched my thirst. But that seemed as if it had happened days ago. Now we were landing somewhere in America, in the U.S.A. The date was December 19, 1956, in the middle of the afternoon.

Finally, the landing gear touched the runway; the buildings around us were blurred until the plane slowed down and finally stopped in the middle of the airport. Some people saw the sign "Newark." Nobody had ever heard about it, and then someone said

— *It is in the State of New Jersey.*

Buses were waiting for us at the bottom of the stairway for getting off the plane. It took some time to get our circulation return to normal and slowly, the crowd was moving forward, down the stairway and into the buses. Only a few of us had any luggage.

The buses slowly approached a distant building away from the main terminal. There, we were "processed" in alphabetical order.

— *My name is Pick György,* — I said. The uniformed Customs Agent looked up at me and asked,

— *Your name?*

— *My name is Pick György,* — I repeated.

He had a photograph of me in his hand, and said:

— *Where were you born?* — I did not understand a word. Fortunately—next to the agent—a woman spoke both Hungarian and English. She translated for me,

— *Hol született?*

— *Budapesten,* — I answered.

— *He was born in Budapest.*

— *Birth date?* — came the next question. I was looking at her while she said

— *Mikor született?* —I responded –

— *1934 március 28,* — which she immediately translated as

— *He was born on March 28, 1934.*

A few more questions were asked, translated and answered. Then the man gave me a piece of paper to sign, it was a 2x3" card, green color, number 3119, stating: *"It is your permanent residency card,"* which was also duly translated.

Even while feeling so exhausted, something flashed through my mind.

— *My God! I am now a permanent resident of the U.S.A.!*

The agent rose and extended his hand with

— *Welcome to the United States!*

I shook his hand and slightly bowed my head. I did not know how to say *"Thank you"* in English.

We were taken to Camp Kilmer, a decommissioned US Army base. During the war it was a major transportation hub for 1.3 million Army soldiers going to the European front. I saw many

white barracks and a lot of people walking around. There, I met old friends, László A. and his wife Ágnes G. I also met one of my favorite high school teachers, "Jano," his real name was Dr. János Strasser. There were always questions, mostly
— *Where are you going from here?*
Many had no answers.
— *Let's keep in touch!*
— *Yes, let's do so!*

But, none of us knew where our semi-permanent of permanent addresses would be.

After a night with about a hundred others arranged in three-level-bunk beds, from the snoring, teeth-grinding and groaning, the noise level was almost constant; I could only get a short nap here and there, when the noise dropped to panting.

The next afternoon, buses of the HIAS (Hebrew Immigrant Aids Society) picked up the Jewish refugees. After an hour-long trip, we emerged from a long tunnel into the middle of New York City.
— *So, this is America!*
Skyscrapers, wide avenues, automobiles and truck traffic that I couldn't have imagined before. Constant blowing of horns; many, many people on the sidewalks; neon signs everywhere. Confusing, confusing... Finally, we stopped at a massive red brick building in Astor Square, the headquarters of HIAS.

Without any explanation, all the women had to stay in the dormitory in the building, but the men were transported to various little hotels in downtown Manhattan. I ended up in the Lafayette Hotel, with a pleasant enough room-mate. We had a chat and went to sleep early.

The next morning I called my uncle Károly Kornhauser, my mother's brother, who by then had morphed into Charles Carleton, MD. In mid-afternoon we were collected and returned to the HIAS headquarters. Soon, a short man with white hair approached me. I recognized him by his *"Kornhauser nose."* He seemed indifferent, neither glad to see me after 18 years, nor showing any interest. He spoke to someone and told the man that he, my Uncle Charles, was going to "sponsor" me. I didn't understand what was discussed, but then Charles said in Hungarian,

— *You don't want to do anything with these Jews.*

I was shocked! These *"Jews"* took care of me in Austria for three weeks, chartered a huge airplane to transport me to the United States and now, as I was told by someone who spoke English and Hungarian, they would provide for us furnished apartments for which they would pay the rent until we could find jobs. These *"Jews"* got me here so fast that I already had my *"green card."* I am permanently welcome here.

And by the way, — *Are you not Jewish?* — All these thoughts raced through my mind, but I was rushed to get out and get into his automobile. A white giant, twice the size of any car I had ever seen in Hungary.

— *What kind of automobile is this?* — I asked, as we were smoothly cruising through the East Side Highway.

— *Cadillac. I have to have a car with prestige for business reasons.*

We crossed the giant double-decked George Washington Bridge to New Jersey. An hour later we stopped in front of his white clapboard house in Wharton, a small town. The question immediately popped into my mind:

— *Is this America, or New York City?*

My aunt Maria and her 11-year-old son, my cousin Andrew, greeted me a bit warmer than my uncle did. That made me feel somewhat better.

Nobody asked me how my life and his family's life were during the Holocaust, nor about the ten years we had lived under the Communist regime.

— *You must forget the past! Learn English as soon as possible and become an American!* — advised Uncle Charles.

I wondered how he knew everything about the world while living and practicing medicine in this town of 4500 inhabitants, half of them Hungarians. Soon I found out that the Hungarians had two churches, one Catholic and the other Reformed. Dr. Carleton and his family became Unitarians and went to church every Sunday. I was expected to go with them to a nearby town, Moorestown, which did have a Unitarian Church. I knew nothing about the Unitarians, their beliefs — later I found out they were very nice people, who in a strict sense, weren't even Christians — but I *knew* I was Jewish and if I did not give up my Jewish identity during the Holocaust and the Communist regime, I sure would not do it in the land of the free.

Hence, my struggle began. My uncle did not believe that a refugee, who doesn't speak the language, should be idle for too long. Using his connections, barely two weeks after my arrival, I was employed as a worker's helper in a small factory. It was physically very demanding work. The bus would come by at 6.30 am. My shift started at seven, moving heavy steel rods and plates of steel to the machinists' stations who then did the grinding, drilling, lathe work, etc. with a half hour break for lunch. A few days after I started my job, a supervisor found out that my hands were not callused and my palms were soft. From then on, my main job was filing iron pieces. There are a million pieces of steel and iron to be filed in a machine factory. Soft iron was the nastiest material, due to its small but sharp shavings. Without safety gloves, these shavings do lodge inside the worker's palms, but those were not provided – today they are required by law for that kind of work.

Even months after I left this job, I was still tweezing out these irritating crystalline devils from my palms. My interminable day usually ended with another "intellectual" activity. At the end of the shift I had to sweep up the floor of the factory.

As soon as I got my first $65 check for the week, Uncle informed me that now I must pay $15 per week for my room and board. For the first three months the "American Dream" turned into a nightmare for me.

In March 1957, the International Rescue Committee –thanks to my Aunt Maria who was working there as a volunteer during and after the Hungarian Uprising and raised money and clothes for the refugees—granted me a three-month scholarship to learn English at Temple University in Philadelphia.

It was a warm and bright Sunday toward the end of March, when Aunt Maria's Buick was speeding toward Philadelphia, with my uncle, cousin and me, along with a skinny mid-size suitcase with *all* my belongings. Maria spoke incessantly;

— *Promise that you will come back often and as soon as the semester is over!*

— *Of course, I will…* — I said disingenuously. Of course, I had no intention of going back; on the contrary, this was the opportunity that I had been waiting for… to escape the extremely constricted opportunities and parochial environment of a little village. I was the product of a big city and most anxious to return to a big city and start my *"American Adventures."*

It was early in the afternoon when we reached the urban campus of Temple University and the four-story Men's Dormitory on the quiet, tree-lined Park Avenue. A tall, twenty-something divinity student was in charge. He knew we were coming and led me to my room furnished for two people. I opened one of the closets. It was my room-mate's, who was away for the weekend. It was full of neatly hung clothes. I noticed a set of Army uniforms, summer and winter tuxedos and assorted sweaters, trousers and jackets.

Across, there was another closet, empty, but with many hangers. I needed only two, one for my spring suit, a product of a Gimbel's basement sale, purchased by my uncle for me, and the double-breasted suit in which I escaped from Hungary.

I guessed that, without a tuxedo I wouldn't be considered good company on campus. On the other hand, I did not come here for a lively social life, but to study the English language.

On Monday morning, someone was knocking at the door. A well dressed, thirty-something man greeted me cheerfully in Hungarian.

— *I am Doctor Bánhegyi and I am the Official Translator and leader of our freedom fighters' group. You came a week later than the rest of the group of eleven university students from Hungarian universities. This will be a very intensive 3-month-long course of the English language and grammar and you are expected to work very hard to learn as much as you can. Your instructors shall be senior undergraduates from the School of Education of the University.*

Later on, I met the other fellows. Some seemed to come from middle-class environments, similar to mine. Others definitely came from working-class families, who had been the darlings of the oppressive Communist regime and were helped in every possible way to become the new intellectuals for the regime.

Apparently, they were not as devoted to the regime as their leaders had imagined. Soon, some discovered that it was too hard to assimilate to a totally new country, with its different culture, values and language; two of them went back to Hungary *"to face the music"* for their defections.

I remember five boys in our group. Years later, I heard about Kerenyi —by far the brightest and hardest working fellow among us, who was a third year medical student in Hungary in 1956. He had a notable career as a Research Professor of Medicine in one of the leading universities in the U.S.A.

On the first day, Miss Gertrude D. Peabody, Dean of the School of Liberal Arts, came to our class to introduce our instructors, pretty, smiling, fresh-faced, 21-22 year-old-girls. Miss Peabody was a warm, grandmotherly type, much beloved at the university. Her family must have been either rich or had very long associations with the University, because our dormitory was named "Peabody Hall."

Thus began my education in English and introduction to *American Culture*. At first, many conventions and common behaviors appeared to be confusing or misleading, even bizarre. Social signals and conventions had different meanings from those in Hungary and caused some embarrassing moments for me, and I am sure, for others.

As an example; here it is considered polite for a man and a woman, unacquainted with each other, to smile at each other, period. In Hungary, if an unfamiliar woman was smiled at a man, she was encouraging him to approach her and start a conversation. A smile was a signal to "break the ice."

It seemed bizarre the way knives and forks are used here. The constant switching of these two implements during a meal struck me as ridiculous. Everyone with good manners in Europe holds the fork in one hand and the knife in the other (lefties included). A simple process: cutting the meat a bite at a time, then pick it up with the fork, etc. No switching!

In the coming weeks most of us were trying hard to pick-up at least the rudiments of the language. I managed to learn a bit of grammar and perhaps a thousand words. I understood more than I could express, but I kept talking in my pigeon English, not at all concerned about correct pronunciation or grammar. After more than 50 years in the USA, I still have a peculiar Hungarian accent. Somehow, they did tolerate my sloppy usage – or should I say butchery – of the American English language.

I thought, sooner or later I would have social contacts with English-speaking people and pick-up the language by reading, listening to it on the streets and, as they say, in bed. Our three months had flown by much too fast. By the middle of June it was over.

A few days before the end of our program I asked Dean Peabody to arrange an interview with Professor Bohn, Chairman of the Physics Department, who very kindly gave me a letter of reference. A few weeks after finishing my course, I was able to use that letter to obtain my first professional job at the Westinghouse Corporation near Philadelphia.

I was working as a Junior Engineer in the Small Steam Turbine Division for twice the money I made as a worker's helper in Wharton.

No one spoke my native tongue, so I had to use English only, which improved rapidly.

Meanwhile, my mother in Budapest managed to send me some of my technical textbooks and a very useful Hungarian-English, English-Hungarian Technical Dictionary. Soon, I found out how outdated my knowledge of steam turbines was, despite my two semesters on heat engines, with the famed Knoudi Professor at the Technical University in Budapest.

In 1957, Westinghouse already had the first generation of computers, using punched cards. Someone showed me how to use the punching machine and "the compiler." I was able to compute stresses in complicated, multistage turbine shafts in a couple of hours. This would have taken me months of complicated hand calculations using the methods I had learned in Hungary.

At the time, I did not know that the "small turbines" we were designing were built for the first nuclear powered naval submarine, the Nautilus.

Late in August, I received a letter from Drexel Institute of Technology in Philadelphia; I was accepted at full scholarship for two semesters and possibly longer. I left my job at Westinghouse, my dear colleagues and wonderful boss, to become a student again.

I struggled very hard from September to March. There were a few Hungarian students in the program. One of them – Peter Fritz – became a lifelong friend. We spent untold hours studying thermodynamics and atomic physics. My grades were very mediocre in the subjects that I already "knew" and for which I earned outstanding grades in Hungary. My English was not good enough. As if my academic record did not give me the "message" loud and clear, I found out that it would take me four years of graduate study to get a Master's degree.

By March 1958, my mother was finally out of Hungary and stalled in Italy. She had been there for 8 months waiting for her visa to the U.S.A. The HIAS notified me that she would probably be able to come to this country by October 1958.

I had run out of time, and the economic situation in this country had deteriorated. I couldn't get my old job back and there was no other possibility in Philadelphia.

Some of my Hungarian refugee friends were restarting their lives in New York City. A few encouraged me to move there, as it should be easier to search for a job in the Big Apple than in Philadelphia. So, on a rainy, cold morning, right after my 24th birthday I boarded a train –destination– New York City.

I had the illusion that New York City, the gateway to the Golden Land, would welcome me with open arms as she had welcomed so many millions before me. What I found was the opposite; most people were disinterested at best, and hostile at worse, except for a few friends. Denes Brach—of blessed memory— was perhaps the best and most loyal of my friends. He was waiting for me at the station and told me that he had found lodgings for me in Brooklyn. Mrs. Wapnish was going to be my landlady; mine was her maid's room next to the kitchen, and most importantly, for only $25 per month.

After a long ride in the Brooklyn-bound subway we got out at the Utica Avenue station near Crown Heights, the heart of the Orthodox Jewish community in New York. The neighborhood was rather drab or more precisely, the color of the Sahara Desert thousands of miles away. But, instead of sand dunes, the tall and massive beige apartment buildings along the dirty streets were desolate and depressing without the wild and beautiful vistas in the African desert. Come to think of it, I don't know how people could live all their lives – or at least a considerable fraction of their lives – in that dirty, grimy, prison-like environment.

Mrs. Wapnish could only speak Yiddish, a language utterly alien to me. Fortunately, her son and daughter lived in the same building and when Mrs. Wapnish and I had to communicate, they interpreted.

Rule No. 1: I could never bring food to her apartment or use her refrigerator, as she was strictly kosher.

I soon discovered that my room was infested by cockroaches, but as disgusted as I felt, that would have to be my home for a while. I was hoping that my $200 would last until I found a job.

Getting a job was difficult. For the first weeks I got up at the crack of dawn and closely studied the wanted ads in the New York Times. I applied for interviews for any kind of job that I thought I could do. Everyone was looking for "experienced" workers. After I was thrown out of 4-5 places as "overqualified," I shut my mouth about my education. When I applied for a manual job, my physical fitness was far more important than my intellectual abilities. I had to sell myself as a self-confident person and I absolutely had to look "experienced." — After about a week, I finally got a job, as an operator of a machine for making plastic bags, the kind used in supermarkets for fruits or vegetables. In those days they rolled off a large drum and I was to produce a fused seam and cut the bag. There were two problems with this seemingly simple operation. First, if one let the fusion step go on for more than a fraction of a second, the result was a burned, stinking piece of molten plastic. The second hurdle was to cut the finished bags to equal lengths. The operation took 2 or 3 seconds and the film for the next bag was already moving into place on the machine.

When the boss showed me the machine and the process, I told him enthusiastically about my years of experience with similar machines. The truth came out about ten minutes later, by then I had messed up about 300 bags. Some were not welded together, others were burned, some too short, others too long. The boss came back and saw the sorry mess I made. He pulled out $10 from his pocket and told me never to come back again. I thanked him profusely. Ten bucks would feed me for a week.

I had three or four similarly short "careers" in various branches of the manufacturing industry. One lasted about two weeks, doing electrical welding on frames of commercial size steam presses, used in laundries to iron shirts. I wasn't completely lying when I said that I was an "experienced" welder. At the university in Budapest I had a one hour practice session in welding. Electrical welding is tricky. If the welding rod is held on the pieces to be welded for more than a fraction of a second, the rod melts and welds onto the pieces. The welder must pull the rod away as soon as the arc is established, and keep the rapidly melting rod's tip about a quarter inch from the pieces to be welded. Simultaneously, the rod must move along the line to be welded. If the rod moves too fast, the weld is no good. The owners were second generation Russian Jewish immigrants and —I guess—they wanted to give me the benefit of doubt. After a couple of weeks and a lot of messed up pieces, they fired me.

To make matters worse, I was a week late with my rent. My landlady turned ugly and in her native tongue called me something I preferred not to know. This attitude had evaporated when I finally gave her the money I owed her, but I learned a lesson: even if I don't have money for food, I better pay my rent.

I hit the nadir of my existence. Denes, when he could afford it, gave me a $10 dollar bill to be able to eat; and I dreaded the end of the month when I had to pay rent and had about $4 in my pocket. I had been unemployed for 3 weeks. As bad as my situation was, the one thing that never occurred to me was to go back to my Uncle's house "defeated." Never! I had not given up hope, not by a long shot. I had heard, *"Many multimillionaires started out as newspaper boys."* — There is no shame in being poor. But starting out as an unemployed? That may be a different matter.

It was then that I met the two younger Horvath sisters, Kati and Mici. Kati was the prettier one and she knew it, although Mici was nicer. Both were in their early twenties. They came out of Hungary in '56 with their older sister Jolan. Kati worked in a beauty parlor. Jolan worked in a photo laboratory.

By the end of June, I was dangerously low on funds without a job on the horizon. Finally, Jolan promised me that she would ask her boss if the photo lab needed a worker in the night shift. They had a job for an "experienced" photo technician in the darkroom. My "experience" consisted of an hour of work with my uncle in his dark room back in the old country. Jolan explained what I need to do. With all that "experience" I applied and was accepted for the job on a trial basis. My shift started at 4 pm and ended at midnight. The photo lab, Berkey Photo, was in Greenwich Village. The work was simple. There were ten little cubicles; each contained a chair and small table with a photo enlarger. Each of us received a hundred reels of already developed film and we were to make positive enlargements. One had to put the film in the machine, focus it and expose the photographic paper. Also, one had to develop a sense of exposure time, depending on the blackness of each frame, longer or shorter exposures were needed. Once the positive was exposed, we had to put it on a moving belt. At the other end, a very experienced technician placed those in the developing liquid and then the fixing solution. If the positive was either over- or under-exposed, he could compensate for it in the developing liquid by controlling the time of immersion. He was simultaneously developing 50 to 80 positives and made few mistakes. After two weeks I was permanently hired at $2 per hour. The shop was unionized and I became a card carrying AFL-CIO member; a member of a labor union in a capitalist country, while never a member of the workers' union in Communist Hungary. That irony stayed with me.

Working the late shift had a great advantage; I had time to look for other jobs. I got in touch with the World University Service. They had nothing to offer, but suggested that I contact the Rockefeller Foundation as it sponsored a small program, "Engineers in the Profession" with the goal to find university and college teaching jobs for foreign born new-comers like me. The jobs were mostly at small southern and southwestern colleges, at such low salaries that no self-respecting American would accept them; hence, the existence of this recruiting program. We did not know these jobs were not very good. For us, they seemed markedly better than being unemployed or doing manual labor in New York.

So, with nine other, mostly Hungarian and Cuban engineers, I became part of the group run by the retired Shakespeare scholar and English professor, Dr. Thornbury, I never learned her first name. Dr. Thornbury's office-mate was Princess Nathalie Troubetskoy, who met with us on Saturday mornings to teach us the English language and a bit of methodology on how to teach others. These one- or two-hour meetings were all the training most of us received in teaching, but this allowed us to include in our resumes that we were "experienced educators and engineers."

There was nothing of a fairy princess about her. In fact, if one met her on the streets of New York, her royal rank would not at all be obvious. She was short, her blond hair was cut to mid-length, her face was heavily made up, she wore bright dresses that looked cheap and were short enough that when she sat, her knees were exposed. One could not tell her age from her face. Only her hands gave a clue to her age, they looked old. But if you looked at her sparkling blue eyes, you saw youth in those, determination and not a little eccentricity.

How did a poor, Hungarian, Jewish refugee strike up a friendship with a Russian princess?

A few Saturdays later, after class I approached the Princess and asked her about her life in Russia. She smiled at me and said,

— *Well, it is a longer story than I can tell you in five minutes, but why don't you come to lunch when you have time and then I will tell you my story and you tell me yours.*

Princess Nathalie Troubetskoy[13] was a true blueblood royal cousin of the last Czar of Russia and a cousin of the reigning

---

[13] **Nathalie Troubetskoy** was born in 1897 in Lublin, Poland and was a member of an old and very influential Russian noble family. She studied art and medicine in Moscow and after serving as a nurse in Russia toward the end of World War I,

monarch of England, Elizabeth II. The Princess, who lived in England before she came to the U.S., knew Elizabeth as a princess and disliked her intensely. "— *She was a little bitch...*" — said the Russian Princess. She liked her next-door neighbor much better, George Bernard Shaw, the Irish playwright.

Three days later, I went to the Greenwich Village address the Princess gave me. It was a basement apartment consisting of a living room and two bedrooms. I noticed the cats first. They were everywhere. I tried to count them, but the Princess told me,

— *There are fifteen cats, plus one old tomcat that belongs to Dr. Thornbury.*

The cats around me were all white with gray hair patches.

— *These are rare Egyptian cats,* — said the princess.

— *Legend has it that their original ancestors were the cats of the Pharaohs. As you probably know, the Egyptians regarded cats as sacred, godlike animals. I breed these—not an easy thing—and sell them for $300 per animal."*

I looked at these furry, four-legged, yellow-eyed and mysterious felines with respect. After all, they were worth almost as much as I made in a month.

---

she and some family members escaped to England where she lived and worked for 20 years, nursing, lecturing and broadcasting. Shortly before World War II, she moved to Rome. After the liberation, the princess served as a nurse to the U.S. 2675th Regiment.

In the early 1950s, a young boy presented her with a shoebox that contained a silver-spotted female kitten. Troubetskoy's research led her to conclude that the kitten was an Egyptian Mau ("cat" in Egyptian). This breed was thought to be extinct. She acquired more cats; Giorgio, a black male and Lulu, a female. The princess used diplomatic contacts to import further cats from the Middle East. In 1956 the princess immigrated to the USA, taking three of her Maus with her to form the foundation for her cattery. The entire Egyptian Mau line traces its ancestry back to just two of these cats, the silver female Fatima and her son Giorgio. I knew both of them.

The Egyptian Mau is a likely descendant of the original African wildcat, domesticated by Egyptians over 4000 years ago.

— *The cats have a special mix of food that I prepare for them and when they get sick I administer antibiotics to them,* — added the Princess.

I also noticed that the cats were tasting the lunch that was in the process of being prepared for us. Noticing concern on my face, the Princess reassured me that the cats were clean, had all their vaccinations and their saliva was absolutely the most potent bacteria killer in the world.

— *Please sit at the sofa while I am preparing lunch,* — requested the Princess. I wore my only good suit, and I noticed that the sofa was full of cats' hair. There was nothing else to do, I just sat down and thought about how long it will take to get rid of all this hair after my visit.

The lunch was delicious and I tried not to remember that the "food-tasters" were cats. At least the stuff was not poisoned, I thought. The cats were all alive. After our lunch, she asked me whether there was any drink I would like to have. I said "coffee" and she prepared a good espresso for me. For her, she pulled out a huge martini glass, filled it with vodka, a few drops of vermouth and dropped in a green olive. She explained that this was her favorite drink, a "very dry vodka martini."

She told me how she had lived in the palace of the Czar in prewar Russia. Her father was a confidant of the Czar. The Princess herself was studying medicine and by the second year of World War I, she had completed her training as a physician. In 1916 she requested to be sent to the front and worked in a field hospital for one year. After the Bolshevik takeover of the Russian government, she and some of her family managed to escape to the West. After the war, she immigrated to England and came to the U.S. in 1956. The Princess was never married, but *"I like men,"* she said, smiling at me while pouring another huge vodka martini for herself...

I became a frequent guest at the princess's place and sometimes she invited me to her favorite Chinese restaurant, where she taught me how to use chopsticks. In that restaurant they knew precisely how she liked her martinis and she always had three. Naturally, when the alcohol started to work in her system, her face became red, her speech had a stronger than usual Russian tinge and she talked faster.

I wondered why she gave me such special attention out of a crowd of eleven men. Then, it dawned on me that almost all of them were married, that I was the youngest and alone, and most importantly, I was interested in and fascinated by her story. Nobody else cared.

There was nothing sexual on my part. She could have been my grandmother. I don't know what she wanted, if anything, beyond enjoying my company. Certainly, she never made the slightest move toward anything that was not completely platonic.

In July, our resumes were completed and sent to as many as a hundred colleges. In August, ten colleges, mainly from the midwest and southwest, such as Oklahoma and Missouri, replied to my applications offering me jobs to teach mathematics or physics to freshmen.

I showed the letters to the Princess. She advised me not to accept any of those offers. She said,

— I have friends in the upper reaches of the Catholic Church. I will get you a better position; just give me your resume. You also want to go to graduate school. These little colleges don't have any graduate programs. In a week, I will have better offers for you than you've gotten so far.

And so it happened. Princess Troubetskoy called her friends, Cardinal O'Boyle in Washington, D.C. and the Archbishop in St. Louis, Missouri. The Catholic University of America in Washington, D.C. had an Engineering School. In St. Louis, there was a Jesuit

University that had a Physics Department. Both schools had teaching positions and graduate programs.

The Princess asked me:

— Which one would you like to go to? I will arrange the interview with the Dean.

— I would like to try the Washington interview, — I replied.

The Princess was good to her word. I had the interview set up for August 22, 1958. Now, it was up to me to prove that I was capable of doing the job for which they were hiring me.

I thought that this interview, and the Dean's acceptance or decline, was going to be based on pure merit and that the Princess merely helped me by opening the door and leaving the rest up to me. Now, when I look back from a distance of more than half a century, and consider my subsequent career path, I must conclude that I was naïve and overestimated my ability to sell myself.

Yeah! I got the job. One day after the interview I received a telegram from Dean Donald Marlow, informing me that I had been accepted into the Faculty of the Mechanical Engineering Department. Of course, it helped the Dean's decision that the President of the University's Board of Trustees, Cardinal O'Boyle, called him prior to the interview, expressing interest in a young Hungarian refugee by the name of George Pick. The Princess did not say a word about it; she only expressed her delight that I got the position. How do I know all of this? Well….because that's how these things were done.

A few weeks later, my photo printer-union member-career ended and my teaching career began. In October 1958 my mother arrived in the USA.

I corresponded with the Princess during the first few months after I moved to Washington, D.C. It was in November that she wrote to me that some poison had gotten into the food supply of her cats and, despite every desperate measure, they all died. A great heart break and a big financial loss for her.

She invited me to visit her in New York for the Christmas holidays, but I couldn't go because I was very busy preparing myself for the second semester of teaching.

Finally, thanks to an unlikely event and crossing paths with an angel, my Russian Royal Blood Princess, my struggles as a refugee were over and I began building my new life in the United States of America.

Princess Nathalie Troubetskoy, wherever you are, I thank you for your help from the bottom of my heart. I have never forgotten your kindness and generosity and the way you changed my life.

FUN WITH THE LANGUAGE
By George Robert Steiner

A Problem with the Window
Some of the panes in the window frame appeared to be a bit loose in our apartment, so I decided to get some putty to fix it. I knew the Hungarian word for it, but I had to look it up in the dictionary. Secure with my new knowledge, I showed up at the nearby hardware store. Those days—pre-Home Depot—these small mom-and-pop stores were still common. I began:

— *I'd like to get some putty...* — since I had never heard the word spoken, I pronounced it something like: puTTi. After all, that's what the dictionary showed...

— *Huh?* — *What do you want?*

— *PuTTi* —I repeated.

— *Hey John,* — he called out for help — *come here and find out what this guy wants!*

This being a Polish neighborhood, some people had experience with new immigrants. John understood me and I was happily on my way to fix the windows...with my *"pudy."*

A Registered Letter
Chicago's downtown, the Loop, had a monumental classical post office building in those days. A modern Federal Complex, designed by Mies van der Rohe, stands in its place today. Architecturally it was a real beauty, but years of neglect and pollution made it look like a sooty monster of a building, its beauty well hidden. It extended over an entire city block, with entrances from four different streets. Under its central cupola there were many windows in a circle, serving various postal functions. I wanted to mail a registered letter to France. — Where do I go, which window will accept it? My two months in the country had not prepared me

for such an important decision. Even in those days, there was a policeman there. I approached him.

— *Sir,* — I said — *I should like to post this letter recommended.*

— *What?*

Well, I repeated it. He just shook his head, meaning: *"OK, follow me!"*

The French word, *"Recommandez,"* designated by the letter "R," usually in green all over the world, indicates "Registered," but I translated the word incorrectly from the French. I was able to mail my "recommended" letter at the proper window.

Sour Candy

My Mother had lived with us for 29 years and eventually made good progress with the language while totally forgetting her German. She told us this story from the early days of her immigration.

There was a little grocery store in our Polish neighborhood, just down the street. In Hungary, she used to buy a certain kind of treat, known as "hard candy" in America. Although the candy tasted sweet, due to certain ingredients it was called *"savanyu cukor"* in Hungarian. When translated word for word, it would turn into *"sour candy."* My Mother was wondering whether that store carried such an item. Dutifully, she looked up the words in the dictionary and at the store she asked for some *"acid sugar."* Even though the owners were immigrants, this request was way beyond their understanding. The three attendants in the store put their heads together. Sugar was the easy part, but why acid? Eventually, they did figure out that my mother was looking for *"sour candy,"* those tart sweets sold in some stores. Problem solved! My Mother smiling on her way home with her "acid sugar" in her purse.

Bad Words

In those days, dirty words were never printed in a dictionary. Upon entering this country, I did not speak English at all and wanted to learn the language very fast. I used every opportunity to ask, probe, investigate about meanings and spellings. The American-born secretary in our office was helpful, but often said:

— *Don't ask me why or what the rules are; I know what is right and what is not.*

I had learned a third of my English from her. Then there was this nice fellow, my friend, Renato, who knew all the rules. I had learned another third from him. The Chicago Sun-Times ran the column by Ann Landers every day. She used a lot of slang and her language was easy to understand. From her came my final third. But when I went to the job-site to inspect my first design, I frequently heard certain words which I never heard or read anywhere else. Being very inquisitive about the language, three months after my arrival, I approached a guy at the building at Lawrence and Marine Drive, a Salvation Army Center these days.

— *Say, what is this f'''n this and f'''n that?*

Almost all objects were preceded by that at that job site.

— *You don't know?* - he asked.

— *No, I don't.*

— *Hey guys, come over here, see this guy, he doesn't know that...*

They all gathered there.

— *OK, don't worry, buddy, we'll help you!* – he said.

— *Do you see that girl walking on the sidewalk?* Then he proceeded to tell me the name of her "parts."

— *Aha!* — I responded to encourage him.

— *OK, now, see that guy over there?* — Then he enumerated his "parts."

— *Now, Bubby, when they get together...*

Transplanted Lives ◆ 155

My English vocabulary was substantially extended in three short minutes.

The Silver Plate

While living in Nice, France, we received numerous wedding gifts and bought many things. It was no longer possible to fly to the U.S. with all that luggage. Marianne's relatives bought tickets for us on the Queen Elizabeth, the largest passenger ship at that time. We were hoping not to get sea sick. — Well, that was not to be. Our D-40 cabin was way down in the ship's bowels and not very far from her bow. In Cherbourg, at 11:00 at night, while we were in bed, we felt the ship moving in a moderate, but steady up-and-down pattern. It was alright for a while, but I knew, trouble was brewing...

The full range of sea sickness hit us by next morning. Our cabin did have a lavatory, but the toilet was at the end of the corridor. I remember reaching the handrail, first on one side, then on the other; the floor was moving under my feet. We could not eat. Food was the last thing on our minds. We spent three days mostly in our cabin. One of those days I ventured out alone and watched a Doris Day movie, "Teacher's Pet," but of course I did not understand any of the dialogs...

On the fourth day the up-and-down and sideways movements stopped and the world around us became calm. I would have liked to have a Coke, known as *"The Symbol of American Imperialism"* in our Socialist society in Hungary, but we had no money. Prior to our departure from Paris, we made last minute calls to my mother and to Mimi, the lady who raised Marianne in Budapest after her parents and sister were killed in Yugoslavia in 1941. We asked the operator at the post office to disconnect us after the 3 minute minimum, because we had no money for another minute; we were totally penniless. So, on the ship, we could not buy anything, but there was plenty of food, if one could stomach it. On the fourth day we felt well enough to visit the dining room, I don't remember whether for lunch or dinner. We were assigned to a table for four. A middle aged couple from England became our partners, who were going to visit their son in Chicago. Even now, I still would not know what to do with 13 pieces of silverware placed for each passenger, I counted them! The menu in this Third Class ("tourist") dining room was a thick, large format booklet with lots of choices. Even though it was in English, I spent a lot of time studying it, just to enjoy this luxury. Then I announced my choice to the astonished waiter:

"Please, bring me a single baked potato," the only thing I could handle.

Night descended on us, our last night on the ship. Our excitement was steadily rising in anticipation of our new life now close at hand. We were overwhelmed. It took some time, but finally we did fall asleep only to be awakened by someone knocking on the door. I was half awake when I opened the door. A young man in Cunard uniform stood there with a piece of paper on a silver plate in his extended hand. Marianne was also awake by then, watching us from her bed. Truly, I had never been in such a situation and it seemed natural to take the plate from his hand and I simply closed the door and was ready to study the paper. More knocks, the guy said something and Marianne gave me her instruction:

— *Give him back his plate!*

Poor guy, he not only missed a tip but even his plate was taken away. I returned the plate and returned to the paper, actually a telegram from her relatives:

"Welcome to America, at the dock Elaine's cousin will wait for you." Indeed, she did.

Transplanted Lives ◆ 157

My first impression of New York from the ship, still a vivid image, was the steady flow of yellow taxis heading north on the West Side Highway. We were approaching Cunard's Pier No. 92 near 54th Street. Soon, we stood before a uniformed U.S. Immigration Officer who checked our passports and visas. It was ironic that this happened in the First Class ceremonial room, directly under a large painting of Queen Elizabeth.

A Tale of A Hotel, a Train and the Windows
Elaine's cousin was a kind, middle-aged woman, Marianne could chat with her. Marianne's English, after years of studying the language privately in Budapest, was good enough to get along although she had trouble at times with what we called the "American accent." People in Europe follow the British pronunciation. I remember the first taxi ride with her. The cab from the West Side piers took us to the Hotel Empire near 63rd Street where we stayed. The hotel is still there, but it is now facing Lincoln Center that did not exist then.

I encountered a strange thing in our room. There was a cover for the window, but instead of a pull-down canvas shade, familiar to me, it was made of metal strips. I wanted to adjust it. I pulled a string up on the side and the shade went up, way up, but when I wanted to lower it, it would not budge. Yes, I am an engineer and I am supposed to be able figure out such things, but, I must admit, I was defeated. There was also a rod hanging on the side, but when I pulled on it, nothing happened. Despite my subsequent successes in this country, on that first morning the venetian blinds defeated me.

Elaine's cousin returned in the morning and took us on a tour of the United Nations. A year and half earlier, during the Hungarian Revolution, we had heard a lot about that organization and now we had a chance to visit those famous rooms where all those silly and ineffective resolutions were made: the General Assembly Room, the Room of the Security Council, etc. I was truly fascinated. I also discovered that the UN issued its own stamps; which cost me a lot of money over time. Then she took us to the Cloisters, those interesting medieval buildings further up in Manhattan.

Then it was time for us to go to the train station. She made arrangements for our luggage with Railway Express and we entered Grand Central Station. I had a small atlas from Budapest with a map of Manhattan. Time and time again I used to look at it in Budapest, imagining my being there, but I never dreamed of walking on its streets. And yet, here we were, in the famous railroad temple; an impressive building at Park Avenue and 42nd Street, with everything underground. We looked up to admire the Constellation on its ceiling, an artificial night sky followed by the sights of many, many artificial creations over the years.

It was time to thank Elaine's cousin and take our places on our train, the Twentieth Century Limited, for its departure for Chicago at 6 in the evening via New York state, Ohio, Indiana and Illinois; arriving at 9 the next morning on the first of May, 1958. By that time the May Day celebration, with its mandatory and nonsensical "Demonstration for the Peace" had probably ended in Budapest, but we were in New York. It seemed to be light-years away.

The coach was extremely hot. It had been sitting under the sun for many hours and we were still a half an hour from departure. Being an experienced traveler by train, I had a solution ready:

Open the window! I was ready for action, but where was the handle? Not on top, not at the bottom. Just then a Pullman porter appeared. Marianne had her first conversation with a stranger in

America, a black man. I am sure they both wondered about each other's accent, but they did make some progress. My wife learned that the window, sorry, cannot be opened. This car was air-conditioned, that is, when the engine (*What's that?*) would be connected, just before departure.

How am I going to adjust to this country when I cannot even open a window? Strange thoughts came to my mind. Fortunately, the "engine" arrived and we did depart. I was looking forward with excitement to watch the city from the train's window, closed or not, but the train traveled in an underground tunnel. By the time we saw daylight again, we were happily rolling north along the Hudson River until we turned west. It was not the most comfortable thing to sleep on the train sitting up, but, *Hey!* we were young and incredibly excited. I remember waking up and shivering. We were in Toledo, Ohio around 2 or 3 in the morning. Was it 2, or 3? No one knew. The clock was set to Daylight Saving Time, but at that time it was not uniformly set in every state. Some changed, some did not. Furthermore, the railroad schedule never changed. *But, really, who cares?* We were approaching Chicago! Gary, Indiana was our last stop.

I still keep a little pamphlet explaining the route of the 20th Century Limited and with this, I announced to Marianne our next stop, Chicago. In half an hour, Marianne, who never cries—although she did cry when we left our Riviera villa—promptly began to cry and continued non-stop all the way to Chicago. For thirteen years she had corresponded with the four people waiting for us at LaSalle Station. Thirteen years of pent-up emotions were about to reach their culmination in that embrace just minutes away.

The train pulled in and as we stepped down, there they were: four people, who changed our lives forever, who made it possible for us to have children and grandchildren born here; who will vaguely know the history of a distant past, what their ancestors experienced a few years earlier in Europe. We had made sure that our sons are fully aware of the good deeds these four wonderful people did for us and for our boys. Their names must be recorded forever: Olga and Emery Sego; Elaine and Emery Gordon. They came from Hungary, Romania and Czechoslovakia, and while childless, they embraced and accepted two young people into their midst: us! Their memory will stay with us forever!

What's My Name?
At birth I was given the names George Robert. George was my parents' choice, but there was a rich aunt who had yet to have children, so my father, in good family spirit, endowed me with her favorite name, Robert, as well. We were at the train station, just minutes after our arrival. Elaine, who had always known me as Gyuri, a familiar form of György, or George, asked me:

— *Do you have another name?*

I was puzzled, so she added:

You know… we already have two other Georges in the family. So it would be nice if we could call you by another name.

Well, I said, *I was also named Robert at birth, although nobody has ever called me by that name.*

Fine, she said, *you will now be Robert.*

Not only did my life change on that May Day of our arrival in Chicago, but my very own name as well.

They drove us to our apartment. I still remember the elevated train right above the road while we were driving north on Lake Shore Drive on a beautiful sunny day. They turned off at a bowling alley, which is still there!

The Gordons owned that apartment building. The Segos lived on the third floor. Emery actually worked in the Gordons' shop, hence their friendship. We got the second floor flat, right below the Segos. All three rooms, living, dining and bedroom, were sparsely furnished. With its full bath and large kitchen, the apartment did seem rather luxurious to us. After they left our apartment, we were alone for the first time in America. Marianne was still struggling with her tears. We needed fresh air. When I tried to open the windows, they seemed strange. Instead of opening toward the inside, like European windows, these had to be raised. Wow, it sure looked different! And they were single panes! I had never seen single windows before. How do they insulate the room? They appeared to be flimsy, and they were, in comparison to well-constructed European windows. Little did I know that insulation was not really an issue in the US at that time. Every place was overheated, not only our apartment, but everywhere.

But that is another story...

THE FIRST TASTE OF FREEDOM — AN IMMIGRANT EXPERIENCE
By Susan V. Meschel

Introduction

Our lives in November, 1956, seemed to be paralyzed by chaos and desperation.[14] The scene was war-torn Budapest, recently occupied by Russian forces to defeat the short-lived Hungarian Uprising. A rather unlikely leader, Bernard Dreilinger, awakened us from our state of apathy. He was the stepfather of my boyfriend, Gyuri. He had lived in France and Switzerland for much of his life and was more worldly and sophisticated than most people we knew. His wisdom and down-to-earth practical sense were legendary. He carefully planned a way for us to escape from Hungary. Bernard found some smugglers to take a group of us to the border area. It took us two days to get near the border, traveling on the back of a truck, riding horse-drawn buggies, and walking in snow and mud in late November. When we noticed the searchlights from the Hungarian watchtowers circling overhead, we tried to become invisible by lying on the ground. After tense hours of crawling over the minefields of the border area, we saw a wonderful green billboard with the advertisement *"Trink Coca-Cola!"* This clearly conveyed to us that we had left Hungary, were now on Austrian soil and free! What freedom meant, I did not really know. It was some abstract idea that would be lovely to have, something we had never experienced.

---

[14] My experiences during the Holocaust and under Communist regime were described in detail in the following publications; YOUNG PEOPLE SPEAK – Surviving the Holocaust in Hungary; FRANKLIN WATTS, INC, New York - 1992.
RED STAR, BLUE STAR – The Lives and Times of Jewish Students in Communist Hungary (1948-1956); EASTERN EUROPEAN MONOGRAPHS, BOULDER, CO - DISTRIBUTED BY COLUMBIA UNIVERSITY PRESS, NEW YORK – 1997.

Life in the Refugee Camp

Austrian volunteers and the Red Cross Staff arranged for the refugees to stay with farmers in the village of Lutzmannsburg, Austria. Our host was a pleasant, kind farmer who was glad to chat with my mother in his native dialect. My mother's family had lived in Burgenland for generations, not far from the Hungarian border, and she was still able to speak the local dialect.

I slept in a tall bed packed with several featherbeds. It was heavenly to sink into such warm and cozy comfort, trying to forget about the anxieties of the previous days. I slept for nearly 16 hours.

Trucks took us to an army camp in an old, somewhat dilapidated castle, called *Judenau*. Our group of refugees was an odd mixture of students, intellectuals, ex-Nazis and a few petty criminals. The latter groups took advantage of the chaos and left Hungary along with the political refugees. The elation of being free was somewhat soured for me by anti-Semitic comments in the camp. One day a large, burly guy yelled at me,

— *Dirty Jews, go to Palestine!*

I was suddenly overcome by rage. Was this the type of life for which I crossed the border? I yelled back at him,

— *You dirty fascist, you killed my father!*

And then with my head bent down like a little bull, I charged into his belly. Being a small girl, this was the only way I could fight. I winded him; he sat down and was unable to speak. I straightened my back, pulled up my shoulders, and walked out of the room with regal dignity. Not a word was uttered in the large room. There was deadly silence.

In the camp we learned to exchange clothing, trade food and information. Our next stop along the road to freedom was the city of Linz, where the HIAS arranged small hotel rooms for many of us. We stayed in the *Hotel Drei Mohren* and received 23 schillings a day for living expenses from the HIAS. This was not very much, but I still did manage to save enough to buy a pair of warm winter boots, my reward for eating goulash for 3 schillings every day. Those boots were my first purchase in the free world.

In Linz I witnessed a strange ceremony, the marriage of my mother and my stepfather. In Hungary, they were married only by Jewish rites to assure my mother's pension after my father, who was killed in the Holocaust. In Austria it seemed suspicious that they had different names. The ceremony took place in a bare, nearly empty office by a casually dressed clerk, who also played the piano and swallowed large gulps of Coca-Cola while officiating.

In Linz, we had to make a very serious decision: To which country we should try to immigrate? How many refugees would each country accept? Where would we have a chance to settle?

My parents wanted to go to Australia, because my stepfather had a childhood friend in Melbourne. My boyfriend, Gyuri's family wanted to settle in Sweden, where they had relatives. It was high drama: Gyuri was as white as a sheet and unable to talk. — I sobbed my heart out, crying that we did not want to be separated. Finally, the four parents reached a compromise: we would all try to immigrate to the USA, specifically to Chicago, where both families had relatives. The issue was still not resolved, for immigrating to the USA was not a simple matter. Gyuri and I decided to ask the local HIAS representative, Eva Eller, for advice. She was a lovely, understanding person, and showed special empathy toward our dilemma. Later, she told me that she had been separated from her fiancée during WW II, hence her sympathy and desire to be especially helpful to us.

Ms. Eller suggested that we travel to Salzburg, to the former US Army Camp Roeder, and try to register for immigration to the USA. My mother and I hitched a ride on a tractor for part of the way. The scene at the entrance to Camp Roeder seemed rather

Transplanted Lives ♦ 165

hopeless. There were thousands of refugees standing in line, all hoping to receive the precious serial number, indicating acceptance for immigration. My mother volunteered to be a translator and they gladly accepted her. She then waved us on as if we were called into the inner office area, and we marched in, ahead of the crowd, and soon obtained the coveted registration numbers. We had to wait for several weeks until our number would be called. We stood in line for bean soup and waited for a free shower stall. We played *Twenty Questions* to pass time, which we called this game *Bar Kochba* in Hungary, after the leader of a Jewish rebellion against the Romans. Our stay was memorable. At Christmas, then Vice President Nixon arrived for a visit. His bodyguards ordered us to applaud, as they said *"the Ruler of the World."* This upset me greatly for we just escaped from Hungary, where we had to applaud all the Communist Party leaders. So, I decided to be stubborn and not applaud. I guess I was testing my freedom. Would they arrest me if I did not applaud? Nothing happened; my rebellion went unnoticed.

After Vice President Nixon's tour, the Camp's administration announced new rules. It was rumored that quotas existed for each religious group, indicating how many members of each denomination may enter the USA.[15] Some of my Jewish friends signed up with the *Tolstoyan Foundation*, because the quota for Jews was assumed to be filled already. The Tolstoyan Foundation was established in 1939 by Alexandra Tolstoy, the youngest daughter of Leo Tolstoy,[16] to aid political refugees, and they did not ask any questions about background, race or religion.

---

[15] This must have been a rumor among the refugees as the Constitution does not allow discrimination on the basis of religion!

[16] Under her leadership, the Foundation became a genuine Bridge of Hope, assisting more than 500,000 people to escape the horrors of war and political persecution and to build a new life in America as free men

166 ◆ *The First Taste Of Freedom — An Immigrant Experience*

During the stressful time of waiting for our serial number to be called, Gyuri and I had a wonderful day in Salzburg. We walked from Camp Roeder to the town in pure glittering snow. The snowflakes were gently falling around us, like a lace curtain. The trees were all covered with crystal clear snow. It was a magnificent sight! We walked, hand-in-hand, all over the city. It was as picturesque as a Christmas postcard. Through the window of a pub I saw a chubby monk drinking beer, a perfect image for the season.

Our Arrival in the USA

We boarded an old army airplane in Munich on the 6th of January, 1957. I fell asleep and missed some of the excitement. First, one of the motors malfunctioned, and then the second one gave up. We made a forced landing in Prestwick, Scotland. The reception at the airport was lovely. They treated us as royalty with tea and cookies. A Scottish lassie taught me my first song in English — *"My bonnie lies over the ocean..."* I reciprocated by teaching her a Hungarian folksong. We continued our journey and landed in Newfoundland, a winter wonderland, all pure white, deep snow and long icicles hanging everywhere. At last, we arrived in New Jersey. Camp Kilmer was a well-organized former army camp and it felt quite luxurious after the straw-filled mattresses in Austria. The cots were comfortable, with wool blankets, real pillows and even pillow cases. The food was also much better. I vividly remember large bowls of oranges and bananas placed for us to eat. Ladies in Red Cross uniforms walked around, trying to teach us some English. They carried a list of the ten most important sentences we should learn in our new country. I only remember the first two:

1. Doctor, please take out my appendix!

---

and women. Her greatest concern was that new immigrants assimilate quickly and successfully into the mainstream of American life, without losing their cultural and spiritual identities. http://www.tolstoyfoundation.org/tolstoy.html

2. What size bra do you wear?

Many refugees repeated these sentences and felt very worldly and knowledgeable. My uncle Andy made a joke of it and embarrassed several ladies with the questions.

Our little group began to splinter as relatives picked us up or made plans for us. Uncle Andy decided to stay in New York and try to find a job with the Manischewitz Company. He imagined that they would be glad to use his expertise, having been the director of the matzo factory in Budapest. In retrospect, this was a very naïve illusion on his part.

We were picked up by my mother's sister and her husband. They drove us back to their home in Aurora, Illinois. There, my education to become an American began. It started with a good dose of culture shock and deep disappointments, which lasted a bit over a year. Everything seemed very strange and I could not accept many of the new experiences. It felt as landing on a different planet. I was living in an American city where people did not walk. Every time my stepfather and I ventured out for a walk, someone tried to offer us a ride. The people we met did not eat fresh fruit. We had some compote, cooked fruit, at dinner and several of our new acquaintances made for me a revolting concoction of some trembling, gelatinous substance in garish colors for dessert, the then popular Jell-O mold.

Girls wore wide and heavy felt skirts with poodle appliqués, gym shoes with thick ankle socks and lots of makeup. Guys wore crew cuts which made them appear as they had just been released from prison.

My Uncle instructed his wife to take me shopping. Not for clothes, even though I did not even own a change of underwear, only what I wore to escape from Hungary.

They bought me a girdle! For me, a girdle! In Hungary, only old ladies with backaches wore girdles. However, as Uncle explained, if

I do not wear a girdle, my hips might sway and I would look like a prostitute.

My girl cousins introduced me to the American custom of shaving armpits and legs, also very foreign to me. I was angry, resentful and disappointed. Where is the freedom if the most intimate details of my body need to be regulated and subjected to strict conformity?

In just a few days I already understood that I was not up to par in being attractive in my new country. The attractive female was considered tall, blond, well-endowed and bosomy. I had none of these attributes.

One evening we visited some friends of my aunt. The host announced that he would like to adopt me. My parents stood in silence, waiting for my decision. How could they think that I would desert them for a room and a few pieces of clothing? Of course, I said, *Thank you, but I will remain with my parents.*

After six difficult days of getting acclimatized, my stepfather and I took the train to Chicago to look for jobs. This also evolved into arguments, misunderstandings and culture shocks.

In Hungary, I was a very good student at the Technical University, studying chemical engineering. I had hopes to continue my studies. However, our relatives and acquaintances, experienced immigrants from the late 30s, told us in no uncertain terms that newcomers, the so-called "greenhorns," always began in sewing jobs in a factory. My mother's job was to sew on 1600 buttons a day for the Hart, Schaffner and Marx Company. I refused to do sewing and began to make the rounds to find a different job. The Jewish Vocational Service provided me with a list of possibilities. One was to scrub the floors in Michael Reese Hospital.

By luck, I found an advertisement of the Toni Company, the manufacturer of the first home-permanent kits. I was hired as a chemistry technician even though I could hardly speak three words of English. They hired foreign workers for slightly lower pay. Most of the employees in the laboratory were newcomers. My boss was Polish, who recited Shakespeare most of the day—in Polish. — I was assigned to test hair samples for the extent of damage to their protein caused by the home-permanent solution, and compare it with the competitor's product. After a few days I was able to perform the maximum number of tests possible with the available equipment. The laboratory was well equipped and they treated everyone well. It was great fun to work in the Merchandise Mart in Chicago and be able to visit the furniture and appliance show rooms during my coffee breaks. These items all seemed like miracles to me, indicators of a life of fantastic luxury and comfort. I was quite proud that as a technician I earned $1.54 per hour, while the adults in my family labored for the minimum wage, a buck an hour.

In addition to my salary, the Toni Company offered other ways to make extra money. We could volunteer as guinea pigs to test new products and be paid for the service. I usually volunteered to test an ointment for diaper rash. They placed a patch of baby urine on my arm, followed by the ointment. In the afternoon we reported whether the patch turned red, itchy, or healed. Occasionally, instead of baby urine, we received samples from older kids. Of course, the patch of urine from older children smelled to high heaven. We could not enter the cafeteria and on those days we were treated royally: the staff served us lunch in the laboratory and gave us perfume samples to be able to go home by subway. All this and 20 tax-free dollars! It was my favorite extra job. With one of these extra paychecks, I bought a swimsuit. This created havoc with my family, who declared that I was throwing away my money and would die in poverty. But the swimsuit allowed me to accept an invitation from a colleague to the pool of the Women's Club at Loyola University. It was a fantastic experience to have fun in the water and it gave me a respite from all the tensions and woes of my new situation.

Visit from the FBI

One afternoon during the winter of 1957, we received a call from the FBI. They wished to come and interview us. As my parents could not yet communicate in English, I was the spokesperson for the family. I knew that President Eisenhower granted parole status for about 30,000 Hungarian refugees with two-year probation.[17] Those who stayed clean were to receive permanent residency status, the precious Green Card.

I understood that this interview was aimed to check our credentials and the veracity of our stories for asylum. The FBI representatives asked numerous questions regarding Communist Party membership, reasons for escaping from Hungary and our contacts in Chicago. I told them that I had been a member of the Communist Youth organization without which one could not attend a university. They knew this, of course, and complimented me for telling the truth. They ended with a strange question: *"Did I know the whereabouts of underground weapon factories?"* I was stunned. I was only a sophomore at a university in Hungary. How would I have such information? I saw my FBI folder, which was quite thick. Many years later I saw that folder again when I applied for a job at the Argonne National Laboratory.

The Woes of Learning English

On North Broadway, near Irving Park Street, there was a YMCA, which offered an introductory English course for new immigrants. I happily signed up with great expectations. There came a chance to learn English. Our young instructor meant well, but I walked out of

---

[17] http://www.immigrationpolicy.org/sites/default/files/docs/executive_grants_of_temporary_Immigration

the third class, crying, and decided that this language was impossible to learn. That week he assigned us to write an essay with the title:

"*From Gadfly to Gadabout*"

Now, fifty years later, after having earned a PhD from the University of Chicago, I still do not understand the meaning of his title! The instructor managed to discourage an entire class of new immigrants from communicating in English.

The World University Service offered an English course for new refugee students at the University of Illinois in Urbana. I got very excited about this chance to learn the language. However, my elation turned into bitter disappointment when I found out that the WUS organization only accepted male students. Despite all my pleas, I was rejected. Gyuri was accepted and I was so envious! I made up my mind to learn the language somehow on my own. I obtained a Public Library card and spent an hour there every day after work reading "Gone with the Wind" in English, side by side with the Hungarian translation. By the time Scarlett said *"Tomorrow is another day,"* I could speak a bit. Twice a week I also attended a 5 o'clock tea dance, organized by the Jewish Family Service. My idea was that if someone asked me to dance, I would be forced to talk. I also learned a lot about social customs and people, which were not particularly pleasant. Among my peers in Budapest, I was accepted and respected. A dance did not mean an invitation to petting or sex. I felt very much like a bird being preyed on. The girls informed me that there is a rigidly graduated scale on what you may allow a boy on first, second and subsequent dates. Such conformity again was repulsive to me, and I yearned to talk to a boy without such calculated restrictions. I dated two boys for a few weeks but it was pure boredom. I tried to talk about it with my mother, *"What would I do with such a guy on a rainy day?"* She had no answer.

My cousins tried to introduce me to marriageable men, and so did my parents, even though they knew that my heart belonged to Gyuri. I vividly recall a date with *Mordie*, an orthodox boy, rather handsome, whose father offered to make me part of a deal. Mr. Schwartz offered to set up my parents in a fish store if I married his son. Mordie invited me for a ride on Saturday to show off his new Cadillac and impress me. When I reminded him that it was *Shabbat*, he shrugged his shoulders and replied that he would drive in a neighborhood where they don't know him. This kind of hypocrisy finished our relationship.

Maxwell Street on Easter Sunday, 1957
My Uncle's cousin owned a hat shop in the old Maxwell Street area. The day before Easter Sunday, she expected many customers to purchase hats for the holiday and needed help. They asked me to help out in the shop. This experience taught me a lot about myself and about business attitudes. I learned that I would never want to sell anything to anyone, ever. To charge double for a measly straw hat with a paper rose, rather than for a plain hat, seemed totally distasteful to me. I did the best I could though.

I vividly recall a Puerto Rican girl coming to buy a hat. She scrounged together her money practically by pennies. I talked her out of buying the paper rose, and Aunt Dora's eyes seemed to shoot poisoned arrows toward me. I also helped to clean up the shop and catalog the hats. They never paid me for this day's work. It was supposed to be "good experience" for me. I had resented this for many years, as at that time we did not even own two chairs to sit on in our apartment. I felt cheated for a long time.

Visit to the University of Illinois.
In the early spring, Gyuri invited me to visit him at the WUS sponsored English course at the University of Illinois in Urbana. It

was great to travel by train for the first time in the USA. To my surprise, Andrew Handler, from our high school was also studying there. Over the years we had coauthored two books already about the lives of our peers, young Jewish survivors of both fascism and communism in Hungary, and he planted the seed for this volume as well. The guys were having a great time studying. I became very nostalgic and went to see the chemistry lecture hall. As I glanced upon the familiar periodic table, I had tears in my eyes; it did not seem likely that I could continue my studies. I loved Urbana, the academic atmosphere was so familiar and friendly, and I felt some of the freedom of the spirit I was missing with my relatives and during my working hours. Once again, I felt accepted as a member of the group, rather than an outsider, sticking out like a sore thumb, rebelling against conformity. It was a lovely weekend and I was ever more convinced that, come what may, Gyuri and I will stay together.

The Critical Turning Point

The turning point in my life happened early in the fall of 1957. I am eternally grateful to Rabbi Ira Eisenstein at the *Anshe Emet* synagogue for his caring and understanding. During that spring, he asked one of the young boys in the congregation, a recent immigrant from Vienna, to take me to visit the University of Chicago. We arrived on a day in late spring and the campus was ablaze with flowering shrubs. I loved the atmosphere and the medieval style buildings. In the Court Theater a student group was rehearsing Oscar Wilde's *Salome*. For the first time in the USA, English was not a chore, an obstacle course, but something poetic and beautiful. I decided that if English can sound like that, it was worth learning. My companion introduced me to Mrs. Vera Laska, the Foreign Student Advisor, who suggested that I apply for a scholarship.

In the fall of 1957, I quit my job at the Toni Company. It was a pleasant job, but I performed the maximum amount of work possible after three weeks and did not want to test hair samples for the rest of my life. I yearned to go back to school. At this time, I had a serious chance. Rabbi Eisenstein asked his congregation to donate my first quarter tuition, which was $240. Today's cost is more than $10,000. I had no official documents as proof of any previous studies, not even a high school diploma. The University of Chicago accepted six Hungarian refugee students on probation; four in the Physical Sciences Division. If we were able to earn a B average, we could continue. During that first quarter, two of my courses were taught by Nobel Prize winners. Harold Urey was the most memorable professor, a kind, absentminded, charming person, who taught physical chemistry. To my delight, I managed to get a perfect score on his final. I am still guarding this paper as a precious memento. The Chemistry Department offered me a research assistantship, which meant that I could even help my parents with living expenses. My project was related to polarography with dropping mercury electrode, a technique that is completely obsolete now.

During this time, I had to deal with yet another obstacle, to find a place to study for my exams. I commuted from the University to our apartment on the North side of Chicago, where my parents embarked on a new venture. They opened our apartment as a retirement home. We already had two ladies occupying the only bedroom, and the three of us camped in the living room. On most days I studied on a bench at the Addison Street beach. The splashing waves of Lake Michigan were soothing to my ruffled nerves. I mournfully complained to my uncle Andy about the problems on the home front. Andy left his job in New York and moved to Chicago to help me. I was always grateful for this gesture of family loyalty and affection.

The native-born students played many pranks on the newcomers. One day a group of us was walking toward Lake Michigan on 57th Street and a student from the Inorganic Chemistry group passed around some chocolates. No one else, but we, the two newcomers took some. These turned out to be chocolate covered grasshoppers! Some surprise!

During the fall quarter, it was the custom among the male graduate students to send a new girl for a bottle of acid. This time, they picked me. I had no idea that one had to pass through the men's room to reach the acid storeroom in the basement of the Kent Chemistry Lab. Luckily; my new-found Canadian friend tipped me off as an older brother. I sang at the top of my voice to give the guys a chance to cover up. My classmates were deprived of the traditional girlish squeals and I also earned a bit of respect.

At Christmas the students organized a party with drinks abundant. Someone offered me a 300 ml beaker of a pale yellow liquid, which I thought was juice and drank it all. I was too naïve... it was whiskey! I promptly got drunk as I never had that much alcohol in my entire life! I went to sleep on the floor of my Canadian friend's lab and determined never to accept drinks from anyone.

A group of us, Hungarian refugee students, were invited to a Thanksgiving dinner to introduce us to this holiday, which turned out to be a wonderful experience. I loved the festive atmosphere, the history and most of the food with the exception of minced-meat pie for which I have not been able to develop a taste. As soon as I could, I learned to cook turkey, make all the trimmings and enjoyed celebrating Thanksgiving ever since.

My first year at the University of Chicago was critical for me. I demonstrated to the Department that I was worthy of their trust. Both, as a student and a teaching assistant, I was able to live up to their expectations. The proof that I could study and become a professional person was very rewarding to me, but this would not have been possible without the kind help of Professors James Parsons, Dean of Students and Norman Nachtrieb of the Chemistry Department. At the University I no longer felt as a refugee, but a person with a home.

Finding the Right Niche

Between December of 1958 and March of 1959 two very important events happened in my life. I married Gyuri, my love of many years, and we moved to Hyde Park. After 56 years, we are still happily together and we still live in Hyde Park. In March, 1959, I earned a Master of Science degree in chemistry at the University of Chicago and was well on my way with a research project for my PhD, which I received in 1962.

We have two daughters and two grandchildren.

Bernard Dreilinger became my father-in-law and a wonderful friend for life. Uncle Andy stayed in Chicago and became a moderately successful accountant. In his later years, he recounted many of our joint experiences as brand new immigrants. He passed away at the age of 93.

After the initial roadblocks, disappointments and culture shocks, I found my niche in the USA. This country offered me choices and opportunities, and I am grateful for those. Perhaps this is what freedom is all about?

HUNGARICAN
By Gabor Kalman

December 14, 1956, my 22nd birthday and I am in a refugee camp in Austria, waiting for my name to be called for the next group of Hungarian refugees going to America.

After crossing the border to Austria, I have spent the past three weeks in Vienna standing in line for various travel papers, running into friends who also escaped after the Hungarian Revolution was crushed by Soviet troops, eating oranges and good chocolate, which I had not tasted for years, and tasting this exotic beverage called Coca-Cola for the first time. I want to make sure that my father, whom I left behind in Budapest, learns that I made it out safe and I am on my way to America.

Vienna, a vibrant, brilliantly lit, elegant European capital, reminds me of long ago Budapest. An amazing contrast to the grim, dreary and gray Budapest I just left behind. As I am about to board a plane for the first time in my life, a couple of kind ladies in Red Cross uniforms distribute small packets with toothpaste and a toothbrush.

I add this to the identical little kit I received when I first checked in with the refugee agency in Vienna.

*

December 21, 1956: Stalin's birthday. I have never been very fond of Stalin, the source of great misery in our lives for the past decade, but his birthday, I can never forget. On this day, year after year, we were forced to march by his enormous statue in Budapest, shouting Communist slogans, deifying our wise father, Yosip Vissarionovich Stalin. This day acquired new significance in my life. I just landed at Camp Kilmer, New Jersey, a former

American military base resurrected to accommodate the stream of Hungarian refugees who arrive in batches day-by-day.

Getting off the plane, we are greeted by a few uniformed Red Cross ladies handing out small packets of toothpaste and a toothbrush. My small collection is growing fast. I left behind my stamp collection, but perhaps this would become my new hobby. No wonder Americans have such sparkling white teeth.

In the mess hall, while puzzling over my first American meal, I spot a classmate from the university in the company of her entire family. I am about to approach her with a friendly smile when I hear her father across the aisle saying in a loud voice: *"Can't we ever escape them, what are the Jews doing here?"*

I am greatly relieved when the next day my great uncle, whom I have never met before, arrives to pick me up. A friend of his drove him from Philadelphia, where he has been living for the past thirty some years. He embraces me emotionally as I am the first family member he has seen in many decades and says: *"Go get your belongings! — I'm taking you with me to Philadelphia."*

I think this rather humorous, for my belongings consist of a small, rather stylish suitcase I purchased at an elegant shop on Kärtner Strasse in Vienna. After I fetch it, it rattles as it contains little else than my ever growing toothbrush collection.

*

As I disembark from the plane which brought me to San Francisco, I carry the same small suitcase that no longer rattles, for it is now padded with some clothing my uncle gave me.

Glancing at the brilliant California sunshine, it does not take very long to realize that the fur-lined full-length loden coat that served me well during the cold border crossing and in winter weather in Vienna and Philadelphia is not appropriate attire for a college student at Berkeley. This is what I am supposed to become, once we cross the Bay Bridge. This feeling is quickly reinforced when I glance at the handful of tall, crew-cut, chino-clad college kids named Bill, Bob, Jim and Joe, who came to welcome me as the poor refugee kid sponsored by their rich fraternity.

What is a fraternity?

*

"7 Palms," a sign across the street as I look out my window. It is a small convenience store named after the seven palm trees gently swaying against the Berkeley Hills. It is incredibly peaceful and quiet here. I feel safe and free of worries for the first time since I was a small child.

The faint gunfire I hear from somewhere is not my imagination, an echo of wars and revolutions, but is coming from the giant television console downstairs where a couple of fraternity brothers are watching a Western.

A new environment, a new country, and a new language that I can barely understand, yet, strangely, I feel at home.

*

— Are you Jewish? — Someone asks me. After the initial shock, it takes me a while to realize that the question is asked out of curiosity and not motivated by an intent to do me harm.

*

For my room and board, I mop the floor and wash dishes at the fraternity. I go to university classes in the morning, take English classes in the afternoon and wash more dishes at a cafeteria across the street at night to earn a little pocket money. I have never washed dishes or mopped floors before.

*

After washing the morning dishes, Lou, the always smiling and kind queen of the enormous kitchen, gives me a little brown bag to take along as I leave for my morning classes. Around ten o'clock, not realizing that it was meant to be my lunch, I sit under a large loquat tree on campus, open the little brown bag and proceed to eat my *tízórai*[18], my mid-morning snack. As I sit there and watch the crowd of students going by, I realize that not only my fur-lined coat, but the suit I am wearing, the very same one I wore when I left Budapest, as well as the nice leather briefcase, my sole border crossing accessory, do not quite match the quasi-uniform look of the crowd around me.

Perhaps the professors do wear suits with ties and carry elegant attaché cases, but these students carry their books and notebooks under their arms. No briefcases, no bags.

The little brown paper bag contains a sandwich, an apple and a cookie. I eagerly bite into the sandwich, but instantly gag upon finding it has an unfamiliar taste and a rather strange texture.

Curious... I carefully separate the two square slices of soft, cottony white bread and puzzle over the brown pasty substance that glued those together. Then I quickly recognize that it must be a fraternity prank as I remember the big jar of lubricating material they showed me just the day before to use once a week to grease the large electric kitchen appliances. Since I have no money to buy other food, I eat the apple and the cookie, re-bond the slices of bread and carry the grease sandwich with me the rest of the day. When I return after my English class I can explain with my still nearly non-existent English that I am no fool, and cannot be tricked. This met with roaring laughter from the brothers gathered around me.

— *It is peanut butter!* — They roar... — *if you'd have eaten it all your life, you'd most likely be as tall as we are.*

---

[18] Literally, "for ten o'clock snack" in Hungarian.

To this day, I don't eat peanut butter. If I tried it, I am sure it would taste like industrial grease.

But would I really be taller?

*

Learning a new language seems easier than eating the new cuisine. Steak and salad are blood and grass. In the coffee shop, the waitress asks whether I'd like the coffee black. I am somewhat puzzled and innocently ask what other colors do they have?

Tonight I am wearing my refugee suit, because a couple of my new friends, Bob and Jim, I am slowly learning how to tell them apart, are taking me to the best restaurant in San Francisco to show me that not everything is blood and grass. The Blue Fox is fancy and very expensive, $5 for a meal! — Delicious? — I am not sure yet.

The strange monstrous creature they serve at Fishermen's Wharf in San Francisco appears decidedly menacing. Is it going to eat me before I even have a chance to taste it? It is a huge lobster! But unlike my previous encounter with peanut butter, we make peace and have remained on very friendly terms ever since.

*

How do you take classes at a world famous university without having even a rudimentary knowledge of English? — Not easily. I find science classes the easiest. I quickly learn that if I mispronounce Hungarian words like *fiziologia*, it becomes physiology. But I am not as lucky with everyday language in the kitchen. And I have never heard of—let alone tasted—ketchup. The best language school is the sink-or-swim method of living among 60 fraternity guys. I did not need to look up *"blind date"* in any dictionary.

*

Upon my arrival, my great uncle in Philadelphia instantly translated my name and decided that I would be called Gabriel in America. In Berkeley, no one has ever known anyone named Gabriel, and when I tell them that my name is really Gabor, they all smile and say;

— Oh, like Zsa Zsa?

I quickly change it back to Gabor and learn to mispronounce it properly.

*

When leaving Budapest, I said good-bye to my father and we agreed that once settled I would send for him to join me.

Today a letter arrives telling me that he suddenly passed away.

*

The fraternity is closed for the summer. All the brothers went home. I am working in an aluminum foundry to make enough money to pay for a rented room and food. I need to learn the language faster, because pouring hot aluminum is definitely less pleasant than washing dishes.

*

American coffee just does not taste like coffee to me, no matter what color it is. Then I discover *Cafe Mediterraneum* where I prefer to study and mingle with foreign students, who also patronize the place for the only decent coffee in Berkeley. But it is on the other side of campus, so I decide to roast green coffee beans I discovered on the shelf of a supermarket. I purchase a proper frying pan and begin to roast the coffee just as I remember the way we used to do it in our home in Kalocsa[19], when I was a child. Since I do not have a kitchen, I use a hot plate. As I am inhaling the delicious aroma of freshly roasted coffee, the door

---

[19] A small town along the Danube, about 90 miles south of Budapest.

suddenly flings open and three firemen, dressed head-to-toe in firefighting gear, complete with axes, charge in, demanding to know where the fire is. They are totally bewildered when they catch sight of the slightly smoking coffee beans in my frying pan on the hot plate.

— *What are you doing?* — they ask.

— *Roasting coffee* — I respond, and it slowly occurs to me that they have never seen this process before, just as the neighbors, who called the firemen, have never smelled the slightly smoky aroma of freshly roasted coffee. They leave only after making me promise never to roast coffee again.

*

The little espresso machine is gurgling and as the aroma of fresh coffee drifts down the hallway, colleagues from neighboring labs and offices drift in for their afternoon cups.

They are G.I.s and officers, for I am in the US Army in Washington, DC. My work is related to the space program. I was drafted straight out of grad school.

*

Whatever gaps remain in my continued effort in acquiring a second language, those are quickly filled by my rapidly expanding G.I. vocabulary. The sink-or-swim method used in the fraternity a few years back is working again.

*

I am in the uniform of the United States Army as I am sworn in as an American citizen. The lieutenant, my colleague and superior, is my witness.

For dinner, we are having rare steak and green salad.

*

I am a veteran now, enrolled in graduate school on a scholarship at Stanford. I shock everyone, friends and relatives, when I announce that I am switching from pharmacology to film. Why did it take all this time to find out that I want to be a filmmaker?

*

San Francisco in the sixties… I was wearing an Afro (more like an *Isro*), love beads and bell bottoms. Allan Ginsberg at North Beach, reading his poetry; Alan Watts on his houseboat in Sausalito. I am right in the middle of it all. Literally, for I am producing and directing for a television series at the California Academy of Sciences in Golden Gate Park. After work, there is a happening to attend.

*

The taxi driver in Budapest greets me in German. When I respond in Hungarian, he catches my foreign accent and asks where I come from. I live and teach in Los Angeles now. I am back in Budapest as an American Fulbright Scholar, teaching a course on the American Documentary Film.

*

55 years in America. Not quite retired after nearly 30 years of teaching as a university professor, I am about to release my new film:

Gyöngyi Mago, a high school teacher in Kalocsa, discovers that once there was a Jewish community in her town and takes her discovery to her classroom. Fighting hatred and prejudice, she teaches tolerance to her students. She is the main focus of my film, but this rare individual provides the lens to rediscover a vanished world. The world I left so long ago.

This is from a former colleague, Mark Harris, himself an award winning filmmaker:

> " 'There Was Once ...' is a beautifully crafted and affecting film that reminds us how the past continues to live in the present and the importance of remembering."

FIRST STEPS
By Marianne Revah

I've decided to call my story First Steps, but I seem to have fallen into my own trap. When should the count begin?

Let's just say that I left Hungary in search of my brother, Peter, who had crossed the Austrian border two months earlier. I was worried because I didn't know his whereabouts and had a premonition that he was in danger and I had to help him. Crossing the border illegally, with strangers, arriving in an unknown country where you don't speak the language, have no place to stay and not a penny (I mean a Groschen) to your name is more of a leap than a step and therefore it is not within the scope of this story. I promise to write about it some other time.

That being the case, let's start counting from the time I stepped off the plane that had flown us from Schwechat, Vienna's airport, to Montreal, with stopovers in Shannon, the Azores and Newfoundland. I remember having breakfast in each of these places, as we were making our way westward. Planes don't "make their way" you might say; they just fly, but this one was an antiquated four-engine WW II troop carrier. Yet the passengers were all very young, high school and university students, who had escaped from Hungary in the wake of the October revolution. Their motives varied: some were freedom fighters, others were freedom seekers.

My motives were twofold. I had had no intention of leaving my country unless the heroic uprising was marred by antisemitism, so I flinched when I heard a fellow student at a meeting recount how some Jews had been beaten up in the countryside,

"...but that was in the order of things..." he said. Yet the overarching motive for fleeing was to find my brother. I did find him eventually, laid up with a broken arm in a Traiskirchen hospital in Austria, but quarantined due to an outbreak of cholera.

Welcome to Canada

My very first steps on Canadian soil were taken in Newfoundland. After yet another nourishing breakfast, we were shown into a big barn-like structure, packed with clothes, generously donated by the inhabitants, and each of us was to choose an item. Imagine a teenage girl who had left home with nothing but a school satchel containing "love letters," family photographs and a pale blue satin embroidered nightgown, intended to be worn sometime in the distant future on her wedding night, and not even a change of clothes!

I looked around, astounded, picked something warm and sensible, so much so that I don't even remember what it was, but on my way out I noticed a red corduroy dress, my favorite color, with gold buttons. This was too much of a temptation!

The man at the door noticed my embarrassment, as I showed him both hands, holding the clothes. I didn't speak any English at the time, it was all sign language, but judging from his smile and nod, clearly he was saying,

It's OK to take both! There was more to this message than the sudden ownership of a red dress. It conveyed to me this country was to be a good place where they understood people without words. Back on the plane, I asked my brother what he chose. Triumphantly, he showed off his trophy: a brown leather pilot's cap!

We landed in Montreal where the slices of white bread and the lunch-meat— was it Spam?—served on the plane and carefully stowed away by us during the flight, were taken away at customs. How were we supposed to know about a ban on importing meat into the country? And more importantly, how would we know where our next meal would come from?

This incident reminded me of an event that took place a couple of weeks earlier, on my second day in Vienna. On the first day, I had spent all my money on a telegram home, informing the family that I had arrived safe and sound. After a night spent on a broken cot in a shelter, I finally resigned myself to collecting some money from a refugee aid center. Next to me in the queue a woman was eating a bread-and-butter sandwich wrapped in a paper napkin. Suddenly, and without a word, she handed me the half eaten sandwich and I wolfed it down. Was it so obvious that I hadn't eaten for two days? Thank you, lady! Food has been precious ever since, as you will no doubt surmise from this story.

Let me add one more food related incident! At the refugee aid center they gave me a little money; just enough to purchase a train ticket for Traiskirchen and buy some bananas for Peter. I'd never eaten a banana in my life before, but resisted the temptation all the way to the hospital. It took all my powers of persuasion to force my way into the hospital plus my nonexistent knowledge of German to actually find my brother. There he was, very pale, lying on his back under a white blanket. Happily I placed my precious gift on the cover in front of him and he said,

"These bananas are green." I suppose he didn't want to show his emotions.

Montreal

Montreal was fully "booked" by other refugees, so we were driven to Saint-Paul-Hermit, an army base, with a spanking clean linoleum floor and a strong smell of disinfectant in the barracks. The already familiar cotton-white square bread was now followed by other novelties. Meat and gravy that we named "general sauce," accompanied by "creamy whipped potatoes." Why would anyone whip potatoes, especially if they were already creamy? And "garden fresh peas." We could never check out the garden bit, as there was nothing but snow all around. Then came a real riddle: it was glistening and trembling and came in green, yellow and red, capped by a tiny blob of white stuff. Our first encounter with Jell-O!

We discovered an entirely new idea of eating in which taste was secondary, compared to color. A few months later—this will be another story—Anne and I were squatting in front of the kitchen cupboard in search of vegetables for dinner. With the acuity of a twelve-year-old, she explained that the main idea was always to choose colors that went well together, such as peas and carrots.

In Saint-Paul-Hermit we had to fill out some official documents and among many questions there was one about religion. To my mind, the reason was quite practical: let each church or synagogue take care of its brethren. Nevertheless, some Hungarians managed to collect subsidies from several religious communities, including the Maltese Order of Knighthood. Others were hesitant to admit they were Jewish so soon after the war. One girl had suffered so much from Jew-baiting in an Austrian refugee camp that she lied about her religion. A few months later, all alone with her problems, she committed suicide in a hotel near Kingston, where she had found a summer job.

My brother and I joined a group of Jewish students and Oskar, bless his soul, became our leader. He was an "older" man, perhaps in his late thirties, who spoke English and knew his way around. Seeing that we were ill equipped for Canadian winter, he decided to use his budget to buy galoshes for all the boys. That was another mystery for us. How could anyone possibly find his own galoshes among ten identical pairs lined up on the landing or at the front door? It must have been yet another strictly Canadian aptitude, just like orienteering – a sporting competition on foot to complete a tricky course in the least time.

As I was the only girl in this group, Oskar broke all the rules by buying me a pair of little red boots with white fake fur lining. This was definitely a good country!

I did own a winter coat, but it was a bit torn by barbed wire as I was crawling under the fence from the Hungarian side of the border into no-man's land. The following year it was replaced with a tent-shaped mouse-gray wool coat from the States, followed by a bottle-green overcoat from Argentina, all gifts, until I could buy my first Canadian car coat at a smoke sale. (Another puzzle: what can they possibly sell in that shop? Smoke?) Although I had no car to match it, the red coat with white fake fur lining, you guessed it, looked just right against the snowy background. It was a first step toward blending in.

The next steps led me to a detention center for undocumented immigrants on Saint Antoine Street in old Montreal, apparently the only place that still had room for Hungarian refugees. We always had our meals in two shifts, first the inmates, then the refugees, the two groups being separated by steel bars in the middle of a long corridor. We didn't really mind sleeping in large cells with bunk beds. Being in jail was even fun, especially watching people's reactions upon hearing our address, situated, in every sense, on the wrong side of the tracks.

Not only were we free to come and go as we pleased, but even had a 5-dollar weekly allowance from the Jewish Immigrant Aid Services (JIAS) that we had to pick up in person. There was a downside to it as on the way "home" we spent most of it on taxis, in order to escape the blasts of cold, damp wind that slapped our faces every time we turned a corner. It was February and global warming hadn't been invented yet.

Little by little we would brave the freezing streets. With some change in our pockets, we roved into small, dank shops, where elderly Polish immigrants sold rich chocolate cake.

"How come they're still working?" I asked my friend Paul.

"They're putting money aside for their old age," I answered.

"But they'll never be any older than this!" he countered. Montreal turned out to be a different place altogether, when we girls were moved into the YWCA on Sherbrooke. The Y had everything, even a party room! Carefree Canadian girls were wearing makeup and shirtwaist dresses with full, swinging skirts and shiny patent leather pumps. There I was; staring at all this nonchalance and elegance from upstairs, not excluded, just an onlooker. The girls were dancing rock-n- roll. They would kick off their pumps, swinging, swaying and sliding with self-confidence in their stockinged feet. "Western" dances had been banned in Hungary as they constituted a political statement. Any student caught in the act at a school dance would be instantly reprimanded and sent home with potential consequences. Secretly I admired the culprits for their skill and daring, but I never indulged in "imperialist" dances.

You might wonder why all this is important. Let me explain!

In those days, nylon stockings were rare treats in Hungary and if you were living in Miskolc, rather than Budapest, you would have to know someone lucky enough to have the necessary travel documents, passport and visa, in order to cross the border into Czechoslovakia, the nearest country where nylon stockings were manufactured in those days. The idea behind COMECON meant a division of labor within the socialist block, whereby Hungarians would shop for industrial products in Czechoslovakia, while Czechs and Slovaks would buy food in Hungary. They would eat their fill and take home as much food as they could possibly carry. In those days, the Hungarian joke was that from time to time the Czech national anthem should be played in Hungarian supermarkets so that while the tourists stood at attention, the locals would get to do their shopping.

If you didn't know anyone who could travel, you'd wear old silk stockings, mended by some woman sitting in a cubbyhole under a blinding bare bulb, repairing "ladders" with a fine crochet needle and a great deal of dexterity. A sign reminded the patrons to kindly wash their stockings before depositing them. Once repaired, the stockings were as good as new until the next run. Some women I knew would wear kid gloves to put on their stockings, so as to avoid inadvertently pulling a thread with their fingernails.

I guess you get the picture: In a strange country, the slightest incident can carry enough meaning to last a lifetime. Kicking off your shoes in public showed a blatant disregard for probably expensive footwear, total trust in the smoothness of the floor (no shards) and an unusual amount of self-confidence regarding the whole act. In those days, a Hungarian greenhorn had none of these.

Nevertheless, our living standards greatly improved when we were put up at the Y. The boys had their own living quarters close to McGill in a fraternity house baptized Petôfi House, after our great national poet. We all had English classes in a church basement taught by devoted teachers using the direct method which I gratefully copied years later when I arrived in France and became a teacher of English myself.

"What method are you going to use?" asked the manager of a chewing gum factory in a Paris suburb. What method indeed, I didn't know a word of French.

"The direct method, of course," I answered brightly. Thank God the interview took place in English.

Back to the church basement, where I was a complete beginner, trying to concentrate on the lesson rather than my future boyfriend's burning black eyes. We were divided into three groups. My brother was in advanced English, so much so that a couple of months later he scored 98 percent on his entrance exam at the

University of Toronto Electrical Engineering Department and was admitted directly into fourth year.

(Thank you, Aunt Emmy, for speaking seven languages, being a brilliant teacher, reading millions of books in English and spending entire afternoons introducing Peter to the subtleties of English literature, while I was roaming the countryside on my bicycle, swimming on the school team, rehearsing in the drama club, or just hanging out with my schoolmates.)

Was it the Hillel Foundation or JIAS that arranged Friday night invitations for Jewish students in Montreal? Or did the members of the Jewish community volunteer to invite us? Whoever took the initiative, obviously did mean well. Our hosts were kind and generous, but somehow totally aloof. The houses we visited seemed identical: thick, white wall-to-wall broadloom, a fashionably upholstered couch in pastel shades, a couple of assorted armchairs and some books in matching colors.

Our hosts would be sitting around a large, well-laid table. After the chicken soup, pot roast, kugel and stewed fruit, they would invariably tell us about some family members who made good, success being measured in dollars. We'd just arrived from a socialist country and this kind of reasoning was as strange to us as a wall-to-wall carpet. For us, achievement meant a university degree, the publication of a book of poetry, a gold medal in sports, but money had nothing to do with it. Our people had small salaries, rented apartments, potted plants and lots of books.

Towards the end of the meal the question would come up about getting a job, but there was rarely an offer, mostly a glance at the want-ad section of the local paper,

Look at all these wonderful opportunities!

My brother and I never found any jobs in those newspapers.

As we were leaving, in the entrance hall there would be a bag of clothes, mostly fine hand-me-downs from their children, hardly worn at all. Occasionally, we would find a 5 or 10 dollar bill in our coat pockets. These people were warm-hearted and generous, but they lived on another planet. There was hardly ever a question about what kind of individuals we really were, how we ended up in Canada and what we wanted to do with our lives. Were they too polite to show curiosity? Were they afraid to hear something shocking or unexpected to which they wouldn't know how to react? After a while we stopped attending these filling, yet unsatisfying dinners.

One day as I was waiting for my weekly allowance at the JIAS, a gentleman asked me if I needed any help. I told him I wanted to work and find a job for my brother as well. He gave me an address and I ended up in the basement of the Jewish General Hospital disinfecting hypodermic needles. He also recommended Peter for a job at Northern Electric.

I wore a long white lab coat down to the floor and had edifying conversations with my fellow immigrant workers, in Russian, about the way Stalin had starved the peasants into submission, killing millions of Russian peasants who didn't want to join the collective farms. This was certainly not what we had been taught in history classes back home! How embarrassing... In high school I actually wrote an essay on the poetry of Soviet minorities, singing Stalin's praise. A new world was opening up in front of my eyes. There was so much to learn and so many steps to be taken!

Life taught us lots of lessons. One day at the hospital, a secretary asked me what I intended to do later on. When I said that I wanted to go to a university to study psychology, she and her colleagues burst out laughing. Even if I had had the right vocabulary, I wouldn't have been able to defend myself. As it turned out, life itself answered her question.

A number of Canadian colleges and universities organized interviews for us, offering opportunities for the right students to pursue their education. The University of Western Ontario had delegated the Dean of Men and a Hungarian speaking professor of psychology to do the interviewing. When my turn came, I had no inkling that they were actually carrying out a mission which was about to change the course of my life. But that happened later...

The next step was Kingston, a breezy city by Lake Ontario where some of us were offered a chance to continue English classes. Once again we were put up at the Y and there I discovered that a healthy diet consisted of a little mound of cottage cheese on a lettuce leaf, decorated with a few pieces of canned fruit. Now why would people willingly starve to death in the land of peace and plenty? To keep my teenage stomach from rumbling, I would purchase big bags of McIntosh apples, the only extra food I could afford, since I no longer had a weekly allowance. However, there were small jobs, like cleaning windows in cottages, using Bon Ami. And the memorable experience of diving into the innocent-looking and inviting, but actually treacherous lake on a deceptively beautiful day in May. The water was ice cold and you had to be a true survivor to come out of it alive! (Had I known the term, I would have shouted Mayday!)

Be as it may, I learned my lesson the following year on the lake when Murdo said whimsically,

"You've got to enjoy it whether you like it or not!" That was a new piece of Canadian wisdom.

As I said, my life was about to change dramatically. It was triggered by a letter from a university professor and his wife, offering me room and board and the possibility of continuing my studies, in exchange for help with light housework and four children. That was a turning point in my life.

Would I like to go and see them and decide whether the proposed arrangement would be mutually satisfactory? It would mean a short train ride from Kingston to London, Ontario. They would meet me at the railway station and I could recognize them by the lady's red straw hat.

As I mentioned earlier, before actually leaving Montreal, we had been interviewed by different colleges and universities inquiring about our future plans. Since we knew next to nothing about the standing of these institutions of higher education, decisions were sometimes made on an emotional basis. For example, Peter and I were offered scholarships by the University of Alberta, but as soon as we mentioned this in a letter to our family, their instant reaction was expressed in telegraphic style,

— Don't go there! It's too far from Hungary and too close to the Soviet Union!

When I was interviewed by the two envoys from the University of Western Ontario, I truthfully answered that I'd be happy to attend Western, unless both my brother and I could obtain scholarships from another university, in which case I'd gratefully decline Western's offer. It was thirty years before I actually discovered that the representatives of the university were asked by this wonderful Canadian family to find a refugee girl they could take into their home. The envoys made a report of the interview. In the Dean of Men's words,

— *Apart from those big brown eyes, it was your honesty that got you into Western.* Meanwhile my brother accepted an offer from the University of Toronto.

I got to spend many a weekend visiting my brother in Toronto and discovering why Steven Leacock, a famous Canadian humorist, and a native of Toronto, said that if he had a choice, he would prefer to die on a Saturday. Everything was closed on Sunday, except Hungarian restaurants.

I wonder if anybody still remembers Ogilvy's clothing store. Not only was the shop closed on Sundays, there was even a curtain pulled behind the glass pane to prevent passers-by from window shopping which was considered almost as sinful as the real thing. It calls to mind the signs in New York: "Don't even think of parking here!"

Talking about parking, in order to save money I'd ride with a fellow student and share the gas. Seeing an ad on the University College notice-board in my first year at Western about a "two-tone car," I thought it should be easy to spot a German (Teuton) car in a Canadian parking lot! You have to be humble if you want to learn a language properly.

After I moved in with the MacKinnons—Murdo, Elizabeth and their children—I no longer attended English classes outside, but became an object of total immersion, soaking up English like a sponge. From the very first word, which was "sideboard," until Criticism History, a course in honors English that I wasn't meant to attend, words came to me endlessly, by turns meaningful and mysterious. Archetypal poetry was for a long time, visually, like an archway through which I could walk into English romantic poetry. Taking a class at Western to become a swimming instructor, I couldn't for the life of me understand how the "body system" would prevent anyone from drowning, until I realized, much later, that the instructor was talking about the "buddy system." Recommending me for my first summer job at the London Life Insurance Company, the professor very kindly said,

— *She's extremely intelligent* — and I thought he was really exaggerating because I wasn't "fluent" at all. It turned out that the only word I thought I understood in this sentence was "stream" and I imagined it had to do with fluency. Flowing like a river...

I did get the job though and it was very boring. We weren't allowed to talk during working hours. Nevertheless, I ventured to say,

— *Hi, how are you?* — to a fellow sufferer, a girl about my age, and she answered,

— *It could be worse but I don't know how.*

I was overjoyed. How could anyone pack so much grammar and humor into such a short sentence? I knew I was going to love English.

With my new family I acquired new responsibilities. Soon after my arrival in Hyde Park, a small village near London, Ontario, the parents decided to go away for the weekend, leaving me in charge of a big house, four children, a dog, a horse and a considerable expanse of land all around the property. Cheerfully, they waved good-bye from the front door. There were no kisses, no tears, nothing that, to me, would have indicated the hardships of separation. (I was four years old when my father went to war and he never returned. Separation is a dark notion to this day.) This was a different world in which people had trust in each other and a conviction that those who went away would also return and everything would be all right. And so it was. The children went about their business, I closed the back door for the night, let Beauty, the white mare get drunk on cider from rotten apples on the ground (prohibition never applied to horses anyway), half-heartedly allowed Tiny, the eponymous British dog, lick the rest of the gravy from the pan as did Elizabeth, but then I scrubbed the pan extra hard.

I learned an entirely new notion of health and hygiene from Elizabeth, the children's mother. A physician's daughter, she used her own brand of placebo:

— *Just mix a bit of salt and sugar in a teaspoon and give it to Marion if she complains of a headache.*

She also had a special approach to flu. The treatment consisted of bed rest, along with a diet of clear soup and dry toast. I don't remember ever taking any medicine. On this occasion, I was installed in Anne's room, the loveliest one in the house, because it boasted a four-poster brass bed and—on the window sill—a colorful population of Plasticine™ figures, carefully created by Anne. Her bedroom sometimes doubled as a guest room. This is where she composed her philosophy of life, absorbed the essence of English literature and drew from it all wisdom far beyond her years.

As I was nursing my flu, as a special treat I could occupy Anne's room, and Murdo brought me some books to read. If the Reader imagines that after about my four months in the country, he picked out children's books, detective stories or God forbid, magazines, he or she is completely wrong. I was offered Bacon and Chaucer. I don't know if I actually understood anything, but I do remember "the evils of the cave" and I'm still convinced that "the human mind is no dry light." As for Chaucer, when I started English 20 in the fall, carrying my edition of the book with two inches of poetry and four inches of footnotes on every page, I suddenly realized that all the other students were using a modern version of the text! *"In mottelee, and hye on horse he sat,"* sounds beautiful, but what on earth is a "mottelee?"

Murdo probably believed that it was good for me to do things the hard way and I still live by his credo. One day when I asked him what subject I should choose for an essay in English literature, he replied,

— *Whatever you know the least.*

Among a myriad of other candidates I picked Pope, about whom I really knew nothing. After due preparation, I handed in my essay, but Dr. Fleck wasn't duped. Aware of my ignorance he began his comment with the words,

"Your suave style cannot hide the fact that..." I was so happy that I never even read the rest of the sentence. Suave style! Thank you, Dr. Fleck, you made my day!

It is now time to get back to Elizabeth who looked after everybody in a quiet, purposeful manner. She prepared a tray for

Murdo on bad-back days or whenever he needed a bit of peace and quiet; laughed away the small kids' tantrums, paid special attention to Cathy who was "high-strung" (I always thought of her as a delicate musical instrument, like a violin) and found the most efficient way to wake me up in the morning without even appearing to do so.

"Marika, would you bring me your waste paper basket?" Just where did she learn this gimmick? Why on earth would she need my waste paper basket at half past six in the morning? As a matter of fact, she didn't. But once you got out of bed on a winter morning, with the window open about two inches and walked across the cold linoleum floor in your bare feet and went all the way down to the newel post, she taught me the word, you were certainly awake and unlikely to burrow deep again under the blankets.

The notion of time in Hyde Park was everything it wasn't in Miskolc. It had its own authority and value.

"We're clock watchers," Elizabeth said, looking at the big brown clock on the kitchen wall. Clock watching was not the same as bird watching or whale watching and often had immediate practical implications.

"Put the roast in the oven at 11:13!"—never a round figure, always written in pencil on a piece of paper, probably because of my blank expression. Then somehow the timing made sense, lunch became complete with gravy, two vegetables and an apple pie for dessert. You can't cut a pie into seven pieces, there was always one left on the serving plate and I learned the expression,

Would you like a sliver?

In Hungary, time was an enemy. The Stakhanov Cult , , ruined the health of miners and factory workers all over the country. At school we had a terrible system called "The quarter to eight movement." Albeit classes began at eight o'clock, students had to be present by a quarter to eight the latest. Precisely at that moment, two specially appointed school mates would stand at the door and write down the names of those who didn't respect the system and arrived a couple of minutes later. In my opinion, the system was basically dishonest and didn't really show how punctual you were, but whether the two "scribes" were your friends or not. I never really adhered to it.

In Canada time took on a new meaning. Going to university meant that I had to be in the car at seven thirty sharp because Murdo was leaving and I had to live by a "quarter to eight" code of my own whether or not I had any morning classes.

Just the same, English expressions were sometimes baffling. One day I surprised my new family by tidying up the living room, which was quite a feat because the youngest children, ages 3 and 5, had lots of toys lying about. The good deed was immediately acknowledged, using the expression:

— Good for you! — to which I replied:

— Why me? It's good for the living room!

Sometimes the whole family was trying to guess a word missing from my vocabulary. One day a rather conspicuous friend had to be picked up and I said they couldn't miss her because she was … she was… until triumphantly one of them guessed just the word I was searching for: "a landmark!"

Three-year-old Marion had a far better command of English than I did. More surprised than impatient, she asked me,

— Marika, what language do you speak? A little bit of English, but what else? — Fortunately, her father came to my rescue. There I was, with summa cum laude high school-leaving diploma in pocket (allowing me to skip Grade 13), nonplussed by a toddler!

Already at that age, Marion used language with precision and feeling. She didn't accept a broken Arrowroot cookie, because she realized that ideally, the two pieces should somehow be joined together and that's why she didn't just ask for a whole cookie. No, she said, she wanted a "together cookie." While we are on the subject of cookies, I might as well point out that it was her brother John raiding the cookie jar, because he could already climb on a chair to reach it.

Hardly a year later, Marion was a bit upset and her father picked her up to comfort her,

— Marion, did I hurt your feelings? — She shook her head slowly,

— No, but you broke my heart!

Meanwhile Cathy, a bright little blonde, was busy concentrating on her scrapbook relating the royal visit to Canada... Nothing could be further from the Marxist theory according to which class struggle was the mainspring of history.

Thus every word had its own story. "Omen" was certainly not "the last word of a prayer," as I surmised from the vocabulary test on the entrance exam, but for me it turned out to be prophetic. The rest of the test probably showed some promise, because I did get into Western with a scholarship, after just seven months in Canada. At the same time I was informed that no allowances would be made for being a newcomer; I would be judged just like any other student and would lose the scholarship if my average dropped below a B.

The fall of 1957, lo and behold, turned me into a frightened freshman or "frosh," wearing a beanie for an entire week — under duress — and forced to watch a Frankenstein movie for the first (and last) time in my life. But I loved Western for what it was and what it meant to me.

This was obviously a very big step forward, followed by many others. However, in order to enroll at Western, I was required to study two foreign languages. French and Spanish were out of the question because there weren't any courses offered for beginners. This is how, in addition to Russian, I had to take German. Here you have a perfect example of the difficulties awaiting me. How do you translate Goethe from German into English when you understand neither?

Certain hardships can be expected when you flee your country and leave your language behind. You also become separated from your family, your friends, the familiar tastes, smells and customs. You acquire possibilities, but no certainties. You cannot take anything for granted and have to fend for yourself. You become an acrobat without a safety net. The future is no longer plotted for you. You're empowered and accountable, but through the effort to reinvent yourself, you might run out of pebbles and never find your way home. Just where is your home?

CRISS-CROSSING THE ATLANTIC

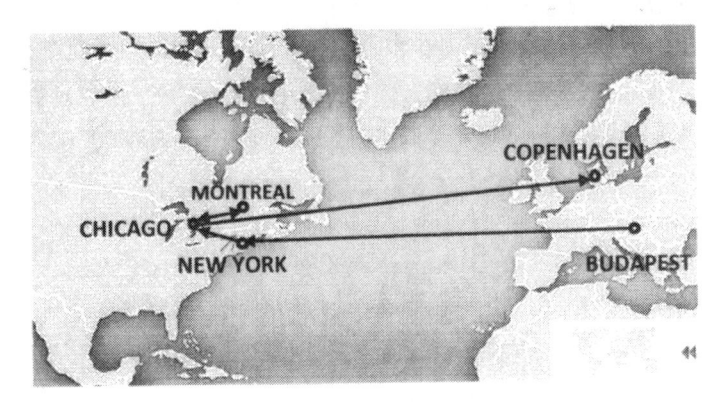

Marietta Vig's paths

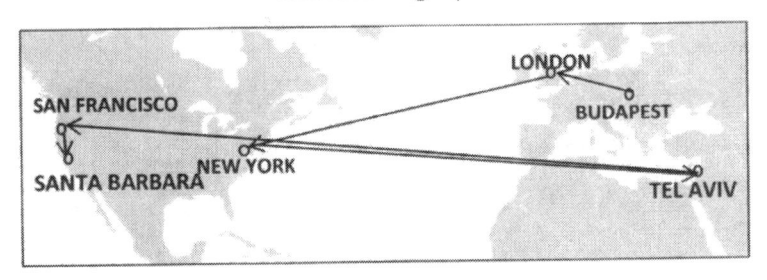

Andras Szekely's paths

THE STORY OF MY TWO IMMIGRATIONS
By Marietta Vig

Adventures in the USA
In 1978 I was a 32-year-old divorcee, still living with my parents and grandmother. I was already working as an architect, but neither had my own apartment, nor my family. I really yearned for a child of my own. I met with many of my friends every Friday evening at the synagogue of the Rabbinical Seminary of Budapest. According to rumors, there were spies among us to observe us and report, whatever they chose, to the authorities. But I was not concerned as I had no interest in politics and naively thought that I was so unimportant to the regime that they would not bother observing me. After thirty years, I found out I was mistaken. After the political reforms the so called "Regime Change" in the 1990s, the government allowed access to the formerly secret personal files. In 2009 I found a 133-page file on me, including my participation in Jewish events between 1972 and 1979.

An acquaintance at the Seminary introduced me to his distant relative, a young man who immigrated to USA as a child in 1956 and came to visit Hungary with the specific purpose of finding a Hungarian Jewish girl to marry. He fell in love with me and wanted to marry me immediately. Since I also very much wanted to be married, my internal alarm did not go off and I would not listen to the concerns of my parents either. I wanted to get away from their protection. My fiancée did not promise me riches, but a normal middle-class life in Chicago, which was sufficient for me to emigrate. It took an entire year until the Hungarian and the US authorities gave me permission to leave the country and enter the USA.

On August 1, 1979 I arrived in Chicago via New York. Prior to the journey, someone introduced me to a lady who was a Chicago resident and was traveling with two small children. She asked me for my help with the transfers. When we parted in Chicago, she gave me her phone number and asked me to keep in touch. Later, she became my savior.

My husband's behavior was very strange and alien to me. After a few days I realized that I could not and would not live with him. There were not only cultural and behavioral differences between us, but I had a strong suspicion that he was mentally ill. After two weeks of married life the moment arrived for my liberation. I contacted my fellow traveler and asked her to pick me up on a day my husband would not be around. Luckily, I escaped with my two suitcases and flew to Montreal to my uncle's family. My relatives were annoyed and blamed me for my unsuccessful marriage. They also worried that my husband might pursue me in Montreal.

From Montreal, I got in touch with my father's former classmate who immigrated to the USA in the 1930s. Tibor and his wife, Anni, greeted me in Chicago and accepted me in their home. I felt assured that they would help me settle in Chicago. After a few days, they planned to travel to Denver for vacation and they decided to take me along. Less than a month after my arrival in US, I left for a vacation in the back seat of a tiny VW among much luggage and a smelly, old and sick dog. We stayed at motels. Anni put away a fair amount of whiskey every night, while assuring me that my life would be on the right track and they would help me along. In two weeks we drove to Denver to Anni's family and then back to Chicago. I was not able to enjoy the wonderful scenery, for I was practically in a coma from fear for my future. Back in Chicago, I accompanied Tibor every day to his place of work in the city. It was easier to access the Jewish Family Service and search for a job from there. I began to call the numbers my Rabbi, Professor Scheiber gave me in Budapest. One of his former students realized my situation and she gave me some practical items for my first home. They invited me to their home where, for the first time since I left Hungary, I felt as a human being and not an unfortunate, abused wreck. I grew fond of the family, their two darling daughters, the charming grandfather and the cultured, cheerful parents. The feelings were mutual and we have remained friends ever since. I also called the owner of an architectural design firm. They had no openings, but gave me the numbers of three or four other architectural design groups and mentioned that in one of these I would be able to speak with a Hungarian engineer. Again, I was lucky. This engineer immediately set up an appointment with his boss and they offered me a job. I remain grateful to him for the job, and I remained a close friend of his family. My work helped me a great deal in adjusting to life in America, quite a change from my earlier life. There were people from various ethnic backgrounds at work; I was only one of many. My "Savior," who helped my escape from my ex-husband introduced me to several young Hungarian immigrants who arrived in the US only a few years before me. They did not work in their professions but became house painters under the supervision of Gyula, a Hungarian master painter. Gyula and his wife, Carol, did help those young men and me as well. They invited me for a few very pleasant weekends while I did not have to stay on the South Side with Tibor and his drunkard wife. On the weekends when I stayed behind, the only pleasant activity was to walk the dog with Tibor along Lake Michigan, since I could not go anywhere by myself. I felt much like a mistreated dog.

Anni became more and more antagonistic toward me. Despite her promises, as I found out, she contacted my ex-husband, although she knew my reasons for leaving him. My ex-husband would not dare to visit me on the South Side.

I did not have to pay for room and board. After my second monthly paycheck, with Carol's help, I found an apartment on the

North Side. Tibor and Anni were annoyed because I did not stay on the South Side. Before I was ready to move, Anni accused me of killing their dog and she threw me out. She took my belongings to Carol and threw them on the floor of the living room. Carol and Gyula welcomed me in their home until I could move into the rental apartment. Gyula and the boys helped me move. Three months before, I arrived with two suitcases, now everyone gave me stuff to live independently; I only had to buy a bed, some sheets and pillowcases.

My first night in my first home was quite traumatic. For the first time in my life, I slept alone in an apartment; I hardly slept as all the strange noises kept me awake and scared.

It was not only the noise, but my doubts whether I could overcome the difficulties far away from the protection of my family and their familiar surroundings. After the first awful night, I began to think in more positive terms. This did not last long, because on the third day, while I was at work, my apartment was burglarized and they took all my pitiful new possessions. But luckily, on the same day, my Hungarian friends delivered the packages I mailed from Budapest during the previous summer. I sat on the edge of the bathtub and sobbed, as I did not even have a chair. My friends changed my lock and reported the crime to the police. As this happened on a Friday, they took me to their home, so I would not be alone over the weekend — I cried for two days. The thought occurred to return to Hungary. This was a complicated legal problem, as I received permission to immigrate to the USA by marrying a citizen. Since I left him, the justification for my stay became blurred... There was the danger of deportation. I did not want to be deported; I would rather leave on my own. I did not plan to return to Hungary, but did not see my future in Chicago either. The burglary intensified my desire to return to Hungary. Had there been an opportunity, I would have boarded a plane immediately. But there was no such opportunity and once again, my friends helped me to begin anew.

Slowly, I began to shape my independent life. I worked, began to get adjusted to American customs and took care of my own affairs. My self-confidence improved as I gained independence. Chicago was no longer scary. I even began to like it. I registered at the Jewish Community Center for an English course where I met immigrants from Russia and Israel. I had new friends who were not from Hungary. Toward the end of 1979, for the first time in my life, I invited friends for dinner. When I arrived, I could not cook at all, but now I had a cookbook. I invited two Hungarian Jewish couples, the M's and the S's, who were of similar age and came from Budapest in 1956. In the course of the evening we discovered that three of the guests attended the same Jewish High School. Perhaps I was able to reciprocate their help and affection by accidentally getting them to be acquainted. They did not know each other even though they had lived in the same city for more than 20 years. They have remained close friends.

After four months in Chicago, the New Year began. I got adjusted to my new, independent life without relying on my family. My parents and my grandmother were terribly worried about me. Their letters and infrequent phone calls rather than encouraging me, depressed me. My uncle in Montreal provided neither financial nor emotional support. He stayed annoyed for putting myself into such a situation. I did not expect financial help from him, but emotional support would have been nice. It no longer hurts because it forced me to solve my problems and view my future more positively.

The next obstacle was my divorce. My husband wanted a quick divorce for two reasons: his fear of my demand for financial support, and revenge. He was hoping the divorce would cancel the legal basis of my US residency and I would be deported. His fear had no basis. I did not expect financial support as he was a total stranger to me. I neither feel grateful to him for bringing me to the USA, nor guilty for leaving him. He was dishonest with me. He never told me about his serious health issues. I found out later that we would never have a child due to his long psychiatric treatment. Since I was not a political refugee, the Jewish Family Service had not been helpful in the past but in this instance they did recommend a lawyer. My husband agreed to assume the blame for the divorce, as long as I paid the cost. His miserliness was greater than his desire for revenge. I paid off the legal expenses on installment. This was stressful but it freed me from my fear of deportation.

I worked, met with friends, acquaintances, and grew to love Chicago. I began to feel at home. During the summer my father came to visit. It was a pleasure to host him and show him my new home. He did witness that I was able to live independently. A year after my immigration, I left for a vacation in Budapest.

Life Among the Danes
The vacation began with a detour; a week with a friend originally from Budapest, who was living in Denmark. This visit changed my life. We decided to move in together in Denmark, for he had lived there for twelve years already, and his life was much more settled there than mine in the USA. In October 1980 I moved back to Europe, to a small town in Denmark. I planned to stay for six months, as it was shown on my visa. I was less ambivalent and fearful than when I arrived in Chicago. I was much calmer. The previous year gave me a healthy dose of self-confidence. It was easier in one sense, yet more difficult in another. It was easier because I did not need to tackle the legal issues alone. The difficulties stemmed from the differences between the two societies. America was open, multifaceted and inclusive while the

Danish society was quite closed and homogeneous thirty years ago. In Chicago, I never felt as a foreigner. In Denmark, everyone was blond and blue eyed while I was a brunette with dark eyes. The Danes are very polite and reserved. I felt they looked through me and looked down on me. Usually there was no basis for these feelings. For example, however hard I tried to learn this very difficult-to-pronounce language and did everything I could to speak it correctly, people often switched to English in the middle of a conversation. I interpreted this as my failure to make myself understood. This was possible, but they might have tried to be helpful. The Danes like to speak English and are proud of their good command. This is no longer a problem for me. My accent was never an issue in Chicago, where almost everyone or at least their ancestors came as immigrants from somewhere. Accents were treated as normal and most people were not bothered by sloppy grammar. The Danes expected their immigrants or refugees to be like them. They expected complete assimilation to render the country uniformly Danish. Fortunately, some people do accept a multi-ethnic society today. My integration required me to learn Danish as well as I could, and get acquainted with Danish history, music, literature and art. I am also familiar with the current political issues. After six months of intensive language study, I was able to find a job in an architectural design company, where I was surrounded by Danish colleagues all day, learning the language quickly. My colleagues were polite and reserved compared to my former colleagues in Budapest or Chicago. I would describe them as "luke-warm." The women accepted me in their club, where we shared magazines, which also helped with my vocabulary and encouraged me to read in Danish. We had lunch together in the company's cafeteria and once a month took turns to host the group for dinner. I learned a great deal from them about cooking, knitting, customs and family relationships. Despite this pleasant collegiality, these women caused the most unpleasant experience I ever had in Denmark. Suddenly I became persona non grata with them. The invitations stopped and they barely said hello. I never found out the reason. Twenty-seven years later I still don't understand what was behind this. I would handle the situation differently today by confronting them and asking for the reason. I did not do it then and I still feel a thorn in my side.

I thought it might have happened because I was a foreigner. Since then I learned that among Danes a friendship may cease without any disagreement. It is difficult to accept this.

After the company was downsized, I found a job with the National Danish Railway Department as a design engineer. We designed bridges and walls free of noise pollution. I stayed there for ten years. I am a member of two non-political organizations: the Danish Chapter of WIZO—Women's International Zionist Organization—and another organization interested in the issues of retirees. I have friends through my husband and through my work and hobbies. We always told our Danish-born son that he is Danish. He was born here, went to school here, but his roots are in Hungary, because his parents came from there. He understands this and has never had an identity problem. He likes Hungary and enjoys visiting there. We speak Hungarian at home and our son learned the language by hearing the spoken word. We thought it was important that he should be able to talk to his grandparents, our relatives and friends. Several Danish acquaintances thought it odd that we speak Hungarian at home. I explained that we prefer to talk to one another in our mother tongue and this does not diminish our integration. Some did accept this, others did not. My son had a very good friend in kindergarten and we also became friends with his family. When my son was about twelve, the boys abruptly ceased to be friends. We did not understand this. His friend tried to reestablish the relationship and the boy's parents also extended several invitations, but our son was adamant. At last, he told us that his feelings were hurt, because the family made unkind remarks about our speaking Hungarian and the boy even imitated my accent. This was the only incident which affected me more deeply. When I chat with strangers on the street, on a bus, in a store or at the pool, they ask me where I came from. I usually respond with the name of the town where I live. In Danish, one could interpret the question as where am I coming from at the moment. A few months ago I had a conversation with a lady at the pool. We talked about recent street repairs. She asked me where I came from and I replied, from Hungary. She laughed, as she only wanted to know how I came to the pool. This shows our heightened sensitivity as immigrants and our tendency to be defensive. Whenever I had any problem at work or anywhere elsewhere, I always attributed this to being a foreigner. It might have been the case at times, but I realized that many problems are not associated with being foreign born.

Why Not Return to Hungary After the "Regime Change?"
After 1990, following the political reforms in Hungary, we were asked whether we would return there. My reply was, No, because we are at home here.

We really feel at home in Denmark, where we spent the larger portion of our adult lives. I have a few relatives and friends in Hungary with whom I stay in touch.

About ten years ago, mostly for financial reasons, we thought about returning to Hungary permanently, but for many reasons we decided against it.

The practical reason: after several years of unemployment I found a job in a Hungarian establishment. My position is not as a professional engineer, but they need my knowledge in Danish, Hungarian and English, and my familiarity with Denmark. I realized in this Hungarian work environment, how alienated I had become from them since I emigrated from there. The opinions, attitudes, morals and relationships of my Hungarian colleagues are farther from me now than those were toward the Danes thirty years ago. Another reason for my resistance to return to Hungary is the currently wide-spread antisemitism and racism there. In the name of freedom of speech, people openly express their anti-Jewish and anti-Roma sentiments. The Jobbik Party in Parliament holds about a fifth of all the seats and it is ultra-right and growing. Their opinions follow the philosophies of the Hungarian fascist Arrow Cross Party during WW II, led by Szálasi. They divide the people into two groups: "true Hungarians" and those whom they view as emotionally alien, the Jews and the "criminal" Gypsies.

My family was not observant. Since I was born after WW II, they did not raise me in a religious atmosphere. My parents fasted on Yom Kippur, but I did not have to. On Passover we always had chicken soup with matzo balls, but I knew nothing about the meaning of Passover. As the communist government frowned on any kind of religious activity, it felt natural that we did not observe the Jewish holidays and customs. I felt Hungarian, this was my mother tongue, and I was raised with Hungarian culture in Hungarian schools. They rob me from my Hungarian identity when they refer to citizens of Jewish origin as "emotionally alienated."

My search for my roots yielded some relevant information. My maternal ancestors moved to Hungary in the early 18th century from Germany. On my father's side, my great-great-grandfather had lived in a north-eastern county of Hungary since the beginning of the 19th century. I would like to know whether these ultra-right politicians, who question the right of others to be called Hungarian, could prove that their ancestors entered the country with Árpád. — Even if they could prove it, this does not give them the right to deny the self-identification of others and spread hatred and fear. I still think of myself as Hungarian, because despite my feeling at home in Denmark and having been a Danish citizen for thirty years, I was not educated here and Danish is not my mother tongue. Denmark is my home. I accepted its customs, which are not very different from what I grew up with. This makes my life easier and reduces any pressure to compromise my principles or my personality. Over the years I have observed the behavior of the Danes in many different situations. I often find their attitudes more appealing than those of the Hungarians in similar situations. I often disagree with my Hungarian friends. I understand their reactions, as once my way of thinking was similar to theirs. I do observe from a distance what is happening in Hungary, but only as an outsider. I often feel they do not want to acknowledge the direction their country is taking, and this scares me. The official view of the Hungarian government and its supporters of the period between the two World Wars is nostalgic. It celebrates it and would like to emulate it. They imitate the customs of that era and adopt its philosophy. That period ended with the murder of 600,000 Hungarian Jews, thousands of Gypsies and political dissidents. In my opinion this is a past to be ashamed of rather than brag about, idealize and wish to revive. Hungary should build its good future, rather than retreat into the past. Stop the hatred and stop looking for scapegoats! The Danes strive for solutions to existing problems and cooperate, with an eye on the future. That is the reason I believe that I would rather be an immigrant here than a stranger in the country of my birth.

As of now, I had lived half my life in Hungary and the other half abroad as an immigrant. I feel fortunate for feeling at home in Denmark where they admitted me and accepted me.

Translated from Hungarian by Susan V. Meschel and Peter Tarjan.

THREE LETTERS FROM ANDREW SZEKELY[20]

The first letter describes his early impressions in Israel in 1971. The second letter is a long suicide note from 1981. The third letter, dated 1994, is another suicide note. Andrew eventually took his own life. He left no one behind, but friends.

Andrew Szekely escaped from Hungary in 1956. He first settled in the UK, where he earned a diploma in electrical engineering, followed by a PhD at the Imperial College in London. In 1964 he moved to New York and worked at AT&T's Bell Laboratories. In 1971 he immigrated to Israel and held an academic position at Tel Aviv University. His first letter from 1971 covers this period.

Andrew married Malka and after a few years they moved back to California where he held an academic position at the University of California at Santa Barbara. They were divorced there.

Andrew wrote the second and third letters about planning his suicide from Santa Barbara in 1981 and 1994. He stayed in touch with many of his old friends from high school and social relationships in Budapest, including George and Susan Meschel. In 1995 Andrew finally took his life. His wanderings in the world did not provide him with a sense of belonging.

Andrew Szekely left behind many friends.

---

[20] These letters were sent to about two dozen of his friends and relatives, whose identities are not available. The particular copies presented here were saved by Susan Meschel and her husband George.

A LETTER FROM ISRAEL, 1971

The London dateline must come as a surprise to you, having last heard of from Israel. Thus, I must start with an explanation, dealing mostly with the difficulties I had in Israel.

Religious Coercion

As I already pointed out in my previous circular letter, the intended democratic structure of Israel has been seriously undermined over the years by the religious coercion of a politically powerful minority, I believe that were the country not at war against a greater enemy, the fight—between those who want a separate church and state, as done in all modern Western civilizations, and those who don't—would flare up in the earnest. You must not be surprised that I feel particularly sensitive about this issue, for I left my native land in 1956 in order to be able to exercise my human rights in full, and having paid this very high price for freedom, I cannot give it up readily.

The arrogant attitude of the orthodox factions came to a head some months ago in what became known as the Ashkelon Motor Race Affair. A foreign (German) company organized this race to take place on the Shabbat, the only free day for Israelis. A few days before the race the religious organizations mounted an all-out propaganda campaign at home and abroad, threatened the organizers to sabotage the racetrack, and finally "donated" a bribe close to 100,000 to the organizers to cancel the race on that day.

You will know, of course, that I'm not the least interested in motor racing, but I am in music, theater, cinema, etc.; all of which are banned in the whole country on Friday nights and before holidays.

Equally important for me is the question of kashrut (dietary laws). Meat is already a problem in Israel, with prices as high as IL[21] 17-18 a kilo of beef, ($2.30 per pound), and the Government is cutting down on meat import. {Pork would be the natural meat, for it is indigenous to Israel, tasty and can be prepared in a variety of ways. However, not only is it suppressed in restaurants (some still sell it though under the pseudonym of "white meat"), but it is illegal to sell it in shops! Yet it still appears in some under the following *"Arrangement;"* (the title of a new book by one of the leading liberal thinkers in Israel, Shulamit Aloni). The municipal food inspector, (Orwell would have called it "Stomach Police"), appears once a week in the shop and cuts off a small piece of the sinful ham or bacon. The shop owner than duly pays him the appropriate bribe of the order of 100 IL ($30). Whereupon the pious inspector departs and everybody is happy.}

Now I know only one recent example in a civilized society of banning a type of food on ideological grounds: the Soviet ban on Matzo for the Jews. It is a telling shame of the Rabbinate that this kind of comparison must be made.

The inedible margarine-based pastries in the University cafeteria are just a small irritation now. While I am writing these lines, an army of dubiously convinced workers are fiercely searching, under rabbinical supervision, for the least crumb of bread in the smallest recesses of the hall, lest it might desecrate the Passover.

In short, the Establishment regards Israel as the exclusive property of the religious minority, or at least consents and complies with its wishes. The religious parties, in turn, ignore the philosophy and ethics of the Jewish heritage and put all the effort into the preservation of its least significant features for a modern society, the laws of the Stomach and the Shabbat.

---

[21] Israeli Pound.

Hebrew

My second major disappointment has its cause in myself, namely the lack of progress in Hebrew. Once the summer *Ulpan*[22] was over I found myself inundated with work, and soon had to give up even part time studies .I manage to somehow arrange telephone calls and minor shopping, but beyond these my knowledge breaks down. The major problem is reading: not only are the letters hard to recognize-many of them look the same and there are numerous styles-but vowels are almost absent except for some substitutes. In English it would look like this:

"Hbrw scrpt *mts v*ls *ntrly, *xcpt whn thy *occr *t th* begnng *r *nd *f wrds.*vn thn*nly twv smbls *r ysd, wth *nds tngshbl phntc vlus"

The * stand for one of the two vowel symbols (aleph and ayin). Imagine reading such sentences when half the words are still unfamiliar.

Worse yet, Hebrew spelling has almost no redundancy in the information-theoretic sense. That is, practically any combination of 3-5 letters is a Hebrew word, and thus if one letter is changed (even if it is an aleph that replaces an ayin and is pronounced the same) a new word results. This, incidentally, makes it possible to construct 3-dimensional crossword puzzles in Hebrew.

The sad result is that after almost 10 months I still cannot read road signs from a moving vehicle unless they are one word or less, cannot enjoy non-English films on the television for which only Hebrew subtitles are provided and I become a bundle of nerves every time another of the interminable printed forms arrives at my desk or mailbox, etc. (A correction from last time: the word God, "El" does have a plural, "Elim." Only the Hebrews' God, "Elohim",

---

[22] Intensive language course for new immigrants.

which is actually "my God", does not. The original—incorrect—information came from an Israeli; the correction from a Hungarian.)

Culture
It comes as a shock to realize that Jews in Israel are not the same as Jews in the Diaspora, especially the young ones. Here they need not excel over the gentiles in every way, and thus their motivation for self-improvement is much less pronounced. Thus the concert hall gives the impression of a meeting room for German refugees from the 30's, the so called opera house is half filled with middle-aged Kibbutzniks, and in the cinemas I always run into some oriental youngsters who come in gangs and shout their comments across the audience. Theaters are closed to me for language reasons, but my friends say I am not missing much. Under public pressure, a daring satirical review had to be taken off the program some months ago after a few days due to threats and riots. Schonberg's Violin Concerto, a famous work by the leading Jewish composer of this century, was recently removed from the program of the Israel Philharmonic Orchestra under pressure by the subscription holders, for being "too modern." Films are banned and censored indiscriminately by a board including several religious representatives. And so I could go on...

I expect you have gained the impression by now that I had finally become disillusioned with Israel, and have returned to England for good. Perhaps you even think to yourself that *"I told him so..."* or *"I could have told him so..."* Fortunately, you are wrong.

I have merely disburdened myself of the aspects of life here that trouble me most. Yet I am not going away. On the contrary, last November I purchased a new apartment and will move in on July 10th. This amounts to a final commitment to stay here.

(Incidentally, this will be my 10th home since 1956 if I count only those where I spent more than 3 months...)

Why am I staying? Because once I singled out the few things that are wrong, all the rest is more or less right. I feel an affinity to the land that cannot be rationalized. The people are not all to my liking, but I do not hate them. (The worst I can say is about the militant orthodox, whom I regard psychologically sick.) My work is very satisfying and meaningful. The informality of life is much to my liking. Everything can be bought, albeit at a high price, and what I cannot buy here my parents or friends bring in sooner or later. Finally, I have had enough of wandering: they made me age inside too fast, and I want to enjoy as best I can what is left. I feel I still have something to contribute, and would like to contribute it here. If, in an autobiography, I would have to give a title to this chapter, it would be *"Squeezing the Lemon."*

So, let me tell you about the rose with the thorns removed.

Apartment
I found my apartment after an intensive search of some 4 weeks, innumerable inquiries and much bureaucratic haggling with authorities, mortgage companies, etc. The story of it is all written up in another article in *Olei Britannia*; "Buying a flat in Tel Aviv" in the January, 1971 issue. In it I also published a list of over 50 apartments for the benefit of fellow *olim*, thus undercutting numerous real estate agents' business in the city. The apartment has 2 and ½ rooms as it is called here — I first worried whether I am getting the upper or the lower half — with a large kitchen, separate bathroom and toilet, balcony and parking space .Gas is centrally provided, central heating by hot water can be installed and I shall do it. The building is almost new (18 months old). Most importantly, however, it has what few flats in Tel Aviv have: a view. It overlooks the "river"—i.e., stream—Yarkon at the northern border of the city,

with a wide belt of tree-lined parks on both sides. It is very near to my present flat and thus also to the University. I have already ordered air conditioners for every room, and will furnish it generously. Oh, the price: IL 63,000 ($18,000), of which about half I paid in cash over several months, the other half is from loans from the British Zionist Federation and the Jewish Agency.

University
My work is very satisfying and challenging. With a dozen colleagues we are building up a School of Engineering and it is no routine matter. I am Chairman of the Undergraduate Curriculum Committee and have been working quite hard over the past few months to put together a 5-year curriculum in 4 years. That is, we want to graduate engineers after 4 years who have a very thorough foundation in mathematics and physics, yet can at once become useful in an industrial environment. I am also on the Undergraduate Admissions Committee, whose work is about to begin now.

Furthermore, as I teach a course on "Technical Writing in English," I was also made responsible for most bulletin and publication entries about the Department that must be written in English.

My other course, Communication Theory, Systems and Circuits, is coming to an end soon. The attendance is rather low but now steady, and I hope that as the department gets better known we shall have more and better students. Meanwhile I was charged with setting up a Communications Laboratory for both undergraduate teaching and research, and this involves acquiring, sorting, filing and absorbing much commercial material.

All my teaching is still in English, although I am being prodded already to think of switching to Hebrew. I still can't see this happen for another year.

Sinai Tour

My most recent experience worth describing was the 6-day tour to the Sinai, organized by the University. Most of it consisted of fiercely uncomfortable rides totaling 2,000 kilometers around the peninsula in a truck disguised as a bus, sleeping out and cooking awful meals from canned food. However, the scenery is majestic and magnificent.

The question of the return of Sinai to the Egyptians, whose legal title to it is itself in some doubt—will be decided by political and military considerations. However, I could not help feeling that Brecht's maxim as expressed in the Caucasian Chalk Circle is applicable: *"The land belongs to the one who loves it and develops it."* In the 60-odd years of its possession the Egyptians did little more than letting the US dig for oil, installed innumerable guns, barriers, minefields, and promoted the smuggling of hashish. In three short years the Israelis made Sharm-al-Sheikh into a promising tourist resort, built new roads and improved the old ones, gave—for the first time—government aid to the Bedouins, and developed the oil fields. Tours go to the Sinai daily, geological and archeological research abounds, and the lot of the Bedouins is improving.

London Trip

I came to London for two weeks to wind up my affairs. (Someone asked me in how many other cities I have "affairs," and whether the one in London is pretty.) I must do a lot of shopping for the apartment, and clear up some banking and legal issues. If you are in England and want to contact me, call my parents' home before the 18th any evening after 5:00 PM (01-998-1789).

Future Plans

To remedy the situation with my Hebrew I decided to sacrifice the coming summer and stay here to attend another *Ulpan* at a higher level. Perhaps I will take a couple of weeks' vacation on the Eastern Mediterranean. Next summer, however I shall be eager to take a job somewhere abroad. If you happen to know of something, such as summer school, short term research project, editing work, or anything similar, please let me know.

Uniqueness
It is said that *"Jews are like any other people, only more so."* Well, there may be something in it. I have lived and worked in 6 countries by now and visited 3 times as many, but only in Israel...

...does the police patrol car driver shout across to you in traffic light when you are studying a map, and gives you the directions voluntarily;

...does the Dean of the Faculty of Science at a University command silence before beginning a speech at a reception in his honor by whistling between his two fingers;

...does an Army major on leave join the truck driver from his Kibbutz to ride around Sinai in his cab for a vacation, but carries his submachine gun with him just in case;

...do Post Offices exist where stamps are not on sale, but they refer you to a nearby shop;

...does the International Operator wish you a peaceful Shabbat before connecting your call;

...does your grocer answer, when you complain that several flies, small stones, etc. were found in the flour after sifting, that *"Of course that's why it says on the packet, sieve before use;"*

...does the seller of your new apartment invite you to move in with them 2 months before they move out, so that you don't waste money on rent;

...do oncoming drivers flash their lights to warn you of police radar traps, as a remnant of the Mandate when the Underground was warned this way against British check points;

...is the section in the Ministry of Health that deals with contamination of food called the "Department of Foreign Objects;"

...do you go to an occupied territory to buy local (Israeli) products at a discount;

...can you buy a locally manufactured airplane, but not a motorcycle or an electric shaver;

...do cinema box offices send you to a ticket agency to buy a ticket for tomorrow's performance;

...do you stay without milk for a month because the milkman is on reserve service;

...are documents stapled at the middle of the top edge, for the Hebrew part needs stapling on the right and the English part on the left.

"*Baruch ha bah*" or in English "blessed is he who comes." If you decide to visit take note of my addresses,

And don't forget that I am still customer for duty free drinks.

Shalom

Andras

The Second Letter

(The second letter was typed in Courier font on a peculiar typewriter and it is shown in the original font, but the lines have been altered to fit the format of this book.)

Easter Sunday, 1982

Dear Friend/Relative,

When this letter reaches you, I am no longer alive, having delivered myself of a life that no longer holds for me any hope of happiness, fulfillment or satisfaction.

Please forgive the pain that my going might cause you. In this letter I shall try to mitigate it as best I can, by showing you how my last step was inevitable, and how there was nothing you - or anyone else could have done to prevent it.

I am writing this in English, even though most of the recipients are Hungarian, partly not to have to write two letters, and partly because English allows me better to distance myself from my emotions. For those of you, who do not know Hungarian; allow me not to attempt clumsy translations of the poetry I shall be quoting.

I am approaching the end of the road because I can no longer live alone, without love, affection, sex, sharing and companionship; with no hope of this ever changing, and no one with whom to talk about it.

Having grown up as a somewhat lonely, only child, I became aware in my early teens that the focal problem of my life is finding a female partner. (A psychologist once described this by the Jungian term "anima possessed.") Thus while I aimed for scholastic and intellectual excellence also for its own sake, my underlying ultimate goal was to present the treasures I so gather, to the woman I love. I was collecting the wealth for what later I recognized as the first five doors of my "Bluebeard's Castle."

After some false starts, at age 31, I found the woman - or more accurately, she found me - whom I was waiting for. She was beautiful, elegant, witty, sensitive, cultured, loving, sensuous, and literate, the list could go on. She was the only woman I ever unreservedly admired - an essential ingredient of romantic love. She had style and quality, and by her excellence she set standards which I never since could match. 16 years ago to the day, at the end of an afternoon Parsifal performance at the Metropolitan Opera, I realized that I loved her and that with her my life's goal and my human potential would be fulfilled.

[I shall call her "X", to protect her identity. Some of you may know her, or think you do. If so, please do not let her know about what happened - we lost touch some time ago and there is no need for this event, a predictable end of a relationship long unimportant to her, to disturb her happiness.]

X could have had any man as a lover, and when she chose me, I felt my years of "waiting and preparing" were vindicated. In the words of József Attila:

> "Már nem képzelt ház üres telken,
> csinosodik, épül a lelkem,
> mivel az árnyakkal betelten
> a nők között Flórára leltem.
>
> Õ a mezõn a harmatosság,
> kétes létben a bizonyosság,
> lábai kigyóim tapossák,
> gondjaim mosolyai mossák."[23]

She brought out the best in me, and began to successfully "de-program" me from the depressive and destructive world view that my mother imbued in me since childhood. By loving me she did more to my self-esteem than all the women and men I knew ever did together. Again, in József Attila's words:

> "Nagyon szeretlek, hisz magamat szintén
> nagyon meg tudtam szeretni veled."[24]

With her I did not have to finish my sentences; she knew what I wanted to say. She

---

[23] **Literal translation by PT:**
It is no longer an imaginary house on a lot, / it is more becoming, my soul is reconstructed, / among the shadows of women / I discovered Flora. She is the dew upon the pasture, / when in doubt, she's certainty, her feet trample on my snakes, / and her smiles wash away my worries.
[24] **Literal translation by PT:**
I love you very much, since with your help / I could learn to love myself.

interpreted my dreams with more insight than professional psychologists. She "read" my voice, even over the telephone, with uncanny accuracy:

> "Kanntest jeden Zug in meinem Wesen
> Spähst wie die reinste Nerve Klingt,
> Konntest mich mit einem Blicke lessen
> Den so schwer ein sterblich Aug
>   durchdringt;"[25,26,27]
> (Goethe: An Charlotte von Stein)

As fate would have it, she was married and had children, whom she feared to expose to the emotional trauma of a divorce. However, by the summer of 1966 she loved me strongly enough to contemplate marrying me, and we even spoke of having a child. It was at this moment that my parents arrived on a visit and promptly threw in all their weight to prevent this happening, for it implied my staying in the U.S. whereas they were established in England to where they followed me from Hungary. They played on my weakness and my bad conscience for having left them behind a

---

[25] This version of her translation is reproduced with the generous permission of Beth Binkovitz.
> You recognized every gesture of my being,
> heard even the purest nerve's cry,
> could read me with a glance, seeing
> deeper than any mortal eye.

[26]Her earlier, somewhat different translation appeared at
[27]http://www2.warwick.ac.uk/fac/arts/modernlanguages/german-studies/goethe/podcasts/24/

decade earlier in Hungary. ("If you marry and leave us in England you will be committing murder" - thus spake a loving Jewish mother ...)

Worn and weakened as I already was by months of jealous pain, sleeplessness and constant fear of whether X will or will not divorce, my parents' misery and exhortations took their toll. X understandably became more and more concerned on seeing my hesitation. When in the spring of 1967 I could no longer stand the torment, I attempted to end it by taking an overdose of barbiturates. Tragically, X telephoned me while I was still conscious and had me "saved" at the nick of time.

After my recovery, our affair continued for a few more months but then, having seen me mostly at my worst, she lost interest and sent me away. (Some time thereafter she did leave her husband, and eventually married a handsome and successful man.) No one, since then, could comprehend the depth of my feeling for her, and no one understood the language of my soul:

> "És lásd, akadt nõ,
> ki érti e szavakat
> de mégis ellökött magától."[28]
>   (József Attila)

It has been my everlasting pain and shame that I never succeeded spending as little as

---

[28] Literal translation by PT:
And notice, there was / a woman who understood the words, / yet shoved me away.

one full day with her, and the brief hours together that we could snatch, were embittered by my having to share her with another man. And so are years of fruitless yearning leading me, like Tristan, to renounce her by also renouncing my life.

My subsequent aliyah[29] to Israel was an attempt to find a "collective home", after losing what could have been my personal one. There I met Malka, a darling, loving soul, who deserved someone much better than me, but did not know it. Although I told her everything I now told you, and did not hide that I still loved X, she wanted to marry me, and I was weak enough to go along, hoping that her affection, good humor and Israeli roots will make up for the lack of romance on my part.

That Israel did not become the home I sought had several causes: first, I was not religious - my Jewishness was more in the intellect than in tradition; second, the University which I joined when I immigrated eventually denied me tenure; finally, after I learned of X's separation I felt I should try for what little chance there might still be for me. So we left, even though Malka and her family gave me as much a sense of a home as they could.

Our separation soon after arriving in Santa Barbara was a natural step, putting our relations on its true basis: friendship and mutual respect. That our marriage failed was

---
[29] Immigration.

totally my responsibility: Malka was always a devoted and loyal wife to me, but she stood no chance against the memory of X: it is not her fault that she could not share my world of opera, drama, poetry, intellectual conversation and outdoor sports.

My last few years have been characterized by valiant efforts and pathetic failures. For self-improvement and enlightenment I tried every trick in the book: EST, Actualizations, Radix, Jungian analysis, Gestalt therapy, drugs (both antidepressant and recreational), reading, psychodrama, meditation:

"I would know my shadow and my light, so shall I at last be whole"

(Michael Tippet: A Child of Our Time)

For finding a partner, I ran the gamut of singles parties, newspaper ads, dating services, blind dates, ad nauseam. I visited Hawaii twice for a woman who eventually rudely snubbed me, and went recently to Budapest to find a wife, but to no avail:

> "Ki szeret s párra nem találhat
> oly hontalan amilyen gyámoltalan
> a szükségét végzõ vadállat."[30]
> (József Attila)

Instead, I continued dreaming of X, spending increasing amounts of time in imaginary conversations with her, going over

---

[30] Literal translation by PT:
Who loves and cannot find a partner / is as homeless as an awkward / wild animal while defecating.

what I should have done 16 years ago to change the course of events, and fantasizing on what might happen that would bring her back to me. The daily events of my own life became the sideshow; the main show took place where she was, and from where I was excluded.

What occasional relationships I had, were unsatisfying: brief affairs where usually I was let go, or longer, sporadic ones with married women, who found in me a source of variation and color in dull marriages. I made a fool of myself running, hopefully, after attractive young women, while no one came even close to X in comparison, not as a lover, as an intellectual partner, a surrogate sister. Yet, my energies were largely absorbed in the search, leaving little for work, socializing or reading. My life centered on the mailbox and the telephone, and only my singing and the affections of my cat kept me outwardly sane.

People in this situation sometimes seek refuge in their work but there, too, I came to a dead end. Back in my teens, under the limitations of the communist regime I did not dare gambling on what I felt to be my vocation: operatic singing. Instead, I opted for "safe" engineering. However, with no emotional outlet in my personal life I sought it-in vain in my profession, and on failing to find it, came to dislike my work and the whole male world of engineering. No wonder, then, that at age 47, when most of my former classmates are well-established professors and the like, I have been struggling in part-time, temporary jobs for years now, spending much time at work and achieving little. The longest I ever held a job was five years; I never reached tenure nor was ever invited to work anywhere.

Meanwhile, thanks to the skills of my last voice teacher, I have been increasingly feeling that had I chosen singing when it was still time, I might have succeeded.

While in earlier years I used to enjoy music, reading, travel, theater, in my enforced solitude (out of my last 18 years for 12 I lived entirely alone) these brought less and less pleasure to me, and I gave them up, one by one. The accumulation of disappointments has made me morose and angry at the world and at people, especially women, for being so inferior, in my eyes, to X. Irrational as this may be, I much identify with the vile Master-at-Arms John Claggart:

> "But alas, alas! The light shines in the darkness,
> and the darkness comprehends it, and suffers...
> O beauty, o handsomeness goodness,
> Would that I ne'er encountered you ...
> For what hope remains if love can escape?
> If love still lives and grows strong where I cannot enter,
> what hope is there in my own dark world for me?"
> (Britten: Billy Budd)

Claggart's destiny is to destroy the one who "shone light on the depravity to which (he) was born"; I rather destroy myself.

On many a lonely dawn, at the "hour of the wolf," when I turn sleepless in my bed, I share the agony of Amfortas:

> "Nur eine Waffe taugt:
> die Wunde schliesst
> der Speer nur, der sie Schlug."[31,32]
> (Wagner: Parsifal)

The weapon that struck my wound was X's perfection; apparently, no one has been able to, or could, heal it.

There is but one intellectual realization I had to reach, to see my way clear. It is this: we do not have a choice between life and death, only the manner of our death and the length and   (sometimes) quality of life we live until then. Now despite the fact that I am in excellent health, financially independent, live in a beautiful town, own property etc., I see nothing in my power to make my life meaningful. No amount of money can buy me a woman I could love, or children for whom working becomes a source of satisfaction. What I shall throw away, then, is just more of the same: loneliness, rejection by women, sexual frustration, loss of jobs, to be topped by the usual health problems of aging. I am on the way to become a

---

[31] One weapon alone will serve: - only the spear that struck you heals the wound.
[32] http://www.monsalvat.no/trans3.htm

pathetic, ineffectual, irrelevant, aging fool, and I despise myself for it.

Some friends have advised me, with good intention, to "compromise;" I have tried to, and it did not work. So now I rather admit that I made one fatal mistake in my life, and have to pay the price for it. I was at the door of the Garden of Eden and could already hear the music from inside, but allowed my parents to drag me back. Most people don't even get one chance for happiness, and surely I have not earned two. I could have flown like a butterfly, yet ended up a caterpillar, crawling in the mud. There is no out, as there was none for József Attila, but the rails in front of the fast train :

"Be vagy zárva a Hét Toronyba
és már sohasem menekülsz."[33]

So you see, my dear friend, I have over the years gradually lost contact with "reality," and you could not have helped. My act is not intended to put blame on you. Perhaps on Hitler, who killed most of my family; or Kruschev, who made me into a refugee; and certainly my mother, who

---

[33] Literal translation by PT:
  You are locked up in the Seven Towers / and you will never escape.
Note: The poet ended his life by throwing himself on the rails in front of a train in 1937.

Transplanted Lives ♦ 237

selfishly destroyed my happiness. But first and foremost, I accuse myself for having been a coward, shirking responsibility and expecting from X to bail me out. I believe I had the potential to be a man of some significance, a loving husband and a good father, but could not do it alone. Instead, I stumbled under a curse of loneliness, hiding my tears behind the sixth door and my women behind the seventh:

"És mindig is éjjel lesz - éjjel -

éjjel."[34]

(Bartók: Bluebeard's Castle)

I don't know when my last day will come, but I can guess how. Some minor frustration, like another snub from a woman, loss of a job, or illness will push me over the edge. I have made all necessary financial and legal preparations during the past year and a half, and am trying to keep my desk clear at work so as to cause the least dislocation to my employers and colleagues.

You may want to mourn my passing in your own way. However, let me tell you that I shall ask for one piece of music to be played at my funeral service, which best expresses the pain of my life: the Lacrymosa from Mozart's Requiem. And please, forgive my weakness and

---

[34] Literal translation by PT:
And forever it will remain night – night – night.

for not setting you an example in tolerating life's burden. What love you have for me, give it to Malka, just as I shall leave her everything I have. Alas, that it had to be this way.

    Andrew

The Third Letter

(The third letter or Postscript was composed in Times New Roman font.)

Postscript
June, 1994

Twelve years have passed since I wrote the preceding pages, but I am still (or again) in the same place, and only a few items need to be added to bring you up to date.

First, what saved me from ending my life in 1982 was probably that around September I met (through a video-dating service!) a very attractive and pleasant Korean lady, with whom I had a relationship for over two years. Unfortunately, we never got close enough to consider marriage, or even living together. (Meanwhile, Malka moved to Oregon some years ago, and last April we finally divorced, formalizing a fact that existed for 17 years. However, we remained good and mutually supportive friends.)

Then, on the day after Christmas in 1985, the unimaginable happened: a graduate student from China walked into the lab where I work at UCSB,[35] and at once I was taken by her. She was married, with her husband still in China, but I learned that the marriage was one of convenience rather than passion. This is the justification I gave to myself for coming on strongly, and very soon I was in love with her and, to a certain extent, she with me. My love was different from that to X, whom I held in awe; S. was 22 years younger than me, and my feelings toward her also contained a part of a father's to his daughter. We were very well matched physically, and did all our sports together: tennis, skiing, swimming, running, aerobics. I also introduced her to the magic world of opera, and she continues to enjoy it to this day. For years I had hoped that our marriage was just

---

[35] University of California, Santa Barbara

around the corner, especially after she moved in with me in 1990, and we even spoke about our future child. (I was anxious to have a child also because this would have been the only way to continue my bloodline: most descendants of my four grandparents died, many in the Holocaust, without leaving any children.)

Alas, a perhaps not unexpected by-product of S's impressive process of personal growth was that she gradually raised her sights regarding a life partner, and after she got her Ph.D. in 1991, she went to live in Berkeley, with the intent of starting a new relationship with a former student colleague. He is her own age, handsome, and professionally successful, and she had been attracted to him for several years.

Her departure was a great blow to me, which was followed by another when she announced in March, 1992, that she was moving in with him. Soon after that I severed all ties with her, because the pain of her having a life without me was too much to bear. Yet, I cannot blame her for choosing someone who is much less likely to make her a widow in 20-30 years, than I would have been. Still, I have been hanging on to a faint hope, since as late as last February she indicated to a mutual friend that if she did not marry her boyfriend, she "probably" would return to me. However, more recent developments convinced me that the chances for this are next to nil.

As soon as she left, I began frantically to try to fill the void she left. I pursued a futile search for a partner through personal column ads, singles parties, computer network bulletin boards, and the like, but with no result. In 1992 I flew a woman here from Texas whom I met through electronic mail, and it was a disaster. Then last November I went to visit another in Hungary, and that did not work out either. Thus since September, 1991, I have been increasingly isolated: I saw fewer and fewer people, and had on average one visitor per month in my home. My phone sometimes did not ring for days, nor did I feel like calling anyone. And when occasionally a woman did show some interest in me, I could not relate to her.

I used to think that I had something unique to offer, but if so, it is not a commodity in demand in Southern California. With my tendency to be attracted mostly to women much younger than myself, but with the age 60 looming only a few months away, my chances of hitting gold for the third time is negligible. If the singles scene is a marketplace, I have a Sachs Fifth Avenue taste with a Woolworth budget. (I am too old, not tall, not handsome, not rich, and professionally not successful, so that most high quality women do not give me a second look.) Yet I find this kind of life is intolerable: there is for me no substitute for a woman, for sex, for a family: behind most successful and happy men there is usually a loving and supportive wife.

I realize that the enormous importance I attach to having a partner is an unusual, perhaps even pathological condition, described by Karen Horney as "morbid dependence," but I have not been able to alter it. I heard it said that we all live our "personal myth." If so, mine is that of the Flying Dutchman, who roams the lonely oceans for years in the quest of a woman who would unquestioningly devote herself to him, and thus relieve his curse. Put less romantically, I seem to have been permanently damaged by my egocentric, "devouring," narcissistic mother, to whom I was all but emotionally surrendered at an early age by my otherwise loving father. I failed to develop the part of my self that can love myself, and instead sought this in a woman. I once put this succinctly in a format borrowed from R.D. Laing's poems Knots:

"Jack fell in love with his image reflected by Jill.
Jill fell in love with the image of Jack she reflected.
Jack loved Jill for reflecting an image he could love.
Jill loved Jack for his loving her reflecting his image."

Consequently, in 1992 my depression got gradually worse, until even psychotherapy was not sufficient, and I started taking antidepressants, which had several unpleasant side effects. (I finally stopped both at the end of last year, since they could not solve my problem.) In addition, I became dependent on sleeping pills, and spent many dawn hours tossing and turning in bed and wondering why, with no one depending on me, I should have to go on living like this. I stopped singing, my favorite pastime and, not enjoying lonely travels, I also gave up on vacations and going to San Francisco or Los Angeles to see operas. Even listening to most music upsets me, for it stirs up emotions, so my record player has been silent for months.

Nor did my self-esteem get boosted by my professional situation: at the tender age of 59, I am the proud bearer of the title (and even this only thanks to the support of a friend!) "Zero salary, Temporary Associate Research Engineer" at UCSB. Since my work efficiency in the past 2 1/2 years dropped to less than half of what it used to be, I was unable to complete my new multimedia learning project, the first version of which was a great financial and professional success. I also dropped my short course organization business, mainly because I could not handle the associated stresses. As a result, my earned income for 1993 was under $5,000. (Fortunately, I was financially fairly comfortable, almost able to live on my investments, especially since I spend nothing on luxuries, which I would not enjoy anyway.)

Had things turned out differently, I would have finished the project working at home - for then I would have had a real home - perhaps while watching the baby. (Despite my age I was willing to undertake such a responsibility, since I am in excellent health, and physically much more active than my peers.)

Finally, my act should be viewed in a historical perspective: on my father's side, my grandfather ended his life during an asthmatic attack. My childhood sweetheart, suffering from a chronic heart condition, killed herself a few years ago, while my first lover twice attempted suicide (and failed) during our relationship; she finally made it in 1984. My mother threatened and attempted it several times, and at last succeeded in 1977, after the man with whom she had a late blooming romance died. And last but not least, Hungary has the highest rate of suicide per head of population, so one might say it was a culture I was born into.

And anyway why should I wait for a "usual" death, which today usually means slowly and painfully wasting away with cancer or AIDS, or perhaps being killed in a burglary, a traffic accident or an earthquake? I would rather fall asleep peacefully, after taking care of all my affairs. There is nothing I see looking ahead but more loneliness, more failures, more despair. Once a good chess player sees that defeat is inevitable, he does not play the endgame. You should thus not view my end as a tragedy; rather, it was my life of yearning, frustration and failures that was the tragedy... the end is a blissful relief from it.

So after living alone for 23 years of the past 30, I again got to the end of the road, and only a miracle could save me from the abyss. If you receive this, it means that the miracle did not happen.

Andrew

P.S. Some time ago I made up the attached Pol Shots™, in the style of Santa Barbara's Ashleigh Brilliant. They express my outlook in a "gallows humor" style which is characteristic of my generation.

I've decided to start a new life soon.

(However, *to do so* I must first end the present one.)

© Andrew Not-So-Brilliant., 1992

One good thing about committing suicide is

that it is a decision I won't later regret.

©Andrew not-so-Brilliant, 1993

In 1995 Andrew committed suicide.

A RETURN TRIP

Gold-Handwerks-Schule

Gold- Gold-Handwerks-

Diploma

Herr Max ......

1938....

RETURN
by Risha Schatell

The stewardess patrols the aisle as I struggle not to scream: Stop the plane, I want off! But I remain silent. This upholstered sardine can won't open till we land and I don't want to be where it's going. What madness brought me here?

My wife, Rose, is sitting beside me reading. Her world, at least, seems peaceful.

The stewardess delivers headsets; a movie is about to start. The screen stares at me, an empty eye. I wave away the headset. The eye comes alive with images. I remove my glasses; the figures blur.

Am I a fool to pursue my certificate from the Academy of Goldsmiths fifty years after I should have received it? Now I ask? Foolish? Try idiotic.

The scene shows our Passover Seder. Every place is filled and tonight all the beds will be occupied, but not all of my family is here. It's a life any sane man would want, yet I've never been happy.

During the Seder I read from the *Haggadah*, and then send the children to search for the hidden matzos. I always give all of them the same prize; nevertheless they hunt for it frantically, shrieking with excitement. The oldest, David, sees it and points it out to the little one, who pounces, screaming

— *I found it! I found it!* — until everyone on the block must hear her. I give her the prize money and a big hug and kiss, looking over her shoulder to wink at David, who watches, laughing. He'll be a doctor in a few years, a fine one. Of that much at least I am certain.

Now the screen shows people being pulled from their homes, beaten, killed, synagogues set afire, windows of businesses owned by Jews smashed in the orgy of hatred and rage known as *Kristallnacht*. I hear the screams, the sounds piercing my being like shards of the broken glass.

They were our friends, our relatives, people we loved like Irma and Karl. They were us. But they betrayed us, and now I'm going back. Even idiocy doesn't fit. Temporary insanity?

I hope it's only temporary.

Rotating my head to ease the kink in my neck, I watch as the screen flashes pictures of my children, babies reaching for me to lift them. I feel again the incredible silkiness of their hair against my cheek, the warmth and terrifying vulnerability of the small bodies melting against my shoulder. I'm astonished still at the fierce protectiveness that consumed me.

The next moment their weddings are flashing on the screen. That's about right. That's how quickly it went.

The screen goes dark. The cabin lights come up. A good life, but one spent looking through a window at myself, my family. No real joy. Why? I close my eyes, weary of the endless questions.

Daylight. We land in Frankfurt. We're driven to the small town of my birth. Some of the streets passing our windows are familiar. But there are empty spaces where buildings stood and new, unfamiliar structures have risen. I'm disoriented.

Rose remains at the hotel for a rest. I'm keyed up. I go for a walk, trying to see everything; trying to see nothing. It's different; it's the same. It's now; it's then. I don't want to be here but it's exciting. I should have been twins.

Everywhere the shop windows display cut glass dishes, vases, goblets. The crystal reflects cold fire, hard edges, the patterns cut with the precision of marching Nazi storm troopers.

Automatically I've headed for our house. It's too far to walk, I flag a taxi. The address rolls off my tongue readily though I haven't used it for half a century. I feel as if the intervening years never happened, but my gnarled hands tell me I'm old. For a moment I'm dizzy. It's good to sit and rest after too little sleep on the plane.

Reflected in the windows of the taxi my parents appear, their arms stretched towards me, imploring me. They scream in silence, the stillness more terrible than sounds would have been. My mother's beautiful long hair has been cut off. They're fighting to live as they breathe in death. If only I can grasp their hands I'll pull them to safety. I try with all my strength, frantically straining toward them, but our hands don't touch. They never do . . .

Did I doze off or was I awake? That nightmare used to be limited to sleeping hours. Coming here was a mistake.

The taxi stops. Our house is a different color, smaller than I remembered. It's a bit shabby, although the windows are clean and the lawn neat. I stand on the sidewalk staring and realize I'm waiting for Rachel to come running, wanting me to lift her and swing her around as I always did. My baby sister who was born laughing, my mother used to say. I'd peek at her between the bars of her crib each morning, waiting for the burst of sunlight when she saw my face. Her joy lit up our lives.

For a moment the pain is so sharp I think I'm having a heart attack. Bending over eases it a little. A lady in front of the house next to ours pauses in sweeping her walk to ask,

— Is something wrong? Are you ill?

She's about the age Rachel would be. Is it possible? Oh, God, could she have..? — The agony is displaced by joy. For a moment I — No. Of course not. She's not Rachel.

I'm drowning in pain, but after an eternity of shallow breathing, it eases a little. I never before fully understood the word heartache means literally a pain in the heart.

The lady stares at me, concerned.

— Are you...? - she begins.

— I'm all right, — I manage to say. — I used to live here.

— Oh, that must have been long ago. We've been here 35 years.

— Yes, long ago. Before the War.

She doesn't ask which war.

— *So now where do you live?*

— *In America, near Chicago, Illinois,* — I tell her.

— *Ah, gangsters* — she says, nodding.

No. Here were the gangsters.

The door to our house opens and a woman descends the stairs carrying gardening implements. She isn't my mother. The fist clutches my chest again.

—What do you want? *Why do you stand here?* — she demands. People are far more suspicious now.

— *He used to live here,* — says the neighbor. — *Long ago.*

The occupant of our house stares at me.

— *What do you want?*

— To look at our house.

— *You're not coming in* — she says.

— No, no, I didn't expect to. But would you — is it possible you know where our family photographs are? Perhaps there's a carton in the attic or...

— *I didn't take them. I don't know anything about them. You come here and accuse me of stealing? How dare you! Go away! Leave me alone!* — She's shrieking.

I can't breathe and fight with her, too, but I'm not ready to leave, so I cross the street, taking small sips of air to ease the pain. I lean against a tree and stare again at our house.

The window on the left was our dining room. The four of us sat at the table, my father filling our plates, my mother saying,

— *As soon as he graduates, he leaves.*

—*This will all blow over* — says my father. — *It's only temporary. People will come to their senses. These people are our friends, our neighbors.*

My mother slices a loaf of bread as if she's cutting away a fast-growing cancer.

250 ◆ *Return*

For the first time in my memory, she disagrees openly with my father. She says,

— It will not blow over. Read Main Kampf and see for yourself. That maniac knows exactly how to manipulate people. He won't stop until he's dead or until all the Jews in Europe are dead. When the boy gets his certificate he leaves. We'll follow as soon as we can.

My father pounds the table so hard the dishes rattle and we jump.

— I said it will blow over. He stays! — he shouts. — Don't you trust your own country?

— It's no longer my country.

My mother's voice is hollow.

— It's full of strangers who know only hatred. The boy leaves. We can't risk his life hoping for a miracle.

My father is silent. Rachel's face is wet with tears. No one asks me what I want to do. Just as well.

The day before graduation, my teacher told me not to return for the ceremony.

— Not graduate with my class? Why?

He explained the school had graciously allowed me to remain but was under pressure not to permit me to graduate.

— This school no longer admits Jews; it certainly can't graduate them.

— But I've earned my certificate. I need it.

He shrugged, repeating it would be better if I didn't appear for the ceremony or there might be trouble.

I went to the headmaster.

— Stay away, — he said. — You got your training, that's all we can do for you.

There would be no certificate of achievement.

A few days later I departed for America, leaving behind the family I would never again see alive.

A dog barks in small high explosions of sound. Startled, I look around. It's a dachshund, naturally.

Rachel and my parents are gone. The neighbors are different. There's nothing here for me. What did I expect to find? This hasn't been home to me for fifty years. Why then do I feel so lost?

I walk over to the main street and take a taxi to City Hall where I have heard my boyhood friend, Karl, is Mayor. When I inquire at the desk for him, I'm told he recently retired, but the clerk telephones him at home. She holds out the phone to me.

— *Come, come,* — says Karl. — *Take a taxi, she'll give you the address—we've moved. Come now. I can't wait to see you!*

Karl greets me with an embrace, a handshake, shining eyes and a flash of gleaming teeth.

Did they knock out Papa's gold teeth before they killed him or after? The fist twists again in my chest.

— *You're pale, Max. Here, sit down, have a drink with me to celebrate your return. Tell me, when did you arrive? Have you seen any of the old crowd? What's happened with you in all these years? Why did you wait so long to come back?*

As he chatters, I look around the room. His parlor is filled with photographs from before the War and after the War.

We make uneasy small talk, trying to catch up on each other's lives without saying too much. I find it hard to swallow my drink.

He tells me about his wife, now dead. There's a son, a daughter, and grandchildren. He enjoyed being Mayor. He had always been sociable, happiest when surrounded by a crowd.

We carefully avoid speaking of the War. But I need to know.

— *Karl, have you any idea what happened to our personal belongings, like family photographs after my family — after they — after...?*

He walks to the window, his back to me.

— No. The furniture the next occupants used, I think. Anything valuable was seized. The personal things were probably burned. I'm not certain. I'll try to find out, but after so many years...

He pours himself another schnapps. I tell him I came for my certificate.

— You never received it?

— Why should refusing me a piece of paper be surprising? Far worse things were done.

— Yes, but such a small thing, such a small, harmless thing.

He takes an enormous swallow of schnapps.

— Don't go back to the old school. It was leveled by bombs.

— I know. When I wrote, the letter had to be forwarded. The records were destroyed. That's why I came back.

— So why do you need the certificate now? — he asks.

— I don't need it. They owe it to me. I want to show it to my grandchildren.

— Can I help?

— Maybe you can. The school authorities require three affidavits from students who knew me and were present during my final year to swear that I completed the required work in the Senior class.

Chuckling, he says,

— I'll give you an affidavit with so many seals and ribbons you won't need more than one. And I can get the others for you very easily. Do you want to see some of the old crowd?

I hesitate. — Not today.

— Alright. How long are you staying?

— Three days. We'll visit England and then go home.

— Only three days? You don't want to see the rest of Germany?

— Yes, but such a small thing, such a small, harmless thing.

— No.

Silence.

— Well, come back tomorrow and I'll have the letters for you. Or should I bring them to your hotel?

— No, no, I'll come. Karl, do you hear from Irma?

— Yes, of course. She lives only a short distance from here. Do you want to see her?

I nod. He makes a telephone call, while I remember my golden first love. She adored me, she said, but she was afraid to marry a Jew.

Following Karl's directions, I find her house. There's a neat lawn, but no flowers.

An old woman with lifeless eyes greets me at the door. Her gray hair is pulled back from her face in a bun. I open my mouth to ask for Irma and catch myself just in time. I know I've aged, but somehow I always pictured her... For the briefest instant there's a glimpse of the radiant young Irma when she smiles. Then it's gone.

Their home is comfortable, practical, and almost impersonal. Everything is beige or brown, sensible neutral colors. Irma fusses with cut glass ornaments on a table, straightens cushions, stoops to pick up a nearly invisible piece of lint. There are engineering books on a shelf, a Bible on one table, no flowers, and no family photographs. The walls display reproductions of Dürer etchings.

I think of Rose's joyful peanut gallery in our home, where she hangs all the pictures of our children and grandchildren.

Irma pours coffee. We talk. —I tell her about my family, my business. She tells me her husband is an engineer. They had no children. They go every year to the same place for their holiday, staying at the same hotel. No, they're not interested in seeing the world. Everything they could possibly need they have right where they are. She's active in their church.

— Do you enjoy that? — I ask.

She's surprised at the question. — It's my duty.

— Do you hear many concerts? The opera? — I ask.

— *Oh, we can get them on the television if we want them.*

I tell her about the certificate but she already knows from Karl.

There's a long pause while I search for a new topic and her hand absently tucks escaped strands of hair into the bun. We listen to the grandfather clock ticking. After several long silent minutes, we say goodbye.

Rose, with her soft auburn hair, is waiting for me in our hotel room, her eyes bright. I kiss her when I come in, surprising her a little.

— *Was she that awful?* — she asks, smiling.

— *Who?*

— *The girl you didn't marry. You saw her today, didn't you?*

— *Yes, and — yes.*

— *I'm glad,* — Rose says, her smile now brilliant.

We hire a car and driver the next morning for a tour. Rose enjoys the quaint old houses, the well-tended parks. We stop in front of my old house and she gazes at it, asking questions.

At the main shopping area the car will wait while Rose selects gifts for our family. She heads for a shop with cut glass displayed in the window.

— *This is very nice, don't you think?*

— *No.*

She studies me for a moment.

— *All right, we'll keep looking.*

We wander in and out of the shops, Rose admiring the wares and turning to me for agreement. I shake my head, finding fault with everything. After a while I say,

— *Why don't we do our shopping in England?*

— *I was just thinking the same thing.*

— *I'm sorry.*

She says, smiling,

— *That's a waste of a sorry,* — as she used to tell the children when they spilled something. — *Save your sorries for important things!*

My chuckle loosens the knot in my chest a little.

After coffee and incredibly rich pastries, I telephone Karl. He has the affidavits. The car brings us to his house.

He can't take his eyes off Rose when I introduce them. I feel a bit smug. Well, more than a bit. Karl insists I look over the papers and decide if they're what I need.

— *They're fine* — I tell him.

He nods, pleased with himself.

— *I'll come with you to see the school official. He's pompous, a petty tyrant. You know the type.*

— *No, I'll manage. If I need help I'll call you.*

He shrugs.

— *Stop by afterward to tell me how it went.*

I telephone to make an appointment as instructed in the school's letter. Rose laughs at the idea.

— *The school no longer exists, and he's so busy you need an appointment?*

The next morning I go to the office of the school official.

He reads the affidavits over several times, checks the notary stamps and my information sheet.

— *I'm not certain you have fully complied with the requirements,* — he says slowly.

— *Exactly which ones have I failed to satisfy?*

— *We must have proof that you did indeed complete the work.* — He plucks at his perfectly-adjusted tie.

Does his wife starch his shirts, his underwear or his brain?

— *You have before you three affidavits stating that I did, one of them signed by a former mayor of this town. What more do you need?*

He reads the papers again, slowly, deliberately.

Finally he says,

— *I'll have to consult with the members of the board. You will be advised of our decision.* — He stands up, terminating the interview.

Still seated, I ask,

— *Do you have a file of our correspondence?*

— *Of course.*

— *Numbered, like this one?*

— *Naturally.*

— *So will your file remain open for another fifty years?*

— *You know,* — I continue, we *have in our city a very powerful organization, the Chicago Council on Foreign Relations. I think they would be interested to hear that I was denied my certificate in Nazi Germany and denied it again fifty years after the Nazis were supposedly out of power.*

He sinks into his chair, staring. I'm beginning to enjoy myself.

— *I know your former mayor will be interested. And the newspapers here and at home.*

He shifts in his chair. Suddenly his suit looks wrinkled; his tie no longer centered. He's smaller, almost shrunken.

— *I'm only five years from retirement. Please don't make trouble for me* — he begs.

It feels wonderful—for a moment. But that makes me no better than they were.

— *Give me the certificate now, or don't, and suffer the consequences!* — I sound starched, too, even to myself.

He slowly extracts a piece of preprinted parchment from a file folder, fills it out, signs it, stamps it and hands it to me. He remains seated. We don't shake hands when I leave.

At Karl's house he asks how I made out with the chief clerk. I show him the certificate.

— I'm glad, — he says. — I thought you'd have a problem with him. That's why I offered to come with you.

We talk a bit, then I thank him for his help with the affidavits. I reach out to shake his hand, but find myself pulling back as if it were on fire.

— How could you? How could you just let it happen? My parents, Rachel, how could you just let them be taken? — I'm astonished to hear myself.

He winces, his face twisting.

— There was nothing I could do. We didn't even know they were gone for two days. By then, your parents were on a train headed for a camp, and the Gestapo had your sister. She had been running messages for... You know, children sometimes — It was thought they were less likely to be caught. — He bites his lip. — There was nothing my family could do, Max. We were all afraid of the Gestapo.

— You poor things, did they frighten you?

— Max, I've been living with it ever since. The shame never stops. Have you never done anything you were ashamed of?

— Yes. I survived. — I take a step towards the door.

— Max, don't leave like this. Can't you understand, we were afraid! We were terrified. My parents kept saying with the inflation we couldn't afford food, and it was getting worse. This man-this crazy man-came along and said he could turn things around. He gave us hope, Max!

— At what price?

— Our souls. But we didn't understand that. At least with him there was a future. We thought we could straighten up with the victims later. Some of us did. — Tried to.

— With dead people you straightened up? How did you manage that?

— We didn't know, Max. We didn't know, I tell you.

I stare at him.

— All right, all right, we had some idea. By the end we knew what was happening but it was too late. Too late for the Jews, too late for us. Max, I'm sorry. I'm sorry. I'm sorry. Forgive me, please! — He's sobbing.

How can I forgive him when I can't forgive myself? When I've never allowed myself to feel anything so I wouldn't feel the loss and the guilt.

Karl's sobbing is quieting now. He waits, mopping his face.

Could he have changed anything? — Could I? — Not alone, but perhaps with the help of others. Some did what they could to protest, like Rachel. They were quickly silenced. No one expected the Holocaust. We were part of Germany. We <u>were</u> Germany. We simply couldn't believe it was possible until it happened, and by then it was too late.

If I had stayed, what difference would it have made? If I had waited till my family could leave, we would all have been killed. How would I have it?

— *God, make it didn't happen,* — I used to pray as a child when I had done something I regretted. But this wasn't my doing. It wasn't Karl's, either. Where does that leave us?

Where we are now: lost.

— *Look,* — Karl says, — *we had a national nervous breakdown.*

— *That's as good an excuse as any, I suppose.*

— *But we were betrayed, too, by our government. We suffered, too. And every day of our lives, every hour, we live with the guilt. We can't make it go away; we can't talk it away or reason or argue it away.* — It hurt to see him begging. — *It's always there. No matter how many great artists we produce, Germany will still be the country responsible for two world wars and the Holocaust, and nothing will ever change that. Do you understand how painful that is for us?*

Pausing for breath, Karl reaches for the schnapps bottle.

I deny his pain as I denied mine. Anger hurts less.

— Are you asking for pity?

— No, for understanding.

— Understanding of something that can't be understood?

— Max, it was fifty years ago. If there were some way for us to live it over, I pray it wouldn't happen again, but we can't. Would we have served the victims by killing ourselves? We'll face what we must when we meet our Lord, but in the meantime we have to live as best we can.

He drains his glass and places it on the table; the sound is an audible period to his speech.

We have to live. That much is certain. There are no answers, but we have to live. I'm exhausted. Wearily I extend my hand. He takes it and holds it in both of his.

— *Come back, Max. Come back for a visit. Don't wait another fifty years. It will be easier the next time.*

In the car to Frankfurt the next morning, we pass shop windows displaying cut crystal reflecting rainbows from the morning sun.

Rose and I board the sardine can again. The same blank eye stares at me. I stuff my glasses in my pocket and stare back.

All this for one piece of paper that changes nothing.

The trip plays out before me on the screen until my neck reminds me of its presence. I rub it, stretch it, turning toward Rose in the process.

— *Got your thoughts sorted out?* — she asks, smiling.

— *I'm struggling with the filing system.*

— *Try chronological.*

Good idea. Then the past will be past, where it belongs, and I'll be free to live the present.

I turn to tell her she's brilliant, and stare at her, seeing her as if for the first time in years. Hair soft around her face, a warm, loving face, lined now, not so smooth as it once was. But the lines around her eyes and mouth are from smiling.

She feels my eyes and turns to me quizzically, waiting.

— *My God, you're a beautiful woman. Why didn't you ever tell me that?*

— *I was sure you'd notice sooner or later.* — Her face flushes like a young girl's. My arm goes around her; she moves closer to me.

— *Max, tell me, did you get what you came for?*

— *Yes,* — I reply. — *I did.*

EPILOGUE

In these recollections we, the authors and editors, tried to give you, our reader, a taste of the human experience of suddenly leaving one's home with hardly more than the clothes on one's back and a small inconspicuous package possibly containing some memorabilia. Our goal was to illustrate the life of political refugees in the late 1950s and their often tortuous paths to grow roots—in some cases for the first time—as they felt alien in the land of their birth.

The escapes from Hungary to Austria were generally tortuous, but successful and most of us found a niche in our adopted homeland. The adjustment did not come without intensive struggles and in one case resulted in tragic ending. Since most of us were students at the time of the 1956 Hungarian Uprising, we attempted to complete our education in the new homeland. By and large we became respected professionals in our fields.

We need to emphasize that none of us regretted the decision to leave and search for freedom. The essay by the unsuccessful attempt illustrates a lifelong regret about his hesitation to take the risk. In these essays the reader could hardly sense any nostalgia for the land left behind.

The storytellers in this book did not yearn for riches, but for freedom from persecution and a chance to live up to one's potential in a sage and fair environment. Most of the refugees flooding into Europe in our time are yearning for the same. In contrast, we were often viewed as heroes for our rejection of communist tyranny, while the current group is often met with skepticism about their motivation. Everyone should have the opportunity to live up to one's potential in a peaceful environment.

We have become useful citizens in our adopted countries and many of us raised children and grandchildren to follow our ideals.

We thank the Reader for being interested in these stories and we hope to transmit a dose of optimism to those who are struggling with growing new roots far away from their former zone of comfort.

BRIEF BIOGRAPHIES OF THE CONTRIBUTORS

As the essays show, most of us managed to find our niche in a free democratic society. As an illustration we would like to show what we have done and accomplished since we left our former homeland and settled in our new, chosen country.

Andrew Handler arrived in the USA in 1957. He received a B.A. from the University of California, Berkeley and a PhD in history from Columbia University, New York, all on scholarships. Andrew had been a Professor of History at the University of Miami in Coral Gables, Florida for 32 years until retirement. He was the author of nine books concerning recent history. Two of these were coauthored with Susan V. Meschel. He was married to Deborah Handler. Andrew suddenly passed away in 2012.

Gabor Kalman arrived in the USA in 1957. After staying with relatives in Philadelphia, he was accepted at the University of California, Berkeley. Gabor studied pharmacy there. While serving in the US Army he received his US citizenship. The work in the Army related to the space program. As a veteran he was admitted to graduate school at Stanford University where he switched careers from pharmacology to film making. During the past 30 years he has taught courses on film in Los Angeles and is an award winning documentary filmmaker. His latest film *"There Was Once..."* is to be released soon. He definitely feels he is American, but occasionally he misspells it HUNGARICAN. He lives in Los Angeles with his partner, sculptor Norman Lloyd and their vizsla, Manci néni.

Susan V. Meschel arrived in the USA in January of 1957 and lived with her family in Aurora, Illinois for a few weeks. After a month she landed a job at the Toni Company as a chemistry technician. In the fall of 1957 she began graduate school at the University of Chicago on a fellowship. Susan received an M.S. degree in 1959 and a PhD in chemistry in 1961. In 1962 she became a US citizen. From 1967 to 1989 she taught chemistry and physics on college level as Assistant Professor at Roosevelt University and the University of Chicago. From 1961 to 1967, and from 1989 to the present, she has been active in research in high temperature solid state materials science at the University of Chicago and at Illinois Institute of Technology. She authored more than 60 scientific papers. In addition to her scientific research she also authored papers on the history of women in the sciences and on the subject of metallurgy in the Bible. She coauthored two books with Andrew Handler. Since retirement she has volunteered at the Museum of Science and Industry and at the Field Museum of Natural history in Chicago. Susan is married to George Meschel, a clinical psychologist, who also became a US citizen in 1962. They have two daughters, Judith and Eva and two grandchildren, Jared and Ashlyn.

Peter Milch arrived in New York in 1957. He earned a B.S. degree from Columbia University, an M.S. from Brooklyn College and a PhD from NYU. He was on the Faculty of Columbia University College of Physicians and surgeons and at S.U.N.Y College of Medicine at Stony Brook. He founded a consulting company—POM Consulting, Inc.—and consulted with several Pharmaceutical Companies in the field of clinical research. In 1964 he married Jaqueline Furman and they have three sons—Stewart, Kenneth and Erik—and eleven grandchildren.

Thomas Muhl started his career as a commercial artist, but he was drafted into the Hungarian People's Army where he became a copyist of masterworks for the brass. With his wife, Andrea, they escaped to the West and after some time in the UK, they came to the US. Tom spent most of his working life as a commercial artist in the US, with several years in Budapest as Artistic Director of a British P.R. firm. Once retired, he dedicated his time to publish his memoir, *Retouching Stalin's Moustache: Arrivals and Departures, Destination Unknown*, Xlibris, Corp., 2002. Many of Tom's paintings deal with the Holocaust and grace the walls of the Miller Center for Contemporary Jewish Studies at the University of Miami. His colorful paintings in an easily recognizable style also depict life in humorous ways. Tom is divorced and he lives in Miami.

George Pick arrived in the USA in December, 1956, and lived with his relatives in New Jersey. In May 1957 he landed a job as junior engineer at the Westinghouse Corporation in Philadelphia. In 1962 he earned an M.S. degree in Mechanical Engineering at Drexel Institute and in the same year he became a US citizen. George taught engineering at the Catholic University of America, first as an Instructor and then as an Assistant Professor. From 1966 he worked as the Manager of the U.S. Navy's High Energy Project Office and later became the Technical Director of the Navy's NATO Seasparrow Office. He authored more than 50 research papers. Since his retirement he is active in volunteer work in Holocaust education at the Holocaust Museum in Washington, D.C. He is married to Letty Pick.

Marianne Revah-Barta was born in Budapest, spent a few years in Gyöngyös and graduated from high school in Miskolc. She arrived in Canada in 1957 and in the same year began to work toward a B.A. and an M.A. in English language and literature at the University of Western Ontario, followed by an M.A. and a teaching fellowship at the University of Pennsylvania in Russian. She continued her studies in Paris with a Diploma in Translation, an M.A. in applied linguistics, a D.E.A.[36] from the Sorbonne, and a Diploma in Interpreting from ISIT.[37]

---

[36] Diplome d'etudes approfondies or DEA (Diploma of Advanced studies)
[37] Institute Superieur de Interpretes et Traducteur

She lives in Paris, France, with husband David Revah, PhD, a scholar of the Hebrew language and literature. They have two children, Danielle and Alain and two grandchildren, Max and Carla. She has been teaching English and training interpreters since her arrival in France, but makes her living mainly as a conference interpreter, working for the French Government, European institutions and the private market. Her brother, Peter, a registered professional engineer in the province of Ontario and a highly respected Professor of Electrical Engineering at Ryerson University, died in 1998.

The MacKinnons are her only remaining family in Canada.

Risha Schatell was born in Chicago. She attended the School of the Art Institute and Northwestern University. She interviewed Mr. Leo Bacharach—alias Max in the story—which affected her profoundly. She hopes that the story allows the reader to walk in his shoes sharing his experiences and his rebirth.

Leo Bacharach was born in Germany in 1917. He was the son of a kosher cattle dealer. He trained as a jeweler in one of the finest art schools, the *Zeichenakademie* in Hanau, Germany. Hanau is near Frankfurt. He graduated in 1934. He immigrated to the USA in 1936 and lived with an uncle. He worked as a jeweler specializing in gold and platinum smithing and started his own store in Chicago in 1944. His wife Audrey was also a specialist in jewelry design. He died at age 93 in 2010.

Michael Simon arrived in the USA in 1956 following his escape from the defeated Hungarian revolution. He continued his education at Pennsylvania State University and later received an M.A in photography from Rochester Institute of Technology. Michael taught photography and later became Chairperson of the Art Department at Beloit College, Beloit, WI. He authored a book on the

History of Photography in Hungary. More recently another book had been published about his photos: The World is Beautiful: The Photography of Michael Simon., Ed. T.H. Wilson; Beloit College, 1998. Since retirement he is active in his community in Maine, teaching courses on photography and world history. He is also active in planning student exchange programs. Michael is married to Carol Simon and they have two children and four grandchildren.

George R. Steiner arrived in the USA with his wife Marianne in 1957. A Hungarian immigrant from the Transylvanian town of Nagyvárad hired him in his firm and also allowed him to take off time for his studies of architecture at Northwestern University. He earned his M.S. degree there. The office specialized in reinforced concrete design of high rise buildings. Each architect in the firm had to design every part of the building from foundation to the roof. As a Registered Structural Engineer he became Vice President. In that firm he was responsible for the design of 29 major structures, among them high rises with 56, 47 and 32 stories, a large extension of the Art Institute of Chicago and a synagogue in Glencoe, Illinois. After several years he became an associate of another firm. During seven years there he was the project engineer of several buildings, including a Hilton Hotel in Philadelphia and a major shopping center. After four decades of design work he landed a senior advisor position at the McGraw Hill Publishing Company. This turned out to be a fourteen year dream job, which involved meeting top leaders, many manufacturers and traveling to most of the states in the USA. After 52 years of work he retired. George and his wife Marianne have two sons and five wonderful grandchildren.

Yes, we had luck, but we also had ambition and good people around us. The "American Dream" really worked for us and we are grateful for the opportunities this country gave us.

Andrew Szekely, after escaping from Hungary, first settled in Leeds, UK, where he earned a diploma in electrical engineering. He subsequently earned a PhD at Imperial College in London. In 1964 he moved to New York and worked at AT&T's Bell Laboratories on digital speech processing. In 1971 he settled in Israel where he held an academic position at Tel Aviv University. He married Malka there and after a few years they moved to California, where he held an academic position at the University of California at Santa Barbara. He and his wife divorced there. In 1995 Andrew committed suicide.

Peter Tarjan arrived in New York Harbor on December 31, 1956, but could only set foot on American soil on January 1 for lack of a Navy tugboat. Thanks to his uncle's friends in Boston, about a week later he was working as a totally unqualified metallurgical X-ray technician at MIT. With his first paycheck he went to meet his cousin, Van, a Korean veteran studying on the G.I. Bill at Purdue, where Peter received a scholarship and graduated with a BS EE "with distinction" in 1959. After earning an SM EE from MIT in 1960, he worked for the General Electric Co, in Syracuse, N.Y. for 3 years. He received the Ph.D. from Syracuse University in 1968. For the next 19 years he worked for Cordis Corp. and its CRC subsidiary as Chief Scientist in Miami, FL and then joined the faculty of the Biomedical Engineering Dept. of the University of Miami as Chairperson for 10 years and later as Professor until 2009 when he retired. His name appears on 23 US Patents and 21 technical book chapters, many juried articles and as editor of Children Who Survived the Final Solution, iUniverse, 2004. Peter has been married to Susanna Moross Tarjan for over 51 years and they have two sons, Joshua and Aaron, and three grandchildren, Noah, Miles and Oona. Peter is a volunteer docent at the Lowe Art Museum and a frequent speaker about the Holocaust in Hungary at schools and other venues.

János Várkonyi was born in Budapest in 1935. He attended the Technical University in Budapest. János became a member of the Communist Youth Organization (KISZ) as a requirement for employment. He was a member of the technical staff of Zrinyi Press for most of his career. He married Katalin Normann in 1960. They have a daughter, Judit, and a granddaughter, Anna Eszter. The family lives in Budapest.

Marietta Vig was born in Budapest in 1946. She studied at the Technical University of Budapest and earned a diploma in architectural engineering. She remained in Budapest until 1979 and then immigrated to Chicago, USA. In 1980 she moved back to Europe and settled in Denmark. She married Andras Szekacs and they had a son, Peter Alexander in 1983. Marietta held a position as architect for 17 years with two firms. In 1997, due to economic changes in the Danish Railways, her position ceased to exist. After some years she found an administrative position at the Hungarian Embassy in Copenhagen, Denmark where she continues to work at the present time.